Copyright © 2016 by Donald Hughes
All rights reserved.

ISBN: 978-1-944680-22-0

Dedications

I dedicate the following pages to healers everywhere, of every race, every belief and profession. We naturally think of doctors and therapist as healers but I am also talking about every human being who tries to make another person's life a little better. We are all capable of doing this, and we all do even without thinking about it. There are days when even something as simple as a smile can heal a heavy heart. So to all you healers out there, whether you know you are doing it or not, I dedicate this book to you.

I also give dedication to that inner healer in all of us. Some rediscover this healer early in life, and others, like me, take a little longer.

I also want to give special thanks to *The Man in the Gray House*. I consider him not only one of my fist healers I also consider him my first spiritual guide. I share a couple pages about this man at the end of this work.

Acknowledgements

I acknowledge my mother who held our family together pretty much all by herself. I thank her for the patience and gentleness she exuberated.

Next, with hesitant breath, I acknowledge Shorty, Charles, my father. I am not so much thanking him for the good things he gave me as I am for the tough things he did. If it were not for his torture, I don't think I would be the spiritual person I am today. If I didn't like who I am today, I would not be able to acknowledge him.

I want to thank Siw Hermanstad, who helped me with ideas for the cover and ideas for fonts. Also Sharon Boyles, Christine Lee D.C., and all those who encouraged me often during the process of forming Fresh Morning Breaths.

I offer deep gratitude to Alison Teal, the therapist who worked with me energetically. She helped me rescue many parts of my young childhood and inner children, frozen in trauma from the past. Also for recommending Lynda Caesara.

Lynda Caesara, what can I say? I grew so much while taking her two years of energy class. Not only was I able to see my own growth, it was so amazing to see the growth of all the other people in our class. I also want to thank Lynda for recommending Jesse and Norma, who teach the third and fourth year classes.

Many thanks to my daughters, Michelle, Jaime and Yizi, who have, at different times, encouraged me to be the best I can be. I want to also thank Yizi for her illustrations of the Chakras and Core, and for taking the photo for the back cover.

Most of all I want to thank my wife, Luyu, who has shown me I am more capable of giving love and receiving love than I thought would be possible in this lifetime

Introduction

In 2009, I shared my first morning thought email. Later, I would come to call these morning thought emails, *Fresh Morning Breaths.*

A worker came to me saying he was going to quit. Later that morning, I sent this person a Buddhist quote and my commentary on the quote. After reading the email, he came over and thanked me; he added, "It helped." The next day, I sent another quote with my commentary to two people who were complaining about how their supervisor was treating them. This time they both thanked me. The following day I did not send them an email. Later that morning, the first guy came over and said: "You can't stop now."

From that day on, each workday, I have tried to send out a positive morning thought. First, it was just the two detailers. Then a few more asked if I would send it to them. Sometime later, I added my daughter Michelle. Later she asked me to add a couple of friends. Now there are around fifty people on the *Fresh Morning Breath* list.

The purpose of *Fresh Morning Breaths* is not to say the quotes shared are correct. Nor are my shared thoughts to be taken as a correct. The quotes, my thoughts, are only offered up to stimulate the reader's own thoughts.

In some ways, I have always had a positive attitude. But I certainly did not always have it together. To say the early years of my life were a struggle would be a huge understatement.

One of the things I received from the early years was agoraphobia. Another thing I received was PTSD. I would say because of these two ailments, I struggled in finding true happiness and inner peace from childhood until just the last few years.

In 1979, I was introduced to Buddhism. I think Buddhism helped me cope with day-to-day life, but did not heal me. Buddhist thought was, and is, an important part of my journey, but I feel it did not give me the inner peace I feel today—not that it doesn't for others.

In early 2010 I took my first Ipsalu Tantra class. It was later in a Level Two Ipsalu week-long retreat, after having locked energy released, I felt I was closing in on a path to healing. One lady assisting in teaching the class mentioned that I was ripe for healing and should continue my inner work. She suggested that I work with a therapist she knew and gave me Alison Teal's name.

I called Alison and set up an appointment with her. By our third session, she told me I had PTSD. For the next year, Alison helped me go back and free the frozen energy from the early years of my life. Working with Alison was a time of great healing for me. Near the end of working with her, she mentioned I should continue my energy work with Lynda Caesara.

Following Alison's advice, I signed up for Lynda's energy class. In the next two years, I learned how to set boundaries, work with my own fight-or-flight patterns, and work with other fight-or-flight patterns people use. Feeling I had received much from Lynda's class, I continued on in a third year energy class. I am now in my fourth year energy class with teachers who have been, and still are, students of Lynda's.

I feel I have experienced most of my healing in the last five years. I am nearly sixty-two years old as I am writing this. For me, this shows none of us are ever too old for a healing process.

I began Fresh Morning Breaths to support a couple of coworkers. It turns out that they have supported me along my own spiritual journey more than I could have imagined. Fresh Morning Breaths will show some of my own healing process and perhaps guide a few who may feel they need it to find their own healing and spiritual journey.

Since the writing in many of the morning thoughts were shorter than others, I have not tried to keep them in the same chronological order in which I had emailed them. Instead, I tried to format them to fill pages evenly. Also, the emails were sent out over a few years, and as new people were added to the list, some of the thoughts were repeated in slightly different ways. I hope any repetition only brings the reader to contemplate more on the given subject.

My vision reading *Fresh Morning Breaths* is one breath—or one page—one day at a time, preferably in the morning.

Life is not so much reality as it is interpretation! I hope the following pages will help others find the best possible interpretation for their lives.

Dony Hia

Around Any Corner...

In life, we never really know what lies around the next turn or corner. The following five photos were taken in Tibet after I walked around the corner. The first photo shows what first caught my eye when I made the turn. The next photos, I believe, speak more in volume than I can put to words. I don't think any need words, but I wanted to explain why I call the series of these five photos "Around Any Corner." The group I had gone to Tibet with had already left, and I was alone in there. While I have to admit there was some fear for me to do this, I decided to walk the back streets of Lhasa alone. It turned out to be a great experience, and I believe that on these back streets, I was able to take some of my best photos. These five are among my favorite. I hope you enjoy them before you read your first morning thought.

Nothing at All…

It would seem that the void and the nothingness of the mystics in not a repelling spiritual poverty but an ocean of indescribable wealth, a treasure-house of unearthly beauty. Nothing is all; darkness is light; suffering is joy.
~ William Johnston

    Mr. Johnston is correct, darkness is light, and suffering is joy; high is low; ugly is beautiful.

    In order for us to know something, we have to have something to compare it to: light to dark; wide to narrow.

    In order to have all, you have to have nothing to compare it too. In order to have nothing, you have to have all as a comparison.

    Nothing contains all! Sometimes I feel Nothing.

Best Wishes for Peace Profound
Love for All
Dony

What I am not…

One of his students asked Buddha, "Are you the messiah?"
"No", answered Buddha.
"Then are you a healer?"
"No", Buddha replied.
"Then are you a teacher?" the student persisted.
"No, I am not a teacher."
"Then what are you?" asked the student, exasperated.
"I am awake", Buddha replied.
~ Thich Nhat Hanh

From what I understand, while the Buddha was alive, he never claimed to be anything more than an awakened man. If one reads the oldest Buddhist text from the Pali language there are no, or at least very few, miracles attributed to Gautama Siddhartha of the Sakya Clan in India (known today as Buddha). The Pali texts are said to date back to about 300 BC, which is a little over 200 years after Gautama's death. If you read these texts, you can see Buddha was as much, or more, psychologist than prophet. It is in the rise of Mahayana Buddhism and the Sanskrit language, about 100 AD (or later) that miracles were attributed to Buddha and other Buddhist prophets.

Since Gautama taught that he was only a man who found a way into enlightenment, this means that we can all find our own way. Buddha more or less said, "I can point you in the direction, but you have to traverse your own way." He said not only humans, but all beings have the same Buddha nature that he had.

I have a feeling that if you lived at the time of Jesus you may have not seen any miracles, and like the Buddha, these miracles would have started showing up in writings 150 or plus years after his death. Yes death. As with Buddha or Jesus our core is never born and never dies.

Best Wishes for Peace Profound
Love for All
Dony

Find your core...

A Love that Is Unshakable Spiritual self-confidence fills one's heart with a love that is not dependent on external circumstances for its fullness. It's a love that is unshakable, unmoving, and indestructible. Such love—a love that transcends yet simultaneously embraces the world—is what compels human beings to evolve, from their own deepest depths, and to become better citizens of our world and our cosmos. Knowing the mysterious source of that love is knowing before thought that life is good. That inherent goodness is who we really are.
~ Andrew Cohen

Chogyam Trungpa Rinpoche (1939-1987), I believe, for western students changed the term Buddha Nature, our core, to *Basic Goodness*. At the core of all beings is Basic Goodness. Even the worst-seeming people are good at the core; the bad stuff resides in layers above the core.

Best Wishes for Peace Profound
Love for All
Dony

Things are not as they appear...

Know all things to be like this: A mirage, a cloud castle, a dream, an apparition, without essence, but with qualities that can be seen. Know all things to be like this: As the moon in a bright sky in some clear lake reflected, though to that lake the moon has never moved. Know all things to be like this: as an echo that derives from music, sounds, and weeping, Yet in that echo is no melody. Know all things to be like this: As a magician makes illusions of horses, oxen, carts and other things, nothing is as it appears.
~ Samadhi Raja Sutra

Monks, we who look at the whole and not just the part, know that we too are systems of interdependence, of feelings, perceptions, thoughts, and consciousness all interconnected. Investigating in this way, we come to realize that there is no me or mine in any one part, just as a sound does not belong to any one part of the lute.
~ Samyutta Nikaya, *Buddha Speaks*

While none of us are the One, each of us is a perfect reflection of the One. Together we all add up to One. It is only we who feel we are divided into separate ones; there really is only One.

Lately, through energy work, I sometimes see colors on people. I like to believe I am seeing the colors of their auras. The first time this happened was in Kentucky when I was doing energy work with someone who I now consider a close friend. I saw her face and hands turn lavender. Yesterday at the end of the session with Alison, while she was moving her hands and talking, I saw her hands turn deep purple. I have also seen reds, greens and yellows on people. People's colors change depending on their moods or where they are spiritually at any given moment.

    I like to think that if all beings dropped their flesh, all that would be left would be a rainbow of colors: dancing energy. Things are not as they appear!

Best Wishes for Peace Profound
Love for All
Dony

Just a couple stories to touch hearts…

There was a blind girl who hated herself because she was blind. She hated everyone, except her loving boyfriend, who was always there for her. She said that if she could only see the world, she would marry her boyfriend. One day, someone donated a pair of eyes to her. She could see everything, including her boyfriend. Her boyfriend asked her, "Now that you can see the world, will you marry me?"
The girl was shocked when she saw that her boyfriend was blind, and refused to marry him. Her boyfriend walked away in tears, and later wrote a letter to her saying - "Just take care of my eyes dear." ~ Author Unknown

Smile!!!!
She smiled at a sorrowful stranger. The smile seemed to make him feel better.
He remembered past kindnesses of a friend and wrote him a thank you letter.
The friend was so pleased with the thank you that he left a large tip after lunch.
The waitress surprised by the size of the tip and bet the whole thing on a hunch.
The next day she picked up her winnings, and gave part to a man on the street.
The man on the street was grateful; for two days he'd had nothing to eat.
After he finished his dinner, he left for his small dingy room.
He didn't know at that moment that he might be facing his doom.
On the way he picked up a shivering puppy and took him home to get warm.
The puppy was very grateful to be in out of the storm.
That night the house caught on fire. The puppy barked the alarm.
He barked till he woke the whole household and saved everybody from harm.
One of the boys that he rescued grew up to be President.
All this because of a simple smile that hadn't cost a cent.
~ Barbara Hauck

Last night, when I got home late from our MSSF (Mycological Society of San Francisco) meeting, I walked into the house and closed the front door. By 10:15 I was in bed. I wanted to fall asleep fast because I knew I would be getting up at 4:30 to meditate. Just as I was drifting off to sleep, Marpa started meowing, and I would say almost yelling. I yelled from my bed through the closed door for him to stop, which he did for a few moments. Then he started up even louder. This time I yelled, as loud as I could, "Marpa I am trying to sleep, and if I have to get up I am going to throw your butt outside." Marpa being true to himself just got louder.

So I jumped out of bed, opened the door and walked out of my bedroom. I saw a shadow on the floor near the back door. It was Tilo, and he had a look like *someone is in trouble and I know it is not me, so I will just chill in the back of the house*: out of sight, out of mind.

Then I looked to my right and I saw Marpa looking quite proud and satisfied, walking towards me. I looked past Marpa and saw the front door to my house was wide open. I guess I had not closed it hard enough. Instantly my frustration turned to gratitude. As I closed and made sure the door was locked, both Marpa and Tilo climbed onto the couch to go to sleep. I gave them both a kiss on the forehead, told them I loved them. I went back to bed and fell right asleep.

Marpa touched my heart last night, so I wanted to share a couple of stories I thought might touch other hearts. Whenever your heart is touched, you are awake.

Best Wishes for Peace Profound
Love for All
Dony

Only one, not two, not more...

Practice for the New Millennium:
1. Spend five minutes at the beginning of each day remembering that we all want the same things (to be happy and be loved) and we are all connected to one another.

2. Spend five minutes breathing in and cherishing yourself and, breathing out and cherishing others. If you think about people you have difficulty cherishing, extend your cherishing to them anyway.

3. During the day, extend that attitude to everyone you meet. Practice cherishing the "simplest" person (clerks, attendants, etc.) or people you dislike.

4. Continue this practice no matter what happens or what anyone does to you.

These thoughts are very simple, inspiring and helpful.
The practice of cherishing can be taken very deeply if done wordlessly, allowing yourself to feel the love and appreciation that already exists in your heart.
~ 14th Dalai Lama

We are all interconnected, and how we touch one life in some way touches all lives. If one smiles through the day, even when a little sad, the smiles when returned to you may just fill your heart with joy. Certainly nothing to lose by trying it.

Best Wishes for Peace Profound
Love for All
Dony

Wild nights...

Thought shattering itself against its own nothingness is the explosion of meditation.
~ Jiddu Krishnamurti

All last night my mind seemed to be dancing in the subconscious realm. Maybe Champa's cook undercooked the morel mushrooms.

Short versions:

First dream: At Max and Penny's house, I was in the house and most other people were outside where there was a pool. All the sudden, the sky turned black and there was lighting and thunder. The electricity went out for a moment and then came back on. I said not to worry; it was only a storm.

Then Penny said, "Your brother left holes in the pool." Next, she jumped into the pool which was supposed to be about five feet deep. She sank out of sight, and I was in the water now. I wanted to dive down and find her before she drowned, but I was fighting to get my wallet out of my pocket before it got wet. My hands seemed to be tied, and I was thinking I couldn't let her drown. At that moment, she rose headfirst and was just fine. Her clothes seemed not even to be wet.

Next I dove down into the water to where a hole was; I could see the blue lining of the pool was ripped and flapping at the spot where Penny sank. I then swam around for about ten minutes looking at other tiny tears in the lining of the pool. I was watching people swim above me. They seemed to be amazed at how long I could stay under the water and not drown.

Second dream: I leaned on Penny's butsudan (type of shrine) and broke it. In the dream, it was a very simple butsudan with an eighteen-inch shelf and then some smaller six-inch shelves. I was trying to repair the butsudan with Superglue, but I was getting the glue all over the place. Even though I was in the living room,

I got some Superglue on the refrigerator. As I tried to wipe it off, it was removing the white paint from the refrigerator. I managed to make the missing paint, match some other missing paint, on the refrigerator. When I was done it looked more like art than just peeled paint.

Third dream: I was in a nice part of a town where there were a lot of old craftsmen houses. I was standing outside of one, and I saw several small heads starting to rise out of the earth. Then I saw the hands starting to rise. A few moments later, several children started to rise from the earth. Even though no one was there, I heard a voice say a man had done an experiment, and these children were the result. I felt these children would grow into healthy happy beings.

So last night was a burst of color and images, not an explosion of meditation.

I was amazed at how much the storm in the first dream looked like the news today of the tornados that happened yesterday. I had not seen or heard about the tornados yesterday.

I really do enjoy dancing in the energy of the subconscious mind.

Best Wishes for Peace Profound
Love for All
Dony

Silence is not Golden, It is clear light…

Words stand between silence and silence: between the silence of things and the silence of our own being.
~ Thomas Merton

From moment to moment I remember with astonishment that I am at the same time empty and full.
~ Thomas Merton

There is a silent self within us whose presence is disturbing precisely because it is so silent: it can't be spoken.
~ Thomas Merton

There are three meditations I do: Analytical (where I read and study what others offer and then reflect on this), Chants and Silence.

I believe it is only through silent meditation that you can recognize the silence (Gap) which Merton spoke of. The first two meditations, for me, are for the material world. Only in silent meditation, seeing moments of no thought, can I sense the *so silent*.

All phenomena are varying vibrations of the same basic building blocks (String Theory). Rosicrucians believe it is electrical charge and magnetism that determine what the basic building blocks will be built into. For instance, a human being is vibrating at a different rate than a rock yet made up of the same basic vibrating energy.

Even thoughts cause an electrical discharge and create a small vibration which start the snowball moving. Chants create a stronger vibration, and most schools of mysticism believe certain chants vibrate with the same vibration as certain protective energies or deities.

I believe in the void (the Cosmic Mirror), the vibration has not begun. In the gap between two thoughts, one may experience this non-vibration by connecting with the Alaya Consciousness (stored consciousness).

Best Wishes for Peace Profound
Love for All
Dony

Letting go...

Mind has a self-fulfilling mechanism. Be alert to it. You are happy, the mind says, "of course, you are happy, it is okay, but what about tomorrow?" Now already the mind has distorted, destroying this moment, it has brought tomorrow in. Now tomorrow will come out of this mind, not out of that blissful moment that was there.

In this moment, if you can be your total being this moment, then there is no problem. This is the supreme accomplishment. It has no hope, it need not have. It is so perfect there is no need for hope.

Hope is not a good situation; hoping always means something is wrong with the you—that's why you hope for the "against," for the opposite. You are sad and you hope for happiness; your hope says that you are sad. You feel ugly and you hope for a beautiful personality; your hope says you are ugly. Show me your hope and I can tell you who you are, because your hope immediately shows who you are: just the opposite. Drop hope and just be. At first, if you try this, just being, this will happen:

At first the yogi feels his mind is tumbling like a waterfall; in midcourse, Like the Ganges, it flows on the slow and gentle. In the end it is a great vast ocean where the lights of son and mother merge in one.
~ Osho

This is a very tricky one because we have been programmed to hope for the future. Karma is not hope; if one is living right, in the moment, one need not hope or worry about the future or past. This does not mean suffering will not come, because we have all made causes in the past which may cause suffering. But if we know we are living right, and this means living by our hearts, not by what someone or some book says, the future will naturally evolve into enlightenment. And if there is suffering that will be enlightening, it can also be joyful. To me joyful suffering means I know I am paying a debt and I do not pull back from it. I know everything is impermanent and when the debt is paid the suffering will dissipate on its own.

Best Wishes for Peace Profound
Love for All
Dony

Open and flexible...

An empty canvas is a living wonder—far lovelier than certain pictures.
~ Wassily Kandinsky

An empty book is like an infant's soul, in which anything may be written. It is capable of all things, but containeth nothing. I have a mind to fill this with profitable wonders.
~ Thomas Traherne

An empty mind is full of potential.
~ Zen Saying

When we leave our mind free of hope and expectations, it is much easier to be accepting and flexible to whatever arises in the moment. For instance, last evening I placed some morels in water to get ready to head out and buy a few wine glasses for tonight's dinner party.

I have eight chairs and plan on having eight people. Just before I was about to leave, there was a knock on the door, and a friend and her daughter were standing there; they both had big smiles. My friend was holding a bottle of wine and a bag with something in it. I looked, smiled and said, "You know dinner is tomorrow." The emails subject had read "Thursday night morel and prawn dinner." My friend laughed and said, "I guess I wanted it to be today because I can't make Thursday." I invited them in and said I would cook a smaller portion of the dinner tonight. After convincing my friend I really wanted to do it, she offered to help.

With help, everything came together rather quickly and we had a nice dinner of: baked morels and prawns covered in butter, pesto pasta with trumpet mushrooms and sun dried tomatoes, asparagus with a sauce made of mayonnaise tabasco, soy sauce and curry. Everything went together so well that the three dishes seemed to have at least ten different flavors. I felt for dessert some mango rice from Champa's would be perfect. I walked across the street and placed two orders. My friend picked it up, and it was a splendid finish for a great meal. I am sure she exaggerated, but she said it was the best meal she had had.

Since my friend and her daughter came twenty-four hours early, it opened two chairs, so I invited the owners of Champa Garden Restaurant for tonight's dinner.

All of this came together because we were open and flexible. If any of our minds had thought, *well, this can't happen because the morel and prawn dinner is tomorrow,* there would not have been such a great dinner and great evening last night.

Best Wishes for Peace Profound
Love for All
Dony

A few thoughts from Buddha...

Holding on to anger is like grasping a hot coal with the intent of throwing it at someone else; you are the one who gets burned.
~ Buddha

You will not be punished for your anger; you will be punished by your anger.
~ Buddha

To be idle is a short road to death and to be diligent is a way of life; foolish people are idle, wise people are diligent.
~ Buddha

An insincere and evil friend is more to be feared than a wild beast; a wild beast may wound your body, but an evil friend will wound your mind.
~ Buddha

In some Buddhist thought it is believed we tend to live mainly in one of ten worlds (listed below). These are not so much actual worlds as they are states of mind.

If we hold anger in our mind we tend to live in a state of self-created hell. If we tend to hold joy in our mind, we tend to live in humanity or even higher.

Notice heaven is not the highest. The reason heaven is not the highest is because we can get caught up in heaven. In the heaven realm we can forget we are all interconnected and lose compassion for fellow man who may be living in a lower world. It is said if we don't try and bring others with us, when our heaven karma is used up, we may fall into one of the lower worlds.

When one lives mainly in one of the four noble realms, this person is less likely to slip backwards. Future births will be advantageous for living mainly in the four upper worlds.

Each world also contains the possibility of the other nine, and it is because of this that we can evolve higher. This teaching is for living in relative reality. It is said in absolute reality, that we are all already Buddha. The universe is a perfect reflection of the cosmic mirror in every moment.

Best Wishes for Peace Profound
Love for All
Dony

Six realms of Desire
1. Hell
2. Hunger
3. Animalistic
4. Arrogance (or anger)
5. Humanity (or passionate idealism)
6. Heaven (or rapture)

Four upper Worlds
7. Learning
8. Realization (or absorption)
9. Bodhisattva-hood
10. Buddha-hood

The Big Thought...

What Is Evolution?
Whenever I explain what evolution is, I say simply this: Evolution is a cosmic process that is going somewhere in and through time. And we are all part of that process. This simple fact is potentially life-transforming, but it›s also hard to grasp at a deep level. The process that created us is moving. We tend to see the world around us as static. But it›s not. It›s going somewhere. We're going somewhere. Awakening to this truth about all of manifestation changes the way we see the world around us and our place in it. The biggest and most important part of this awakening is that we discover our power to affect where the process that created us is going. We realize the ultimate reason for our own existence: to be a spiritual hero, to boldly take responsibility for the future of the process itself.
~ Andrew Cohen

We tend to think of evolution in terms of Darwin, something happening outwardly over many generations. Whatever manifests outwardly has already, some time before, manifested inwardly on a spiritual level. Whether it is a new form of art, technology or even a new species, before it awakens in the outer realm of phenomena, it has already manifested in the inner spiritual realm of thought. In the Bible it says, *"In the beginning was the Word, and the Word was with God, and the Word was God"* (John 1:1). I would beg to disagree: in the beginning was thought. Have you ever tried to say a word without a thought coming before it? Even a parrot has to think before it mimics a word. The first thought was probably so powerful it burst out into what we know as the big bang, and this thought has been multiplying and expanding ever since. I think most Physicist believe this thought (universe) is ever expanding. Some believe the expansion will slow down, and then the universe will eventually collapse back down upon itself. The many will really become the One again.

For interesting reading on the universe, type *The Expanding Universe* into your search engine.

Best Wishes for Peace Profound
Love for All
Dony

Only one...

In looking for my mind, I discovered that it seems to be in many different places. Sometimes it is drinking a glass of water, remembering swimming in the summer, feeling the breeze. In this contemplation I observed that the self is more elusive than I thought.
~ Sakyong Mipham

One could spend a lifetime searching for mind or self and will never find it. It is through sitting in meditation that we can realize there is no *self* and no *other*. We may see the watcher but the watcher is not self it is one with the One.

Best Wishes for Peace Profound
Love for All
Dony

A few thoughts from Thoreau…

As a single footstep will not make a path on the earth, so a single thought will not make a pathway in the mind. To make a deep physical path, we walk again and again. To make a deep mental path, we must think over and over the kind of thoughts we wish to dominate our lives.
~ Henry David Thoreau

Thoreau has often been called the first American Buddhist. While he may not have actually been Buddhist, he certainly was influenced by Eastern thought. His time spent in nature is much like what the Buddha supposedly told the monks of his order: "Spend time in the forest in solitude and meditation."

Rick Fields wrote,

> Thoreau died in 1862. When a friend asked him on his deathbed if he had made his peace with God he responded, more like a Zen master than a transcendentalist, which he was not aware they had quarreled. How deeply he had gone, and how closely his friends identified him with the Orientals, is apparent in the description John Weiss gave in 1865:
>
> His countenance had not a line upon it expressive of ambition or discontent; the affectional emotions had not fretted at it. He went about like a priest of Buddha who expects to arrive soon at the summit of a life of contemplation.

Best Wishes for Peace Profound
Love for All
Dony

Tilopa on non-attachment...

Have a mind that is open to everything, and attached to nothing.
~ Tilopa

The problem is not enjoyment, the problem is attachment.
~ Tilopa

It's not the appearance that binds you; it's the attachment to the appearance that binds you.
~ Tilopa

    While my own spiritual practice is evolving within me, I do consider Kagyu to be one of many lineages that helps me understand my own world.

    Tilopa is regarded as the human founder of the Kagyu lineage of Tibetan Buddhism. Kagyu tradition believes Tilopa received the teaching directly from the Buddha Vajradhara.

    While Kagyu is of Tibetan Buddhist lineage, a lot of the Tantric and Yogic practices used in many Buddhist traditions date back to before the time of Buddha. There were many sages and profits in India hundreds, if not thousands of years, before Buddha. Buddha incorporated some of these earlier practices that came before him into his own practices.

Best Wishes for Peace Profound
Love for All
Dony

Find the switch...

Things derive their being and nature by mutual dependence and are nothing in themselves.
~ Nagarjuna

Just as the grammarian makes one study grammar, A Buddha teaches according to the tolerance of his students; Some he urges to refrain from sins, others to do good, Some to rely on dualism, other on non-dualism; And to some he teaches the profound, The terrifying, the practice of enlightenment, Whose essence is emptiness that is compassion.
~ Nagarjuna

A Buddha teaches according to the audience's ability to understand. A person seeking a spiritual life needs to learn his, or her, own nature in deciding what is the best path.

If you realize your nature is more like a cat than a dog, live with the wild nature of a cat and not the loyalty of a dog. Each of us comes into this world with our own nature and gifts, and it is up to each of us to find and develop these gifts. Once we develop our gifts we can share them with the world.

Others can be teachers and guides, but it is up to each being to find their own inner light. Not even a Buddha or a god can give or take this light away.

Find the switch, turn on the light and shine brightly!

Best Wishes for Peace Profound
Love for All
Dony

Freeing souls...

A Confidence That Frees the Human Soul:
Spiritual confidence is the unique and palpable sense of absolute conviction that cannot be affected by external or internal fluctuations. It is knowing before you know that you know. It's the highest gift and blessing that comes only from the deepest insight into the true nature of things, which destroys existential doubt and frees the human soul. It is a confidence that comes from knowing that mystery which is ungraspable. The kind of spiritual confidence I am speaking about is different from any other kind of confidence we might be familiar with because it comes from a very different source and from a very different part of the self.
~ Andrew Cohen

That confidence, for much of my life, was an unknown term for me. I hid it well (never let them see you sweat), but I knew I lacked confidence.

Confident Agoraphobia* is an oxymoron. I was also an oxymoron—I was an Agoraphobic who longed for attention. When in the safety of family or friends, where I could relax, I guess I could be quite entertaining. Drink also helped me with overcoming the fear of the Agora, even at the ripe old age of thirteen. Pot multiplied the fear ten times over; no wonder I was not fond of pot.

I guess if I did have any confidence, it was that I had a good, soft heart. I did not know what to do with it, but I knew had one. Finally, after thirty-two years of Buddhist practice, four years after overcoming agoraphobia, one year of doing intense energy/EMDR work and, most importantly, sharing *Fresh Morning Breaths* with family and friends for nearly two years,

I have gained an inner peace and confidence that in the past I thought I might never know in this life. Thank all of you!

*Agoraphobia: a condition characterized by an irrational fear of public or open spaces.

Best Wishes for Peace Profound
Love for All
Dony

Leaving trails…

I do not know which to prefer
The beauty of inflections
Or the beauty of innuendoes,
The blackbird whistling
Or just after.
~ Wallace Stevens

Some lovely glorious nothing did I see.
~ John Donne

    Often when I see a bird fly overhead, it leaves a trail in my mind just like a jet often leaves a trail in the sky.

    Lost loves can also leave trails in our mind, as can present loves. It seems I have grown as much from losing love as I have having love.

    May I continue to grow!

Best Wishes for Peace Profound
Love for All
Dony

Inside out...

Do not speak- unless it improves on silence.
~ Buddhist Saying

You can explore the universe looking for somebody who is more deserving of your love and affection than you are yourself, and you will not find that person anywhere.
~ Buddhist Saying

We often forget we need to take care of and nurture ourselves before we can take care of and nurture others. Only to the extent to which we have created joy, love and happiness inwardly can we share it outwardly. Also, to the extent we are enlightened inwardly, we can share this enlightenment outwardly.

Still working hard on the innards.

Best Wishes for Peace Profound
Love for All
Dony

It is, what it is…

Some changes look negative on the surface but you will soon realize that space is being created in your life for something new to emerge.
~ Eckhart Tolle

Life will give you whatever experience is most helpful for the evolution of your consciousness. How do you know this is the experience you need? Because this is the experience you are having at the moment.
~ Eckhart Tolle

In relative Reality the past does have some power over the present because the past laid down the foundation for now. I would say the past has less power over the future because how we react to this moment will lay down the foundation for the future. In absolute reality, there is no past, present or future but it is hard for our un-enlightened minds to comprehend this. Even though we only experience it once in a while, we all have moments that are outside of time.

Negative and Positive are another illusion; there just *Is*! It is our ego that attaches good, bad or indifferent; our ego creates subject/object where there is only One and that One is *Now*.

If you are happy, everything before the moment of this happiness seems right. If you are unhappy, everything before this moment of unhappiness seems wrong. Yet, in absolute reality there is no right or wrong; there is just *Isness*!

Best Wishes for Peace Profound
Love for All
Dony

Step over those beliefs...

One day Mara, the Evil One, was travelling through the villages of India with his attendants. He saw a man doing walking meditation whose face was lit up in wonder. The man had just discovered something on the ground in front of him. Mara's attendant asked what it was, and Mara replied, "A piece of truth." "Doesn't this bother you when someone finds a piece of truth, O Evil One?" his attendant asked. "No," Mara replied. "Right after this, they usually make a belief out of it.
~ Benny Liow, *108 Treasures for the Heart: A Guide for Daily Living*

If only we could let go of our beliefs, each moment would be fresh and new, and we would be in awe. Normally we experience something, and for a split second, we are in the moment. Then our mind compares this experience to something in the past or something we want, or fear, about the future and we lose the Awe moment. The older and wiser I become, the fewer beliefs I seem to hold on to.

A student asked Suzuki Roshi why the Japanese make their teacups so thin and delicate that they break easily. "It's not that they're too delicate," he answered, "but that you don't know how to handle them. You must adjust yourself to the environment, and not vice versa." ~ David Chadwick, *To Shine One Corner of the World: Moments with Shunryu Suzuki: Stories of a Zen Teacher Told by His Students*

It is written, the Buddha always adjusted his talks to the capacities of his listeners; he never tried to adjust his listeners to his talks.

Best Wishes for Peace Profound
Love for All
Dony

Erasing patterns...

If only I could throw away the urge to trace my patterns in *your* heart, I could *really see you.*
~ David Brandon, *Zen in the Art of Helping*

Mindfulness is the aware, balanced acceptance of the present experience. It isn't more complicated than that. It is opening to, or receiving the present moment, pleasant or unpleasant, just as it is, without either clinging to it or rejecting it.
~ Sylvia Boorstein

    When I came across the first quote above, it really touched me. My first thought is, is how I see my relationships with my daughters and grandson. I don't try to place anything in their hearts. I joyfully and supportively sit back and watch these three hearts open and blossom like the most beautiful flowers that one can imagine. I feel so blessed and overwhelmed with joy that I can even think I may have helped fertilize these flowers in the slightest way. My eyes are watery but my own heart is as light as a feather. I am at a point in my life where I am able to do this with my friends as well. Thank you All!

    Butterfly, the sun is jealous this morning; an hour before he could climb above the horizon your call lit up my space.

Best Wishes for Peace Profound
Love for All
Dony

This is your day, hopefully there will be many more…

From a Buddhist point of view, the actual experience of death is very important. Although how or where we will be reborn is generally dependent on karmic forces, our state of mind at the time of death can influence the quality of our next rebirth. So at the moment of death, in spite of the great variety of karmas we have accumulated, if we make a special effort to generate a virtuous state of mind, we may strengthen and activate a virtuous karma, and so bring about a happy rebirth.
~ 14th Dalai Lama

This day is a special day, it is yours.
Yesterday slipped away, it cannot be filled anymore with meaning.
About tomorrow nothing is known.
But this day, today, is yours, make use of it.
Today you can make someone happy.
Today you can help another.
This day is a special day, it is yours.
~ Vijaya Samarawickrama, *A Buddhist Reflects on Happy Living*

And then we die! If one truly understands the importance of this comment, it can wake you up right on the spot. It is actually only our flesh and the mind, which we have until the time of death, which perishes; our awareness and a string of consciousness continues forever. How you live now will decide how you will live somewhere in the future. This is not much different than planning for your future in this life.

Best Wishes for Peace Profound
Love for All
Dony

Be thankful you have an empty mind…

*The beauty of life is, while we cannot undo what is done,
we can see it, understand it, learn from it and change.
So that every new moment is spent not in regret, guilt,
fear or anger, but in wisdom, understanding and love.*
~ Jennifer Edwards

*Like it or not, if you look at your own mind you will discover it is
void and groundless; as insubstantial as empty space.*
~ Padmasambhava

    It is because our lives are really empty that all is possible. If there was anything fixed about our minds or surroundings things could not change. The thing that is not changeless is not of us; we are of it. True awareness is changeless, and while we might think it is we who are aware, awareness is much more than any one of us. Awareness is the One.

Best Wishes for Peace Profound
Love for All
Dony

Learning to Fly...

When you have come to the edge of all light that you know, and are about to drop off into the darkness of the unknown, Faith is knowing One of two things will happen: There will be something solid to stand on or You will be taught to fly.
~ Patrick Overton

    The woman with whom I've been working with, Alison, has recommended I do energy work with a woman named Lynda. She said this will develop the natural intuition and psychic powers that seem to be rising in me. I went online and I was amazed at how many people (healers of different types) mention they have studied or now study under Lynda. I talked to her last night and plan on starting classes in September.

    When I woke up, I thought of a recurring dream I had when I was young and full of vision, hopes and dreams. The dream always started with me standing on a cliff, mountain or some other high object. Even though fearful, I would dive off the edge. Always, just a couple of feet before I hit ground or water, I would pull up and take off flying. As I got older, and sometimes recently, I have had dreams in which I am flying and teaching others how to fly. How can I truly teach others to fly, if I don't learn to fly myself? Lately I hear the voice say, "Climb to the Edge." Talking with Lynda last night, not only do I think she will point me to the edge, she will push me out of the nest. I hope for my sake, not hers, I learn to fly.

Best Wishes for Peace Profound
Love for All
Dony

Emptiness and Fullness are married...

I think about the "empty" space a lot. That emptiness is what allows for something to actually evolve in a natural way. I've had to learn that over the years—because one of the traps of being an artist is to always want to be creating, always wanting to produce.
~ Meredith Monk

Don't play with what's there. Play what's not there.
~ Miles Davis

In art classes, they teach students to work as much with the negative spaces (empty spaces) as much as the positive spaces. Without emptiness, there is no fullness. According to Buddhist thought, there is no environment anywhere that does not contain life; even in what appears to be empty space to our naked eyes there is life. Buddhist thought says there is life everywhere; it may not be life as we know it, but there is life everywhere. Even the vibrating atoms that make up dust have spirit in them.

Best Wishes for Peace Profound
Love for All
Dony

Even a Smile...

Thousands of candles can be lighted from a single candle, and the life of the candle will not be shortened. Happiness never decreases by being shared. We are shaped by our thoughts; we become what we think. When the mind is pure, joy follows like a shadow that never leaves.
~ Buddha, *The Dhammapada*

If we just give out one smile in the morning, this smile may multiply to hundreds of smiles by the end of the day.

When we bring joy to someone, they tend to share that feeling of joy. May all reading this feel Joy; and then share that joy!

Best Wishes for Peace Profound
Love for All
Dony

Innards and Outwards…

The only reason we don't open our hearts and minds to other people is that they trigger confusion in us that we don't feel brave enough or sane enough to deal with. To the degree that we look clearly and compassionately at ourselves, we feel confident and fearless about looking into someone else's eyes.
~ Pema Chodron

Know thyself, and thou shalt know the Universe and God.
~ Pythagoras

When I was young, I used to say: if you turned me inside out, the universe would not be large enough to hold everything. Now that I am older, I am convinced this is true with all people. If we turn our awareness inward, we never reach the bottom or an end; we can think anything we want and create any world we choose in this inner world. The more we understand this inner world, the more we understand the outer world. At some point we come to realize that everything, fear, joy etc., we experience in our outer world is an expression of our inner world. When there is joy in our inner world, there is joy in our outer world. When there is fear in our inner world, there is fear in our outer world. If we find enlightenment in our inner world we will find enlightenment in our outer world.

Best Wishes for Peace Profound
Love for All
Dony

Ride the Stallion…

Your Best Friend and Your Worst Enemy
The ego, or individuated self-sense, is both your best friend and your worst enemy. It is your best friend because, in the most positive sense, it represents your capacity to individuate—to see yourself as a unique, autonomous entity and to bear witness to your own experience with some measure of objectivity. Individuation is what makes it possible for you to be a conscious agent of evolution, a vessel for Spirit in action. The more profound our individuation, the more powerfully Spirit can shine through us. However, ego is also our worst enemy. And this is because, for too many of us, over-identification with our separate individuality obscures the deeper and higher spiritual dimensions of our being. It is very important to understand this paradoxical nature of ego if you, as an individual, want to take responsibility for creating the future, as yourself.
~ Andrew Cohen

Look for Buddha outside your own mind, and Buddha becomes the devil.
~ Dogen

Hell is not punishment, it's training.
~ Shunryu Suzuki

    One's mind is like a wild stallion. If you try to tame a wild stallion with the whip and cruelty you may break the horse. A horse with a broken spirit may carry you but it will always do it grudgingly. A wild stallion will always want you off its back. If you tame the stallion with love and treats, it will feel joyful when it carries you wherever you want to go. Don't try and push your ego away; tame it with love and treats. This is the Tantric Way.

Best Wishes for Peace Profound
Love for All
Dony

A few shared thoughts from Tolle…

The primary cause of unhappiness is never the situation but your thoughts about it.
~ Eckhart Tolle

All true artists, whether they know it or not, create from a place of no-mind, from inner stillness.
~ Eckhart Tolle

Time isn't precious at all, because it is an illusion. What you perceive as precious is not time but the one point that is out of time: the Now. That is precious indeed. The more you are focused on time—past and future—the more you miss the Now, the most precious thing there is.
~ Eckhart Tolle

In the second to the last quote, Eckhart speaks of a place of no-mind. In the last quote, he mentions how time is an illusion. Buddhists point out that mind itself is also an illusion. Try as you might, you can never find a mind residing in your body, or out of your body, for that matter. You can find a brain, but that is not your mind. The brain is more of a transmitter sending and receiving thoughts that are in line with its wiring. The thoughts that pass through you are also not yours; like art, they come from and return to no mind (the cosmic mirror, void).

If you want to change your thought process, you have to change your wiring. There are many ways to change the wiring—books, diet, affirmations, and a host of others. I believe a great way to rewire one's self is meditation. Meditation brings us to the place of no-mind.

Best Wishes for Peace Profound
Love for All
Dony

Don't accept on face value alone...

Believe nothing on the faith of traditions, even though they have been held in honor for many generations and in diverse places. Do not believe a thing because many people speak of it. Do not believe on the faith of the sages of the past. Do not believe what you yourself have imagined, persuading yourself that a God inspires you. Believe nothing on the sole authority of your masters and priests. After examination, believe what you yourself have tested and found to be reasonable, and conform your conduct thereto.
~ Buddha

If a practice brings peace and joy to you and others and brings no harm, it is a good practice. If a practice brings peace to yourself but harm to others, or peace to others and harm to yourself, it is a practice you should walk away from.

Tantra embraces the natural energies of the bodies and connects you with cosmic, universal energy. It is becoming one with the other, and the very cosmos itself.
~ Swami Nostradamus Virato

We are already connected because there is only One. We have always been One, we don't have to become one with the cosmic; we just have to remember we always have been. Connecting is remembering.

Best Wishes for Peace Profound
Love for All
Dony

Love Your Inner World, and You Will Love Your Outer World…

Great compassion penetrates into the marrow of the bone. It is the support of all living beings.
Like the love of a parent for an only child, the tenderness of the Compassionate One is all-pervasive.
~ Nagarjuna

Whoever wishes to attain Buddhahood need not follow the various practices but must only practice one thing and that is deep compassion.
~ Chenrezig

This weekend, I started reading the first required book, *Eastern Body Western Mind* by Anodea Judith, for the two-year energy class I am starting in September. The book is 458 pages, and I read 246 pages this past weekend. The book is a good quick read with lots of information. This book is right in line with the work I have been doing with Alison. I would say if you want to know why you are or how you became who you are, I highly recommend this book. The full title of the book is *Eastern Body Western Mind: Psychology and the Chakra System as a Path to the Self*. I have read several books on Tantra and Kundalini that cover the Chakras. These books are usually from an Eastern perspective and often hard to grasp if you have not done a lot of spiritual work. With Anodea Judith's book you need not have any previous introduction.

By reading it, I am getting a better understanding of the work I am doing with Alison. During my next visit Alison is going to do a rebirthing session with me. I am excited and a little nervous all at the same time.

I posted the reading list the for the first year's class. I am sure anyone wanting to understand their inner self would benefit from reading any of the books below. I read *Creative Visualization* by Shakti Gawain 30 years ago and *Waking the Tiger* by Peter Levine in 2004.

We can only show great compassion and love to others to the same extent that we have great compassion and great love for our own being.

Best Wishes for Peace Profound
Love for All
Dony_

Eastern Body Western Mind, Anodea Judith
Hands of Light (Chapters 12&13), Barbara Brennan
Light Emerging (Chapter 15)
Creative Visualization, Shakti Gawain
Boundaries, Cloud & Townsend
The Amazing Power of Deliberate Intent, Ester & Jerry Hicks
The Power of Intention, Wayne Dyer (optional)
Waking the Tiger, Peter Levine
Dancing the Dream, Jamie Sams
Giant Steps, Barry Kaufman
The Tao of Equus, Linda Kohano
Riding Between the Worlds, Linda Kohanov
Growing Yourself Back Up, John Lee
Facing the Fire, John Lee
Raising Great Kids, Cloud & Townsend

It's All Inside...

Within this body exist Mount Meru, the seven continents, lakes, oceans, mountains, plains and the protectors of these plains. In it also dwell the seers, the sages, all the stars and planets, the sacred river crossings and pilgrimage centers and the deities of these centers. In it whirl the sun and the moon, which are the causes of creation and annihilation. Likewise, it contains ether, air, fire, water and earth. All beings embodied in the three worlds, which are connected to Mount Meru, exist in the body together with all their activities. He who knows all this is a yogin. There is no doubt about this.
~ Shiva-Samhita

The microcosm is a reflection of the macrocosm and each of us hold the entire universe within.

The entire architecture of the universe is faithfully mirrored in our own body mind.
~ George Feuerstein, *The Path of Ecstasy*

To the extent you know the universe within you, you know the universe outside of you. Anything you seek outside of you is really already within you; you just need to manifest it.

Best Wishes for Peace Profound
Love for All
Dony

A few thoughts from Osho and from Dony...

The witnessing soul is like the sky. The birds fly in the sky but they don't leave any footprints. That's what Buddha says, that the man who is awakened lives in such a way that he leaves no footprints. He is without wounds and without scars; he never looks back -- there is no point. He has lived that moment so totally that what is the need to look back again and again? He never looks ahead, he never looks back, and he lives in the moment.
~ Osho

We all have scars, some of us more than others. As we let these scars go, it opens up space in us for new positive or negative thoughts; we get to choose.

I have pretty much finished my trauma work with Alison; I have rescued pretty much any little Donny, Duke, or Don that needed to be rescued, and I have opened up a space for any others to walk from the past, safely to the present moment.

Alison mentioned, as I left yesterday, a thick folder in a pretty short time. I am amazed to realize each of us can go back and rewrite our memories. I first learned this in Ipsula Tantra but really fulfilled it with Alison.

Now, that I have worked through my trauma with Alison, I will start working with her on who I want to be now. I hope to enter this process with and empty mind. As Zen Buddhists say, "An Empty Mind is Full of Potential."

Best Wishes for Peace Profound
Love for All
Dony

Silence in the Light...

Silence reveals itself in a thousand inexpressible forms: in the quiet of dawn, in the noiseless aspiration of tees towards the sky, in the stealthy decent of the night, in the silent changing of the seasons, in the falling moonlight, trickling down into the night like a rain of silence, but above all in the silence of the inward soul.
~ Max Picard

    I liked this sentence by Picard; in between each comma, I experienced a different silence. After the last comma, I experienced a deep peace.

    If you can, take two minutes; be very still, very silent, and place your awareness deep within your core. Place your awareness as if trying to experience a different dimension, where there is only a clear light of silence. If you can, you have found the path that can lead back home.

Best Wishes for Peace Profound
Love for All
Dony

Kicks & Licks are not all bad...

Forget like a child any injury done by somebody immediately. Never keep it in the heart. It kindles hatred.
~ Swami Sivananda

There is something good in all seeming failures. You are not to see that now. Time will reveal it. Be patient.
~ Swami Sivananda

The more I seem to walk my destined path, the more I realize each moment has been perfect in and of itself. While moments of rewards and pleasures too were perfect, it was the licks, kicks, feelings of insecurity and loneliness, with perfect timing, that really have polished the spirit within.

I have found a path for my healing; hopefully I can share some knowledge so others can also find their own paths to heal in their own ways.

Best Wishes for Peace Profound
Love for All
Dony

No Ground…

If we're willing to give up hope that insecurity and pain can be exterminated, then we can have the courage to relax with the groundlessness of our situation. This is the first step on the path.
~ Pema Chodron

We try to find a place to ground ourselves to. Whether it be a job, family, money, religion, etc., these are all things that we grasp at thinking we can ground ourselves and find some type of security. In this life, there is no real security in the world; the rug can always be pulled out from under us. We can lose our job, our wives or husbands, our money and even our religious beliefs. The one thing that we can be sure of, and it is on the inside not the outside, is that our watcher will always be there. If we are aware of, and trust our watcher, we can find a deep peace inside no matter what happens on the outside.

Best Wishes for Peace Profound
Love for All
Dony

Dream the Dream...

I don't use drugs, my dreams are frightening enough.
~ M. C. Escher

He felt that his whole life was some kind of dream and he sometimes wondered whose it was and whether they were enjoying it.
~ Douglas Adams

"The world, indeed, is like a dream and the treasures of the world are an alluring mirage! Like the apparent distances in a picture, things have no reality in themselves, but they are like heat haze."
~ Buddha

    I was quite amazed by one of my dreams last night. It started with me dreaming I heard news of an old friend, Rod, dying. I was not sure, in the dream, if the news was true or not. Then I saw a maroon car pulling up alongside me; in the car was Rod's widow, whose face was distorted; she was crying. She stepped out of the car and I consoled her. This is the short version the dream; it actually had much more content. I even said as I was leaving the dream and waking up "this dream is like a movie."
    I went back to sleep, and I immediately started dreaming again. In this dream, I was going out to dinner with a friend. As I was getting dressed to leave, I found some gold jewelry. I put a golden trinket on a chain and put it around my neck. At dinner the guy with me, I don't know who he was, made a comment about the small trinket. I opened the lid on the trinket. The piece became larger and more valuable. Within the piece was the power of Buddha and the sages. It seemed to have the power to attract spirits and help them take on bodies. Then the dream changed and I was going along a road, with old cabins on my right side. I looked in some of the cabins, and I could see couples being brought together to copulate and bring forth their bodies for the spirits. In some cases they were

human; in some cases they were part human and part animals; in other cases they seemed to be otherworldly beings. At this point I half awakened and said to myself, this dream is too good to let go now. Again, this is a short version. There was way too much detail to write down in just a few minutes.

I went right back to sleep and continued dreaming. This time I was standing on ground in the sky next to a wall made of clouds. As I stood there, I could see eight beings standing in the air getting ready to fall to earth to take on their upcoming birth. One of the beings I was seeing was me. Each being was represented by the adult body they would grow into.

As I looked at the eight beings I realized I was dreaming. While looking at the eight I thought to myself, I am dreaming and it seems like I have been dreaming for an hour. I also thought, this dream was so real I can even feel it. I reached out and touched one of the beings with the fingertips of my right hand. In the dream I could feel the fingers touch the being. Next I thought, I am dreaming, and when I awaken I will be the only being that will remember this; the rest of you will be on to another existence where you won't remember.

I awoke feeling blessed for having been able to have such a lucid dream.

Best Wishes for Peace Profound
Love for All
Dony

Silence to sound, and then back to silence again…

If speech is worth one sela (a small coin so-called), silence is worth two.
~ The Talmud

Experience teaches that silence terrifies people the most.
~ Bob Dylan

    Funny how uncomfortable most people can be with silence! Yet, it is from silence that all great works, and not so great, come from.

    If you want to try something interesting, the next time you are listening to someone talk, do more than just listen to what they are saying. Also try to figure out where the sound comes from and where the sound goes when they finish. You might be surprised to realize the sound comes from even deeper than the person talking. You might realize that the sound is coming from the void and then returns back to the void. If you realize this then you might question: Is the sound this person's, or is it even greater than this person?

Best Wishes for Peace Profound
Love for All
Dony

Healing Cycles…

Healing cycles can only be opened up to, watched, and validated; they cannot be evaluated, manipulated, hurried, or changed. When they get the time and attention they need, they are able to complete their healing mission.
~ Peter A. Levine, *Awakening the Tiger*

In Buddhist thought, we are all healing, evolving back to the Buddhas we forgot we are. No being is left behind. Each of us, depending on our Karma, sets the pace of our healing (evolving back to spiritual beings). To the extent we heal a condition, we can point out how others might heal the same condition. Anytime we help another being we are a bodhisattva, ("Awakened Truth" or "Enlightenment Being").

Best Wishes for Peace Profound
Love for All
Dony

Forever young…

It takes a long time to become young.
~ Pablo Picasso

    Yes, it seems the more we learn, study and connect with our core spirit, the younger our heart and soul feels.

We are not human beings on a spiritual journey; we are spiritual beings on a human journey.
~ Steven R Covey

    When we do let go of the flesh, the spirit lives on, recharges and takes on another incarnation. We are forever young.

Best Wishes for Peace Profound
Love for All
Dony

Homesick…

I'm an ex-citizen of nowhere. Sometimes I get mighty homesick.
~ From the movie, *Paint Your Wagon*

    Whether one realizes it or not, we are all homesick to get back to the One from which we all originated. Those who do realize it, on some level, take up a spiritual or a mystical path.

Best Wishes for Peace Profound
Love for All
Dony

Maybe you Just need to change the station…

Character cannot be developed in ease and quiet. Only through experience of trial and suffering can the soul be strengthened, ambition inspired, and success achieved.
~ Helen Keller

No one has a right to consume happiness without producing it.
~ Helen Keller

When I was brushing my teeth this morning, I was thinking about a *Fresh Morning Breath* thought, and for some reason Helen Keller quotes came to mind. Funny how these thoughts float around the universe, just waiting for someone on the right frequency to pick them up. If your frequency is to pick up good, happy thoughts, this is what you will receive. If your frequency is for negativity, that is what you will receive.

What is really great, whether you realize it or not, is that you are in charge of the remote control.

Best Wishes for Peace Profound
Love for All
Dony

Blindly bright is our Orb!

Accept what comes from silence. Make the best you can of it. Of the little words that come out of the silence, like prayers prayed back to the one who prays, make a poem that does not disturb the silence from which it came.
~ Wendell Berry

I really like what Berry says above. The silence (cosmic mirror) has never been disturbed and will never be disturbed. This is one of the laws of the universe. There is also a silent place in all of us that cannot be disturbed or tarnished. If you want to have an idea of what that silence is, imagine a bright white, sun-like orb in the middle of your heart chakra. Imagine, even as brightly as this orb shines, it never uses up energy. There is a dot (tingle) in all of us that is eternal, in the same way the cosmic mirror is eternal. The cosmic mirror is there even before a universe is born or dies.

Best Wishes for Peace Profound
Love for All
Dony

A few thoughts by a few wise people…

Never discourage anyone who continually makes progress, no matter how slow.
~ Aristotle

Flatter me, and I may not believe you. Criticize me, and I may not like you. Ignore me, and I may not forgive you. Encourage me, and I may not forget you.
~ William Arthur

The scars you acquire by exercising courage will never make you feel inferior.
~ D.A. Battista

    I read in the book *The Path of the Buddha* by Kenneth W. Morgan how different people of different mindsets should meditate. It was written some should focus on breath, others on a small object, such as a small round object, others on a candle flame, etc. In further reading, it was written those who are witty should meditate on death. I consider myself somewhat witty and I have meditated on death (in a positive way) for years.

    I often add at the end of a conversation: and then we die. This simple statement always seems to put things in proper perspective, at least for me.

    A few examples: I just lost $70,000, and then we die. I just had the greatest night of my life, and then we die. By this meditation alone, we can keep ourselves from being swayed by blame or fame.

    Knowing that death could come at any moment should be enough to encourage us to live life to its fullest.

Best Wishes for Peace Profound
Love for All
Dony

Start Your Peeling Today…

Inside this new love, die.
Your way begins on the other side.
Become the sky.
Take an axe to the prison wall.
Escape.
Walk out like someone suddenly born into color.
Do it now.
You're covered with thick clouds.
Slide out the side. Die,
and be quiet. Quietness is the surest sign
that you've died.
Your old life was a frantic running
from silence.
The speechless full moon
comes out now.
~ Rumi, translated by Coleman Barks

A person who I have never met sent me an email. Like many of us, she is dealing with stress and in one part of the email wrote, "I just want to jump off the spinning earth for a moment while I take a breather."

We have all felt like this at times and we know we cannot jump off the earth. We can, though, jump into Peace. This peace cannot be found outside by a deity. It can only be found by diving in. We have to go inside and peel the layers away until we find nothing left to peel away. If we can do that what we experience is awe, unconditional love and unshakable peace. We all have moments like this; the trick is to combine these moments into hours, days, months and then to a way of life.

Some say: "Live in the world but not of it!"

Best Wishes for Peace Profound
Love for All
Dony

A few thoughts from Albert Einstein…

I see only with deep regret that God punishes so many of His children for their numerous stupidities, for which only He Himself can be held responsible; in my opinion, only His nonexistence could excuse Him.
~ Albert Einstein

The intuitive mind is a sacred gift and the rational mind is a faithful servant. We have created a society that honors the servant and has forgotten the gift.
~ Albert Einstein

There are two ways to live your life. One is as though nothing is a miracle. The other is as though everything is a miracle.
~ Albert Einstein

    I feel mankind is evolving to the next level, and that is how future generations will survive; and not all of them will live on this planet. This future being, which will be a continuation of us, will think of us as we think of Neanderthals. I also feel this species will require less material, such as food, to exist. If this is not the case, the planet will not be able to sustain so many creatures.

Best Wishes for Peace Profound
Love for All
Dony

Nothing to be done or undone…

In pursuit of Knowledge, every day something is added. In the practice of the Tao, every day something is dropped. Less and less do you need to force things, until finally you arrive at non-action. When nothing is done, nothing is left undone.
~ Lao Tzu

This is the peace of Buddha, the total silence—because there is nothing to achieve, no one to achieve, nowhere to go, and no one to go. Everything empty.
~ Osho

    If we are truly living in the moment, we stop grasping at things we want, stop repelling ourselves away from things we don't want, and we are not indifferent to what we are experiencing. I think if one is bored, one is not in the moment! When we are truly in a moment, there is nothing to be done, except be in awe of the dance of energy that we are all part of.

Best Wishes for Peace Profound
Love for All
Dony

Little or no purpose...

A Greater Purpose
I don't believe the purpose of life is to just be happy. Why would God take fourteen billion years to produce highly evolved sentient life-forms that would ultimately develop the extraordinary capacity for self-reflective awareness, simply in order for them to be able to experience happiness? It's my conviction that we are here for a reason, that there is a grand and great purpose to our presence in this universe, and that none of us are going to truly find what we are looking for unless we get over our misguided pursuit of personal happiness and connect with that greater sense of purpose—that ultimate reason for being.
~ Andrew Cohen

I agree with Cohen, life is more than happiness. I am not so sure we can know our purpose.

We are to the One what a cell, or even an atom is to our body; as above so below. While we know what a cell is, I don't believe a cell knows what we are. I could be wrong, but in relative reality, I don't think so. I don't think a cell knows its purpose in the big picture of our body, the cell may know what it is, maybe not, but it does not know what humans are. It is the same with the Super Consciousness; it may know what our purpose is (in this incarnation), but I don't believe we can truly know. The psychotic is just as convinced he knows the truth as the genius, and they both only know partial truths.

Maybe our purpose is to be aware in the moment. When we are truly aware, there is more knowing; there is also a chance of meeting the knower. It may be that the One can only know the beauty of all through all.

Best Wishes for Peace Profound
Love for All
Dony

The Basic Five Create All…

When we fill the jug, the pouring that fills it flows into the empty jug. The emptiness, the void, is what does the vessel's holding.
~ Martin Heidegger

    Just like our bodies, the universe is made up of the five elements, earth, wind, fire, water and ether. Unlimited combinations of these five elements make up all that is in the universe. There is nowhere in the universe these five elements are not possible. To give an example of this, when a rocket heads into what we would think of as empty space, it carries with it, earth (matter), wind, fire, water, and sometimes life. As there is nowhere in the universe without unlimited possibilities, it is the same with us; as Hermetic belief says, as above so below. If you believe, a manifestation of that belief will follow.

Best Wishes for Peace Profound
Love for All
Dony

Change…

Change the fabric of your own soul and your own visions, and you change all.
~ Vachel Lindsay

We must always change, renew, rejuvenate ourselves; otherwise we harden.
~ Johann von Goethe

    I guess I was somewhat trained for change. From about four to eight years of age we lived in four states. Within these four states, we lived in maybe twenty houses and a few stints on different rivers for a couple of weeks at a time. While I sometimes fear change, I certainly find more growth when change is thrust upon me.

    Lately I have had a strong feeling that a big change is on the horizon and I am keeping my senses open so I will know the right time to take the leap into a new world. My Old Soul keeps saying it is time; it just hasn't said what it is time for, yet.

Best Wishes for Peace Profound
Love for All
Dony

On Help...

If you have come here to help me, you are wasting your time... But if you have come because your liberation is bound with mine, then let us work together.
~ Lila Watson, aboriginal activist

In one sense, we never help anyone. We may offer, but it is up to the receiver to accept our offer. On top of this, I believe that help passes through us from universal love. The more one is tuned to this channel of universal love, the more goodness can pass from the void to the here and now. This goodness cannot be forced, but if the receiver is tuned to the same channel, it will be accepted; if not, it will be refused.

Best Wishes for Peace Profound
Love for All
Dony Hia

A few thoughts on Abundance...

I have the greatest of all riches: that of not desiring them.
~ Eleonora Duse

He has achieved success who has lived well, laughed often, and loved much.
~ Elbert Hubbard

Be content with what you have, rejoice in the way things are. When you realize there is nothing lacking, the whole world belongs to you.
~ Lao Tzu

Abundance is not something we acquire. It is something we tune into.
~ Wayne Dyer

Often, when we are struggling, we turn to the universe or gods and ask for help. We should also turn to the universe or gods daily and offer thanks for the abundance we have in our lives. Abundance is *out there*, and more so, *in there*: one has only to choose abundance.

Last night I had a dream of a huge python, twenty-five feet long. A lady I knew put it in her car to take it home. We were at a party near an ocean. I thought she should put in the trunk instead because it might squeeze her to death.

On the way to work, I heard that they killed a python in Florida that had a seventy-six-pound dear inside. Funny coincidence, or was I tuned into the radio waves?

My grandma used to say, if you dream of a snake and you don't kill it in your dream, you have an enemy. If Grandma were alive today, I would tell her: Grandma we choose to have enemies or not and I choose not to.

Best Wishes for Peace Profound
Love for All
Dony

A few thoughts on Death (#2)...

One regret dear world, which I am determined not to have when I am lying on my deathbed is that I did not kiss you enough.
~ Hafiz of Persia

Destroying is a necessary function in life. Everything has its season, and all things eventually lose their effectiveness and die.
~ Margaret J. Wheatley

Each night, when I go to sleep, I die. And the next morning, when I wake up, I am reborn.
~ Mohandas K. Gandhi

After your death you will be what you were before your birth.
~ Arthur Schopenhauer

Hafiz, thank you for reminding me to kiss the world today, and the world thanks you for kissing me back.

Margaret, I don't think I have even touched upon my effectiveness yet, but after I do I will gladly let go to make room for the next.

Mohandas, I die with each out breath and am reborn with each in breath. Some Buddhists say we die and are reborn three thousand times a moment.

Arthur, I think each being is evolving and after death we are, even if just a small amount, a more evolved spirit than the one who was born sometime earlier.

Marpa is dying, and it amazes me at how long he is holding on. Last night I started to do a practice that I felt would help him move on sooner. I could feel his energy coming up my left arm. His body quivered as he was letting go. Luyu asked me not to, so I used my right hand and felt the energy move back into him and watched the light return to his eyes, and he perked up some. While he barely shows it, I know he is suffering and I look forward to when he decides to move on and lets the suffering go.

Best Wishes for Peace Profound
Love for All
Dony

A few thoughts from HHDL...

There is no need for temples, no need for complicated philosophies. My brain and my heart are my temples; my philosophy is kindness.
~ 14th Dalai Lama

Be kind whenever possible. It is always possible.
~ 14th Dalai Lama

We can never obtain peace in the outer world until we make peace with ourselves.
~ 14th Dalai Lama

Of course, if everyone practiced kindness, the world would be a more peaceful place. Only to the extent that we learn to be kind to ourselves can we learn to be kind to others. Often when we are unkind to someone, or some being, we are actually unhappy, non-accepting and unkind to a part of our own being. I look back and think how funny that we spend twenty-four hours a day with ourselves, and yet we can still be non-accepting. Then again, maybe the problem is we do not actually spend twenty-four hours a day with ourselves; we are often somewhere far off into the past or future.

Best Wishes for Peace Profound
Love for All
Dony

Ah, to dream...

Hold fast to dreams, for if dreams die, life is a broken winged bird that cannot fly.
~ Langston Hughes

Reality is wrong. Dreams are for real.
~ Tupac Shakur

Dreams will show you where you are and where you are going. They reveal your destiny.
~ Carl Jung

When I was young and life was tortuous by day, it was by dreaming at night that I feel I stayed relatively sane.

I learned at a young age our subconscious mind, and memory, does not distinguish between what happens during waking hours or night-time dreams. I realized I could not touch what happened yesterday any more than I could touch what happened in a dream. The only difference is, if there were others in my waking hours, they could have somewhat, but not the exactly, same memory as I have. As far as the dreams, only I can have the memory.

Both past memories and nighttime dreams help me share a memory or tell a story. I feel blessed to be able to remember so many dreams going back from last night to as far back as four or five years of age.

Think of a memory and a past dream; while you have them in mind, try and weigh them. Does one seem to have more weight than the other? In my mind, for the most part, they are both light and fluffy.

Best Wishes for Peace Profound
Love for All
Dony

Happy With…

Each day Daniel Lings father made him write the Buddhist saying:
"He who speaks does not know; he who knows does not speak"
This never made an impression on Daniel.
At 17 Daniel rewrote it: "He who knows speaks in order to know better"
~ Barry Neil Kaufman, *Giant Steps*

Kaufman's book *Giant Steps* is about eight people who Kaufman helped. They range from an autistic child to a drugged out teenager.

He helps each one by being totally accepting and asking questions. Kaufman's questions seem simple and brilliant at the same time. His writing is like listening to music that dances around in my mind. It is a great book. I am glad it is required reading for the energy class.

Kaufman figured out Jeanette's learning disability was a vision problem and her getting sick all the time was something she had subconsciously learned to turn on in order to get out of school. After Kaufman helped Jeanette, Daniel wrote this and placed it in his restaurant under the Buddhist saying.

"To Love Is To Be Happy With"

To be Happy with is to be accepting, and to be accepting is to be loving.

Best Wishes for Peace Profound
Love for All
Dony

Day of Contemplation...

Our intention is to transcend superficial differences that divide us – race, religion, politics, beliefs and culture – to acknowledge, experience and honor the bond that unites us all as one interdependent organism. We also intend to evolve in both consciousness and action so each of us learns to perceive the whole, relate to others in wholeness, widen our definition of 'we' to be all inclusive and become evolutionary leaders for a peaceful, holistic, sustainable world.
~ Unknown

A nice thought for me is this: There comes a time on this planet when there are no veterans because in the future wars will be a thing of the past. Of course, I don't see this in my life time, but I do imagine it in my inner world.

If nations, instead of using money on their militaries, used it for feeding hungry people of the world, on education and medical service (both physical and mental health), there would probably be fewer veterans because there would probably be smaller militaries, which create veterans.

I do not want to take anything away from the veterans who served their countries, but it would be great if we were celebrating Feeding the World Weekend, Teaching the Children Month, and Mental Health Day today, just like we do Veterans Day.

Best Wishes for Peace Profound
Love for All
Dony

Discover Your True Self...

Each of us is here to discover our true Self, that essentially we are spiritual beings who have taken manifestation in physical form, that we're not human beings that have occasional spiritual experiences, that we're spiritual beings that have occasional human experiences.
~ Deepak Chopra

The physical world, including our bodies, is a response of the observer. We create our bodies as we create the experience of our world.
~ Deepak Chopra

Once we truly believe, we create our body and the world we live in; there is no room for victim mentality. We naturally take on the responsibility for our lives and actions. Our lives truly can be as rich as we can believe they can be.

A while back as I was working on a walking stick. I kept feeling energy at one spot in the middle of the stick, at a point where a knot slightly looks like a Ganesh to me. When I completed the Morel Walking stick, I placed on grips I had carved on each side of where I felt the energy. As I held this spot, I was compelled to chant the words Om Hia for several minutes. When I finished, I looked up Hia on the web. The first thing that popped up was Hiawatha, a Native American word that meant Iroquois Captain. Since then I feel that Hia is my own inner captain or guide.

In high school, when I was dabbling with artwork, my girlfriend at the time said, "If you ever become an artist, you need to have a signature that is different." She suggested I sign my drawings using Dony.

This is why, for some writings now, I have been using the name Dony Hia. For me, it means Artful Guide.

Best Wishes for Peace Profound
Love for All
Dony

True Strength is Gentle…

Horses may be prey animals, but they aren't stupid, and they aren't weak. They're beautiful and powerful and proud of it, but they know they must remain sensitive, responsive, adaptable, and observant to avoid being eaten. They also know, as the old saying goes, that true strength is gentle, and true gentleness is strength.
~ Linda Kohanov

    I love this saying, "true strength is gentle, and true gentleness is strength." Growing up as I did, I am not sure how responsive I was. But I know I was sensitive, adaptable and observant in order to survive and keep a relative amount of sanity. When I was young, I thought my gentleness was a form of weakness and maybe even cowardliness. Looking back from today, I see it was always a gift. When I think of all the people out there who struggle to survive, and yet stay gentle and kind, I see there is a lot of good in this world.

Best Wishes for Peace Profound
Love for All
Dony

A few thoughts on suffering…

The suffering itself is not so bad, it's the resentment against suffering that is the real pain.
~ Allen Ginsberg

Suffering also has its worth. Through sorrow, pride is driven out and pity felt for those who wander in samsara; Evil is avoided, goodness seems delightful.
~ Shantideva

We can only hold as much joy as the pain and suffering that we've had carved out of us.
~ Unknown

    Character is built through overcoming suffering, not from trying to avoid suffering. Nirvana and Samsara are one, not two; you cannot have one without the other. You cannot have joy without something to compare it to: sadness. One can actually hold joy, even bliss, deep inside while suffering remains on the surface. "The waves on the surface of a body of water do not disturb the depths" is often used as a metaphor with Buddhist teachers. What happens with the flesh does not disturb the spirit at the core.

Best Wishes for Peace for All
Love for All
Dony

It's Okay to feel sad…

It's okay to be unhappy. If you feel it, you feel it. It's not bad—there are no bad and good feelings
It's just an opportunity to understand what you're thinking.
~ Barry Neil Kaufman

    Often we try to numb or block out unhappy or sad feelings. In doing this, we take our selves out of Now by trying to think of ways, or things, to remove the sadness. In recent years I not only stay with the unhappiness, or sadness, but also try to dive deep into it. Doing this I can find a deep joy below the sadness. I have found that below the sadness there is a loving heart, which has the right to be sad in certain moments. I think if you dive deep enough into your heart, at the center you will only find peace and joy.

    In a little over an hour I will be sitting in my energy class. Of course, I have no idea what it will be like today, but I believe it will be another powerful class.

Best Wishes for Peace Profound
Love for All
Dony

Tilopa was a Tantric...

One should not give or take, but remain natural, for Mahmudra is beyond all acceptance and rejection.
Since alaya is not born no one can obstruct or soil it. Staying in the unborn realm, all appearances will dissolve into dharmata, and self-will and pride will vanish into naught.
~ Tilopa

When Tilopa says not to "give or take," he means with hope of results. Such as, you donate something hoping to achieve good karma. This is not a gift. You are bargaining; you are being selfish. If you give from the heart, it is good. If you give from somewhere else, it may not be.

Our witness (our awareness), which is not born, and does not die, is one with the alaya consciousness (eighth consciousness). In the gap between 2 thoughts we reside in the alaya. Nothing in the universe can soil our basic being, which is awareness.

This is what Eckhart Tolle calls "living in the Now." When we are aware, we are here Now. It is only our human mind which tries to get outside Now. We never do get outside of Now, and when one awakens, one laughs and realizes "Ah, it was always Here Now."

Best Wishes for Peace Profound
Love for All
Dony

Living on the Edge...

What does it take to use the life we already have in order to make us wiser rather than more stuck? What is the source of wisdom at a personal, individual level?

The answer to these questions seems to have to do with bringing everything that we encounter to the path. Everything naturally had a ground, path, and fruition. This is like saying that everything has a beginning, middle, and end. But it is also said that the path itself is both the ground and the fruition. The path is the goal.

This path has one very distinct characteristic: it is not prefabricated. It doesn't already exist. The path that we're talking about is the moment-by-moment evolution of our experience, the moment-by-moment evolution of the world of phenomena, the moment-by-moment evolution of our thoughts and emotions. The path is uncharted. It comes into existence moment-by-moment and at the same time drops away behind us.

When we realize that the path is the goal, there's a sense of workability. Everything that occurs in our confused mind we can regard as the path. Everything is workable.
~ Pema Chodron

We already have everything we need. There is no need for self-improvement. All these trips that we lay on ourselves - the heavy duty fearing that we're bad and hoping that we're good, the identities that we so dearly cling to, the rage, the jealousy and the addictions of all kinds - never touch our basic wealth. They are like clouds that temporarily block the sun. But all the time our warmth and brilliance are right there. This is who we really are. We are one blink of an eye away from being fully awake.
~ Pema Chodron

My friend Siw emailed me and asked how I make a decision when I am in doubt. I don't think Siw would mind me sharing the answer with all of you.

Siw is a friend who I love dearly and whatever decision she makes will be right in the moment. May the universe guide Siw to make a decision that will be her shortest path to awakening!

Good Morning Siw,

I usually meditate on whatever it is, think about it deeply for a moment, ask the universe for guidance and then try to let it go. The answer usually seems to come from my gut, not my head.

Of course, you really don't have time to let it go, so I would sit for five minutes just letting the question float through your consciousness, and then try to let an answer just come to you.

You know, Pema Chodron says we are not really living unless we are living on the edge. Do you feel yourself living up there with a comfortable salary? Or do you feel yourself living in a town where, while you might not make as much money, you could challenge yourself to do something you love?

I am toying with the same question and know I am not living on the edge.

Alison suggested if I want to make a career change, I might make a great life coach. I am waiting for any signs to guide me, but I do have some time.

I will send wishes your way that an answer comes to you quickly.

Hugs, Dony

Best Wishes for Peace Profound
Love for All
Dony

Neither All Bad, Nor All Good…

What we have to learn, in both meditation and in life, is to be free of attachment to the good experiences, and free of aversion to the negative ones.
~ Sogyal Rinpoche

There is a famous saying: "If the mind is not contrived, it is spontaneously blissful, just as water, when not agitated, is by nature transparent and clear.
~ Sogyal Rinpoche

It must be twenty-five years since I first read Sogyal Rinpoche's book on living and dying. I enjoyed the book so much I bought his book on CD. Yet when I awoke this morning, Sogyal Rinpoche was the first person to come to mind when thinking about whose quotes I should use for today's morning thoughts.

Years after I read Sogyal Rinpoche's book, he became controversial. There have been many Buddhist teachers over the years who have been controversial. Chogyam Trungpa is another who comes to mind.

I imagine for centuries in Tibet there have been many great teachers who were controversial. It is said Marpa, the translator, drank too much and beat his students. It is also said Milarepa, who is one of my favorite characters in Buddhist literature, through black magic caused a roof to cave in on relatives who stole his inheritance.

I think this shows we should rely more on the teachings than the teachers, who are human like us.

Best Wishes for Peace Profound
Love for All
Dony

Be Aware of Your Gurus and Their Teachings…

Flint has the potential to produce fire, and gems have intrinsic value. We ordinary people can see neither our own eyelashes, which are so close, nor the heavens in the distance. Likewise, we do not see that the Buddha exists in our own hearts.
~ Nichiren Daishonin

The problem in Western society is that you don't look at life and death as a whole. You isolate death. That's why there's so much fear.
~ Sogyal Rinpoche

Both of these teachers have helped many people but have also been controversial. My first Buddhist practice was Nicheren's Buddhism, chanting Nam Myo Ho Ren Ge Kyo. While I still chant this chant every now and then, I left his teachings because his writings condemned almost all other Buddhist sects. From what I have read in the earliest teachings from the Pali text, Buddha always said never to slander another's teachings.

I have also found joy in Reading Sogyal Rinpoche's work, and I have found his teachings very useful and have shared his tapes and books. Sogyal Rinpoche had a ten million dollar civil suit filed in Santa Cruz by a woman who says Sogyal Rinpoche, author of *The Tibetan Book of Living and Dying*, "coerced" her into an intimate relationship. The Dalai Lama approved the case against Sogyal Rinpoche.

To me, this shows the teachings can be more useful than the teachers, and one should take what resonates in one's heart and leave what doesn't. It is written Buddha said on many occasions do not take the teachings on anybody else's word, not even his. One should test any practice and if it helps you and does not harm others, use it. If it doesn't, leave it.

Best Wishes for Peace Profound
Love for All
Dony

Crazy Wisdom...

Don't accept, don't reject. There is nothing to do in fact. You are not asked to do anything. You are simply asked to be loose and natural; be yourself and let things happen. Then the whole world is going on without you: the rivers go to the sea, the stars move, the sun rises in the morning, the seasons follow each other, the trees grow and bloom and disappear, and the whole is going on without you—can't you leave yourself loose and natural and move with the whole? This is sannyas for me.
~ Osho

All major religions have a list of rules to control the masses and to raise funds to keep the organism growing.

Buddhism, Jainism, Taoism, Lao Tzu turn one more to the inside than many other religions but still, they have a long list of how one should live. I believe Tantra (both Buddhist and Hinduism Tantra) not only have the fewest rules, they try to undo the mind of rules so one can live more naturally.

Of course from the outside, a Tantric might seem a little crazy; then again, I am sure any great mystic appears a little crazy to the masses.

I am sure most people of their times thought, Jesus, Buddha, Muhammad, Moses and a host of other mystics were crazy. I want to learn crazy wisdom.

Best Wishes for Peace Profound
Love for All
Dony

Thoughts from Emerson...

A chief event of life is the day in which we have encountered a mind that startled us.
~ Ralph Waldo Emerson

Do not go where the path may lead, go instead where there is no path and leave a trail.
~ Ralph Waldo Emerson

A man is what he thinks about all day long.
~ Ralph Waldo Emerson

I understand Rosicrucians believe all phenomena is just the most basic elements (energy) drawn together in a particular way. In Rosicrucian belief, it is magnetism and electricity which binds the basic elements in any particular way to form what we see as phenomena. They also believe that all matter is endowed with spirit, which I see as the One, or if you like, "Superconsciousness."

Our thoughts create electricity (neurons firing off in our brains), and believe it or not, this electricity can shift energy and this shift in energy is what creates every moment anew. Even little shifts affect the entire universe.

It is as Emerson said: "A man is what he thinks about all day long."

Best Wishes for Peace Profound
Love for All
Dony

Let It Past, At Least That Thought...

When we recognize an emotion, such as strong passion accompanied by jealousy, we are actually breaking down the speed of that emotion. The total sense of recognition is important in both Sutra and Tantra. In Sutra, it is *mindfulness. In Tantra, if we see that nature, and look at it nakedly, we will see the nature of that wisdom. You don't need to logically apply any reasoning. You don't need to conceptually meditate on anything. Just simply recognize and observe it.... We will have the experience of that wisdom by simply being with it without conception. Therefore, recognition is quite important.*

The first step is just simply to observe it. Simply recognize the emotion and then watch it as it grows or as it continues. Just simply watch it. In the beginning, just to have an idea that [the emotion] is coming is very important and effective. In the Vajrayana [Tantric] sense, the way to watch these emotions is without stopping them. If we recognize the emotion and say, "Yes, it is passion," and then try to stop it, that's a problem. Rejection our emotions is a problem in Vajrayana.
~ Dzogchen Ponlop Rinpoche

    I know several people who have moved from California to Seattle to be closer to Ponlop. If I had an urge to leave home and follow a teacher, I guess it would be Ponlop. He is the only person I have met who when he walks into a room, I feel no ego.

    In Tantra, we do not pull away from our emotions. We learn not to let them hook us and pull us out of the moment. As I have written in the past, our thoughts are not our own. Thoughts are always floating in and out of the void, and depending on how we are wired, we tend to catch certain thoughts as they pass through. We can either let a thought or emotion pass through, or we can let the thought grab us by the mind and fling us around as if we were our own private tornado. With practice, we can learn which thoughts we should build upon and which we should laugh at as they pass through our minds.

Best Wishes for Peace Profound
Love for All
Dony

Look Within...

From the Gnostic Gospels:
If you bring forth that which is within you, then that which is within you will be your salvation.
If you do not bring forth that which is within you, then that which is within you will destroy you.
~ Peter A. Levine

Peter A. Levine's book *Waking the Tiger* is one of the books which are required reading for the two-year energy class I am starting in September. I first read this book in 2004, the day before I overcame the agoraphobia that had haunted me for about 44 years. I had forgotten what a great book it is. Not only is every experience you have had since birth within in you, working with Alison, I have realized that every experience of every life is within you. If we open up, we, as humans, have access to everything which has happened since the Big Bang.

Even the Gods envy the experiences humans can touch upon and live.

Best Wishes for Peace Profound
Love for All
Dony

Wide Open Spaces…

Thirty spokes share the wheel's hub;
It is the center hole that makes it useful.
Shape clay into a vessel;
It is the space within that makes it useful.
Cut doors and windows for a room;
It is the holes which make it useful.
Therefore benefit comes from what is there;
Usefulness from what is not there.
~ Lao Tzu

It is the same with our minds; it is the open spaces, not filled up with views, which make our minds useful. If we are set in our ways and believe our way is the right way, or the only way, we often miss the opportunity to learn, grow and evolve.

Like the entire universe, we ourselves are evolving, and how we evolve will determine the world our children's children will be born into.

Best Wishes for Peace Profound
Love for All
Dony

Reprograming...

Body and Mind
Whatever increases, decreases, limits or extends the body's power of action, increases, decreases, limits or extends the mind's power of action. And whatever increases, decreases, limits, ore extends the mind's power of action, also increases, decreases, limits, or extends the body's power of action.
~ Spinoza

The above is a quote from *Waking the Tiger* by Peter A Levine. Whatever is in our conscious mind at this moment will be in our subconscious mind shortly. If you have any doubt about this, look at your dreams. I would guess the way we respond to our world is at least 90 percent, or more, from subconscious impulses. At least part of our subconscious mind is programmed from our conscious mind and our relationship with the outer world. We have the ability to reprogram, to some extent, our subconscious mind. I, personally, have been amazed at how I have reprogrammed parts of my mind working with Alison.

Life, truly, is not so much reality, as it is interpretation!

Best Wishes for Peace Profound
Love for All
Dony

In Us the Future Is Evolving...

The First Tenet: Clarity of Intention
The First Tenet of Evolutionary Enlightenment is called Clarity of Intention. This tenet points directly to the essential nature of the evolutionary impulse itself: the wholehearted, passionate intention to exist, to develop, to become, and to evolve. That impulse is the same uninhibited YES that burst forth as the big bang, which compels the body to procreate and the mind to innovate. When that impulse expresses itself at the highest levels of consciousness, it is experienced as the inspiration that pulls us toward spiritual liberation and enlightenment. It is the mysterious drive to become more conscious. To have Clarity of Intention means to align oneself with the clear and single-pointed purpose of that impulse itself. And the way that alignment occurs, in a human heart and mind, is that the intention to evolve becomes more important to us than anything else in this world.
~ Andrew Cohen

Whether we realize it or not, we are the future of what beings, at least human beings, will be on this planet in the ages to come. Yet, when that future comes, these beings will look back at us and see us much like we see the prehistoric humans.

Best Wishes for Peace Profound
Love for All
Dony

Shrieks of Monkeys...

As surely as we hear the blood in our ears, the echoes of a million midnight shrieks of monkeys, whose last sight of the world was the eyes of a panther, have their traces in our nervous system.
~ Paul Shepard

Funny, in Tibet I shrieked as a monkey tried to take a piece of me; luckily we both went our separate ways unharmed. Yes we have, in our DNA, instincts from eons past which partly determine how we respond to situations. In this life we have voices from the past, right up to this very moment, which determine how we respond to any given situation. Often when we respond to someone right in front of us, we are really responding in connection with an experience from our past.

If we have had trauma, we tend to get caught in a vortex and make the same inappropriate response over and over again. Luckily, we can reprogram our memories and heal the traumas which create these vortexes. *Waking the Tiger* by Peter A. Levine is a great book for describing how Traumas affect us.

Below is the creature I had to hit with both hands as hard as I could as he climbed up to bite my face. He flew about eight feet as I fell forward. I was so glad he turned and ran.

Best Wishes for Peace Profound
Love for All
Dony

Heart Energy...

When you begin to touch your heart or let your heart be touched, you begin to discover that it's bottomless, that it doesn't have any resolution, that this heart is huge, vast, and limitless. You begin to discover how much warmth and gentleness is there, as well as how much space.
~ Pema Chodron

You're the only one who knows when you're using things to protect yourself and keep your ego together and when you're opening and letting things fall apart, letting the world come as it is - working with it rather than struggling against it. You're the only one who knows.
~ Pema Chodron

We have a heart in our chest that weighs a pound or two. We also have a heart that is not material but an energy that is not only inside. This energy here also encompasses what we expand or contract to. When we are secure and loving, we expand this energy heart to touch many. When we are troubled or insecure, we shrink the energy heart so much it can't even be felt by others. Even though we shrink it, it is still capable of expanding again when we open up and relax.

When we feel love for another, and that person feels love for us, the two energies (Auric) fields can merge as one.

Best Wishes for Peace Profound
Love for All
Dony

A Couple Thoughts from Barry…

Gratitude is one of the sweet shortcuts to finding peace of mind and happiness inside. No matter what is going on outside of us, there's always something we could be grateful for.
~ Barry Neil Kaufman

A loud voice cannot compete with a clear voice, even if it's a whisper.
~ Barry Neil Kaufman

    Yes, we can always find something to be grateful for! I find it funny people will concentrate on what they don't have more than what they do have. Success is wanting what you have, not having what you want. It seems I always have just a little more than I need; there is always a little to share.

    Often we hear a loud judgmental voice in our own heads. This is the first voice we should bring down to a whisper and maybe let disappear. If we can create a kind, clear voice in our own head, it will naturally flow out to others.

Best Wishes for Peace Profound
Love for All
Dony Hia

This Guy Really Nailed It…

The Dalai Lama, when asked what surprised him most about humanity, he answered: "Man. Because he sacrifices his health in order to make money. Then he sacrifices money to recuperate his health. And then he is so anxious about the future that he does not enjoy the present; the result being that he does not live in the present or the future; he lives as if he is never going to die, and then dies never having really lived.
~ Unknown

My good friend, and chiropractor extraordinaire, Christine Lee sent out an email with the quote above. As she puts it: "This guy nailed it on the head!"

More and more, I try to live in the moment, trying to just dance with the energy of Now. Of course I can't always do this, but when I do, I feel so much energy and so much alive. I watch things come in and out of my awareness moment to moment. I just watch and try not grasp on to something in this moment which would cause me to miss the next. When we live like this, we can realize seeing a stranger's soul in their eyes as we pass by can be as rich as kissing a loved one.

Best Wishes for Peace Profound
Love for All
Dony Hia

One Is All…

Nothing exist as a block and cannot be parceled up.
~ Kay Ryan

Everything in the universe is interdependent. What happens on one side of the universe affects the whole universe; including our own actions. If we affect the far ends of the universe, think how much more we affect those close to us, or even our neighborhood or town. Of course, since we are not omnipotent we do not really know how our actions will affect the future. What we may think is the right thing may not be right for others. Other times, things that, in the moment, we thought were a mistake turn out to benefit many. One is all, and All is one!

Best Wishes for Peace Profound
Love for All
Dony Hia

Empty But Full…

Beyond intellect within the mind nothing arises. This is the Path of all the Buddhas, enlightened ones.
~ 17th Karmapa

The more we can remove our views of what should be, or should not be, for ourselves and others, the more we can be awed at what is. Our minds can become as they were when we first took on this incarnation: empty of preconceptions but full of wonder and possibilities.

Best Wishes for Peace Profound
Love for All
Dony Hia

Other Being's Feelings...

Through my work as a horse trainer and equine-facilitated therapy specialist, I've observed that feelings are contagious. They expand in predictable ways—even across species lines. "We seem to be standing here in silence tonight, I told Nancy, "but we're actually immersed in a sea of vibration.
~ Linda Kohanov, *Riding Between the Worlds*

Kohanov had discovered what many others had—prey animals are highly sensitive to other beings' feelings. They need to have this to survive. When a predator is sneaking up on a heard, one horse may see the predator, or sense it, and when this horse feels the fear other horses will take off running from vibrations picked up from the first horse.

Human beings who have been traumatizes from violence, such as myself, at a young age often develop this same skill. You actually pick up feelings of others. Sometimes people enter the world with this ability, and everyone has it to some extent. We tend to call this feeling a gut feeling or a sixth sense.

Those who have suffered have healed, and have this empathetic ability to make some of the best therapist and natural healers.

Best Wishes for Peace Profound
Love for All
Dony Hia

One Flower to Another…

I was a late bloomer. But anyone who blooms at all, ever, is very lucky.
~ Sharon Olds

    Long before many of the people reading this were born, I dropped out of college and went to work as a plumbing apprentice. One day I had to go to Curtis Park and remove a cover from a swamp cooler on the roof of a three-story house. Having a fear of heights, I was scared, but not to death; I did not fall. When I finished, I was talking to the lady who owned the house. She was about 65 years old, and she told me she had been born in this house. We were standing in the front yard, and there was this strange tree. The lady told me it was called a monkey tail tree and her father had planted it when she was born. She also told me it first bloomed when the tree was 50 years old. At that moment I thought, wow, the ultimate late bloomer. I thought I was just starting to bloom, at around 20, and was a late bloomer. Looking back, I think if I was even a seedling then I was barely a seedling. Nearly 59 years old now, I feel I and my heart are just starting to form a bud. I hope through the energy work I am doing now, and the deities letting me live long enough, I might produce my own flower in this life.

    I believe when one blooms one performs one's life purpose. I believe I have performed many purposes, yet not the one I volunteered for when I took on this incarnation. May we all bloom!

Best Wishes for Peace Profound
Love for All
Dony Hia

A Few Thoughts from Ken Wilber...

What is it in you that brings you to a spiritual teacher in the first place? It's not the spirit in you, since that is already enlightened, and has no need to seek. No, it is the ego in you that brings you to a teacher.
~ Ken Wilber

There is nothing but God, nothing but the Goddess, nothing but Spirit in all directions, and not a grain of sand, not a speck of dust, is more or less Spirit than any other.
~ Ken Wilber

I have one major rule: Everybody is right. More specifically, everybody — including me — has some important pieces of truth, and all of those pieces need to be honored, cherished, and included in a more gracious, spacious, and compassionate embrace.
~ Ken Wilber

I believe seeking is the ego trying to find its way back home, a place beyond duality thinking. If we did not have natural moments of where we feel oneness, we would not seek.

It seems in both Wilber's and Rosicrucian teachings, Spirit is the basic building block of the universe. Spirit is the vibration that forms all phenomena.

Everyone and everything that takes on form has something to offer and something to teach. Depending on our own vibrations, the frequency we are tuned to, we understand the teachings or we don't in any given moment.

Everything is Guru!

Best Wishes for Peace Profound
Love for All
Dony Hia

Inside Out (2)...

Yet the clinical experiences described by Jung, Freud, and just about every significant analyst of the twentieth century have shown this obsession with all that is light and airy to be a form of escapism, "a refuge for all those timorous souls who do not want to become anything different." The field of psychotherapy as a whole recognizes that a decent into the depths of emotion, as well as into the personal and collective unconscious, always precedes the ascent into greater consciousness, transcendence, and lasting change.
~ Linda Kohanov

    We can only go as far into higher consciousness as we are willing to go into lower realms of our own subconscious mind. I believe if one was willing, and able, to go all the way in to the core of one's being, one would find it is as vast inside as it is outside. At the core is the golden umbilical cord, which connects us directly with the One, the universal consciousness. So, if you could turn any being completely inside out, you would find that the whole universe had resided within, as it does with all of us.

Best Wishes for Peace Profound
Love for All
Dony Hia

A Few Thoughts from Deepak . . .

Whatever relationships you have attracted in your life at this moment, are precisely the ones you need in your life at this moment. There is a hidden meaning behind all events, and this hidden meaning is serving your own evolution.
~ Deepak Chopra

Even when you think you have your life all mapped out, things happen that shape your destiny in ways you might never have imagined.
~ Deepak Chopra

Walk with those seeking truth . . . run from those who think they have found it.
~ Deepak Chopra

    Each of us is on our own journey, and this journey helps the whole universe evolve. This happens even if we don't believe it. Even when we think things are not going right, things are perfect in every moment. And the next moment will be a perfect reflection of how we lived in this moment.

Best Wishes for Peace Profound
Love for All
Dony Hia

Abundance...

Life will give you whatever experience is most helpful for the evolution of consciousness.
~ Eckhart Tolle

It's exhilarating to be alive in a time of awakening consciousness; it can also be confusing, disorienting, and painful.
~ Adrienne Rich

The intellect has little to do on the road to discovery. There comes a leap in consciousness, call it intuition or what you will, the solution comes to you and you don't know how or why.
~ Albert Einstein

Most people dream of traveling the world. While there are many places out there I want to see, I do find pleasure traveling the inner canyons of my consciousness.

If I travel in far enough, I realize we are just an expression of mother earth and father sky. We are brought up from the elements of mother, charged with the energy of father, and we are a dancing energy until mother and father call us home to rest for a while. Then we start the dance all over again, just with different wrappings.

Best Wishes for Peace
Profound
Love for All
Dony Hia

A Few Thoughts from Gandhi…

Freedom is not worth having if it does not include the freedom to make mistakes.
~ Mahatma Gandhi

What difference does it make to the dead, the orphans and the homeless, whether the mad destruction is wrought under the name of totalitarianism or the holy name of liberty or democracy?
~ Mahatma Gandhi, Non-Violence in Peace and War

In the attitude of silence the soul finds the path in a clearer light, and what is elusive and deceptive resolves itself into crystal clearness. Our life is a long and arduous quest after Truth.
~ Mahatma Gandhi

We are taught that in the animal kingdom only the strong survive. Unfortunately, as humans evolved from the lower animals, many humans have not let go of the idea that brute strength should be used to subdue those less strong. Even worse, many nations feel the same way.

If one can go into and experience the core of one's being, which is Spirit, one will not only find that there is no room for violence; this core is also joy and bliss because it is the only door that directly connects us to the One, the Universal Intelligence.

Best Wishes for Peace Profound
Love for All
Dony Hia

Rebel Buddha...

That is the essence and mission of 'rebel Buddha': to free us from the illusions we create by ourselves, about ourselves, and from those that masquerade as reality in our cultural and religious institutions.
~ Dzogchen Ponlop Rinpoche, *Rebel Buddha: On the Road to Freedom*

How wonderful it would be, I thought, if only we could practice the teachings of the Buddha as he really taught them from his own experience – free from the clouds of religiosity that often surround them... Yet it's difficult to distinguish the tools themselves from their cultural packaging.
~ Dzogchen Ponlop Rinpoche, *Rebel Buddha: On the Road to Freedom*

True wisdom is free of the dramas of culture or religion and should bring us only a sense of peace and happiness.
~ Dzogchen Ponlop Rinpoche, *Rebel Buddha: On the Road to Freedom*

Of the teachers I have met, I felt most connected to Ponlop. It was in a house where he sometimes taught that I overcame agoraphobia; I think it may have been because even though he was not there in person, some of his energy was. Also of the teachers I have met, he seemed to have the least ego. As mentioned before, for me, when he walked into a room, I felt no ego, I just felt an authentic, wise, humble being. When I thought about whose quote I should use today, Ponlop came to mind. The first book I read by Ponlop, *Wild Awakening*, was quite an enjoyable and enlightening read.

Best Wishes for Peace Profound
Love for All
Dony Hia

We All Serve...

The spirit intervenes, changing our dance with destiny, delicately urging the heart to open and to serve.
~ Berta Broken Bow

We are all interdependent to one another, and we serve even when we are unaware. We serve when we show warmth and love to others, and we also serve when people think the worst of us.

I like to think of friends and loved ones as gifts, and those who seem to rub me the wrong way as gurus. It is those who we seem to have trouble with who actually give us the most opportunity to grow and expand our awareness of our own minds.

In the dance of energy, we all play our parts.

Best Wishes for Peace Profound
Love for All
Dony Hia

A Few Thoughts on Mushrooms...

I am . . . a mushroom; on whom the dew of heaven drops now and then.
~ John Ford

All mushrooms are edible – once.
~ Unknown

The Smurfs are little blue people who live in magic mushrooms. Think about it.
~ Unknown

In a few moments I am off for an energy class and then a mystical weekend in Mendocino foraging mushrooms.

Each time I am in the forest, there is a mystical connection between myself and mushrooms. Sometimes it starts before I get to the forest. Sometimes I will see one in my mind's eye in a spot I have foraged before. It will be almost as if a voice is calling me. I usually listen to the voice and hours later when I get there, I find a mushroom within feet of where I had seen it in my mind's eye.

I have no idea what the class today, or the weekend, will bring although I do see a spot where the chanterelles are calling me.

My wife Luyu's first Mendocino weekend, she is excited.

Best Wishes for Peace Profound
Love for All
Dony Hia

Dancing With Fear...

Dancing with Fear.
~ Linda Kohanov

I read this line in *Riding Between the Worlds* by Linda Kohanov last night as I was bathing. It made me think of how many times we, as a species, try to pull away from our emotions. Of course, we need fear at times just for survival. There must also be a reason for sorrow, feeling of loss, loneliness, joy and any other emotions we have receptors to feel. The thing we often do, though, is to feel an emotion that is not appropriate for the moment. We often create a fear in our mind for something that hasn't even happened.

While at this point in my life I feel pretty dang successful with a lot of joy in my heart, I also feel I arrived here more from fear than courage. I was agoraphobic (a condition characterized by an irrational fear of public or open spaces) from around 6 to 54 years of age. One of the reasons I dropped out of college was the agoraphobia; the other was a lack of money. Because of the agoraphobia, I wanted a job where I did not have to deal with the public; plumbing was the perfect job.

Because of insecurities and fear, I have worked on my mind since I was a teenager. It is only in the last few years that I have found ways to unlock the energy from the past causing irrational fears.

Is the dance with fears over? No there is a voice deep within which says I should have the courage to follow the artistic calling or healing calling I feel deep inside, yet I fear even this voice.

While many other fears and insecurities are gone, and I feel a richness in my core I thought I may never reach, I still need to dance with the fear that I am not talented enough to take on this artistic desire.

I guess I'll keep growing through fear. I wonder if those reading this might also recognize some of their own fears.

Best Wishes for Peace Profound
Love for All
Dony Hia

Few Thoughts from Big Ben...

Energy and persistence conquer all things.
~ Benjamin Franklin

Content makes poor men rich; discontent makes rich men poor.
~ Benjamin Franklin

Either write something worth reading or do something worth writing.
~ Benjamin Franklin

A house is not a home unless it contains food and fire for the mind as well as the body.
~ Benjamin Franklin

Big Ben is food for the mind; sometimes I have to be careful not to stuff myself.

I feel so blessed to live in a time when there is so much wisdom and knowledge within reach. It would be great if we could feed both the bellies and the minds of the poor throughout the world. I think of all the times that evil men have tried to destroy the knowledge of others. This has happened often, many times, even before the burning of the Library of Alexandria.

Dictators are afraid if the masses have knowledge and wisdom they cannot control them; they are right.

Best Wishes for Peace Profound
Love for All
Dony Hia

A Few Thoughts from Galileo…

I have never met a man so ignorant that I couldn't learn something from him.
~ Galileo Galilei

We cannot teach people anything; we can only help them discover it within themselves.
~ Galileo Galilei

The sun, with all those planets revolving around it and dependent on it, can still ripen a bunch of grapes as if it had nothing else in the universe to do.
~ Galileo Galilei

Galileo spent the last years of his life under house arrest because the Pope felt his teachings went against the Church. Turns out Galileo was right and the Church was wrong. Yes, the sun, whose light is eight minutes away at the speed of light, makes life possible, including grapes, here on earth.

I understand Rosicrucians believe that life is formed from positive electrical energy, negative electrical energy, magnetic attraction and spirit. They also believe the earth supplies negative energy while the sun supplies positive energy. I believe thought is the magnetic attraction forming matter and spirit gives life to matter. In both Rosicrucian and Buddhist teachings, all matter (phenomena) has life. Every grain of sand, every blade of grass, and the entire earth should be regarded as if it were a living breathing being, which it is. Mother Earth, Father Sun. Ahhhh!

Best Wishes for Peace Profound
Love for All
Dony Hia

Dig Deep for the Treasure Within…

Every moment and every event of every man's life on earth plants something in his soul.
~ Thomas Merton
Happiness resides not in possessions, and not in gold, happiness dwells in the soul.
~ Democritus

Look within. Within is the fountain of good, and it will ever bubble up, if thou wilt ever dig.
~ Marcus Aurelius

    It is pretty evident that the richest riches are found within. In the last energy class, we were asked to go into our core. For some of us it was easy; for others the teacher had to help them find and go into their core. With each person, the teacher walked up and said, "Go to your core." It was obvious to me, somehow, she can sense if you are in your core or not. If anyone had trouble, she would pass her hand down in front of them and help them find their core. When it came to my turn, and I dropped right into my core, she asked how I knew this place. I told her it is where I had always gone since I was very young if I needed to ask for help. I told her that if I went any deeper I would see the face of God. She smiled and said, "You got it." It would be nice if these were things we could teach our children in school. Can you imagine if schools taught children to find their authentic selves?

Best Wishes for Peace Profound
Love for All
Dony Hia

A Few Thoughts from Early China...

Be not ashamed of mistakes and thus make them crimes.
~ Confucius

Our greatest glory is not in never falling, but in getting up every time we do.
~ Confucius

Respect yourself and others will respect you.
~ Confucius

Do not do to others what you do not want done to yourself.
~ Confucius

Confucius lived 2500 years ago in China, about the same time that Buddha lived in India. It amazes me at times how much wisdom has been around for thousands of years and how many people in power ignore this wisdom.

As I was telling my grandson, DeShaun, last night, an ounce of wisdom is worth a pound of knowledge. I also mentioned to him if he spent as much time reading as he did playing his games, he would gain both wisdom and knowledge. He continued to play his game, which of course was fine. One can only offer nectar; it is up to the receiver to decide if he or she wants to taste it.

Amazing, these minds of ours!

Best Wishes for Peace Profound
Love for All
Dony Hia

Expanding or Contracting...

The more I realize that I am in the process, and not some finished product coming off the human assembly line, the more I can settle into life with less anxiety and more optimism.
~ John Lee, *Growing Yourself Back Up*

In his book, *The Path Is the Goal,* Chogyam Trumpa conveys the idea that we are in a process and we do not reach a point where we can say, "Ah, this is it"; the journey continues on forever.

In the universe things are either expanding or contracting. Even if the body is contracting with age, our minds and spirits can expand. If we can live within this expansion, even as our body ages, our minds and spirits can feel youth and growth.

Best Wishes for Peace Profound
Love for All
Dony Hia

Reflections…

This being human is a guest house. Every morning is a new arrival. A joy, a depression, a meanness, some momentary awareness comes as an unexpected visitor. Welcome and entertain them all. Treat each guest honorably. The dark thought, the shame, the malice, meet them at the door laughing, and invite them in. Be grateful for whoever comes, because each has been sent as a guide from beyond.
~ Rumi

We think we see others, yet we never do! Even how you see your dearest lover is but a reflection of your own mind. We see someone we don't like: reflection of our own mind. We see someone we like: reflection of our own mind. We really never know the people we like or dislike. We just know small portions of them, things they share while in our presence. Think of how many thoughts go through your head in a day, which you never share with another. Every person you know has just as many thoughts never shared with another. We pick a few things about a person and decide we like or dislike them. The sages see the world as a reflection of their own mind and often love everything about it, even the so-called evil ones.

Best Wishes for Peace Profound
Love for All
Dony Hia

Just Be...

There's no way to describe what I do. It's just me.
~ Andy Kaufman

When an animal feels hunger, it "knows" to eat. When it feels fear, it "knows" to protect itself by fighting or fleeing. When if feels lust, it "knows" to procreate. When it feels affection, it "knows" to bond or nurture or protect. When it feels something, it does something about it. Animals don't block or postpone or suppress the energy working in them. They use it up.
~ John Lee, *Facing the Fire*

    Often Zen monks will describe their lives in much the way Kaufman did his, or even the way Lee describes how animals live. If we can remove our mask and live authentically, we have a lot more energy. When we suppress emotions, good or bad, we create energy blocks within our being and these blocks cause dis-harmony within our being, which in turn opens doors for illness of body, mind and spirit.

Best Wishes for Peace Profound
Love for All
Dony Hia

Lying in the Grass...

Out beyond ideas of wrongdoing and right doing there is a field.
I'll meet you there.
When the soul lies down in that grass the world is too full to talk about.
~ Rumi

    This poem reminds me of when I was nine years old and we lived in Sacramento. There was a field behind the neighbor's house. The wild grasses would rise three or four feet high. I would go to this field and somewhere in the middle, flatten out a bed where I could lay and gaze at blue sky and puffy white clouds. Lying there on a cool crisp Saturday morning I could smell the freshness of the grass and hear the sounds of spring. In that place, I could forget the craziness of the past; Shorty was gone by this time, and I had no fear of the uncertain future. I would lie there and imagine I would someday rule the world. Now it is fifty years later, and this old soul that resided in such a young man is still looking at ruling the world. Only now, it is only his world that he is becoming master of, a world more spirit than flesh.

Best Wishes Peace Profound
Love for All
Dony Hia

Get Out of Your Head…

Denial is tricky. When you're in it, you don't know it; if you could know it, you wouldn't be in it. Denial is the ultimate method of suppressing feeling. It is very hard to overcome. Psychologist estimate that maybe 40 percent of all clients end psychotherapy still in denial—their psychotherapist unable to crack their shell.
~ John Yee, *Facing the Fire*

From what I am learning, doing energy work, one reason regular therapy does not often work on anger is that most therapists only work with the head and not the body. When anger is stored in the body instead of the head, it can change from being an emotional issue and become a physical pain or illness issue. When anger, or even joy, is stored deep in the flesh, the mind may not recognize it as an emotion anymore. In times of fight or flight, the buried anger can rise up and take over, driving the bus; the rest of the time, it can be buried so far below the surface that we don't even see it.

From my own experience, through energy work, when I release my buried anger, not only do I start reacting differently to tense situations, my body feels lighter and healthier.

Best Wishes for Peace Profound
Love for All
Dony Hia

Me, Not Me...

Could I have been anyone other than me?
~ Dave Matthews

Just a few years ago, if someone had told me I would be doing the energy work I am doing now, I would have laughed at the idea. Now I believe it is such a powerful tool that I am at a point where I cannot imagine not learning it. I hope I can get to a place where I can share some of what I am learning.

I want to share a practice, taught to me by Alison and in energy class, that I find healing, physically, spiritually and mentally. Sit comfortably with eyes closed. Think of your name, when thinking of your name, or names, think deeply that this name is you. Feel this name being all of you. Then, starting at the top of your head, slowly scan down your body and energy field, which extends about three feet around you. You might be surprised to find as you slowly scan down your being that you find areas that are not you. These areas are energies from others that have penetrated your energy field. When you notice these, if you are really relaxed and aware, you may notice whom the energy belongs to. Then again, you may not know who the energy belongs to. You will just realize it is not yours. When you notice energy that is not your own, just mentally or visually ask it to leave. If you realize you know who it belongs to, ask it to go home. If you feel you are successful in having the energy leave, Alison would say fill the space with light. In energy class, on the other hand, it would be more apt to invite the energy you left somewhere else to return home.

Both Alison and teachers of the energy class say we should not have anyone else's energy in us; nor should we place our energy into others. Sometimes when we strike out at someone with anger, verbally or otherwise, we may leave a trace of our energy. Also, sometimes when we desire someone, or something too much, we can send parts of our energy out away from us.

I know for many people this may seem a little out there. But before judging, I would suggest giving it a try. You might just find that you release some pain or fill a void.

Best Wishes for Peace Profound
Love for All
Dony Hia

Ground Yourself...

The ground's generosity takes in our compost and grows beauty!
Try to be more like the ground.
~ Rumi

What you seek is seeking you.
~ Rumi

In energy class, the teacher often says one of the benefits of the class will be the act of opening up to your life's purpose.

Mystics tend to believe we choose our births. It seems only natural I became a plumber; I certainly had a lot of my own shit I needed to turn into fertilizer. Now that there are flowers blooming from the compost, it would be nice if there was a way I could start showing others troubles now are treasures later.

Best Wishes for Peace Profound
Love for All
Dony Hia

A Few Thoughts from Plato...

All men are by nature equal, made all of the same earth by one Workman; and however we deceive ourselves, as dear unto God is the poor peasant as the mighty prince.
~ Plato

He was a wise man who invented beer.
~ Plato

How can you prove whether at this moment we are sleeping, and all our thoughts are a dream; or whether we are awake, and talking to one another in the waking state?
~ Plato

Every heart sings a song, incomplete, until another heart whispers back. Those who wish to sing always find a song. At the touch of a lover, everyone becomes a poet.
~ Plato

    I am often amazed at how much wisdom was on the planet thousands of years ago. You had Greek philosophers, you had Buddha and other Indian sages, Confucius in China, the Mayan civilization in the Americas, and great societies in the Middle East. Time and time throughout history the planet has had brilliance only to have warring tribes destroy the wisdom of the sages. More often than not, this destruction has been in the name of religion. It seems the mystical schools, which were not formed into religions, have never tried to destroy the wisdom of other beings.

    My heart sings louder these days than it ever has, and still to my own tune.

Best Wishes for Peace Profound
Love for All
Dony Hia

Play…

The conscious mind may be compared to a fountain playing in the sun and falling back into the great subterranean pool of subconscious from which it rises.
~ Sigmund Freud

The first human who hurled an insult instead of a stone was the founder of civilization.
~ Sigmund Freud

I think most people take their minds way to seriously; they should take their minds out for a good time more often. After that, it would be a good idea to dive in the water and check out the life below the surface. One might find that there is more life in the ocean of the mind than in all the waters on the planet.

The first human who decided he did not want to hunt one day, and said to the person next to him, "If you give me a chunk of that mammoth, I'll tell you a great story" was probably the founder of the first religion. There have been great storytellers ever since!

Best Wishes for Peace Profound
Love for All
Dony Hia

A Few Thoughts on Giving Thanks…

Best of all is it to preserve everything in a pure, still heart, and let there be for every pulse a thanksgiving, and for every breath a song.
~ Konrad von Gesner

Gratitude is the inward feeling of kindness received. Thankfulness is the natural impulse to express that feeling. Thanksgiving is the following of that impulse.
~ Henry Van Dyke

Pride slays thanksgiving, but a humble mind is the soil out of which thanks naturally grow. A proud man is seldom a grateful man, for he never thinks he gets as much as he deserves.
~ Henry Ward Beecher

Thanksgiving is three days away and I know there are already people out there who are dreading going home. Unfortunately, many families are dysfunctional, and getting together once or twice a year is not the healthiest thing for these people. I feel very blessed and thankful for each and every person in my life: those who I am close to and those who I may have struggled with. The ones we struggle with are after all our best teachers.

My prayer for this year: May all those who are struggling and trying to find peace and happiness be able to look within and find it in their own hearts. Inside our own heart is the only place that peace and joy can really be found. If they can't find it by themselves, may someone help point the way!

Best Wishes for Peace Profound
Love for All
Dony Hia

A Little Jung…

The word "happiness" would lose its meaning if it were not balanced by sadness.
~ Carl Jung

The meeting of two personalities is like the contact of two chemical substances: if there is any reaction, both are transformed.
~ Carl Jung

Sometimes I am amazed at how many adults still seek happiness ever after and are not content with happiness in the moment.

There have been so many great people in my life who have helped me to continue to evolve. Some have done it with love and some with pain. I am not sure who I owe more gratitude to. We need the love but it is true that we grow more from the pain. I guess I am thankful for both.

Best Wishes for Peace Profound
Love for All
Dony Hia

Irritations...

Everything that irritates us about others can lead us to a better understanding of ourselves.
~ Carl Jung

The shoe that fits one person pinches another; there is no recipe for living that suits all cases.
~ Carl Jung

    About thirty-three years ago, a Buddhist practitioner said to me, "What we don't like in others is what we don't like in ourselves."

    It is also said that everything is a reflection of our own mind. More and more, I like all aspects of people, even things that used to rub me the wrong way.

    I think that if there are five billion people on the planet there should be five billion belief systems and five billion spiritual paths.

    I think this goes along well with what the mystics believe (which I now consider myself) but rubs many religious people the wrong way.

Best Wishes for Peace Profound
Love for All
Dony Hia

Chameleons…

We are like chameleons; we take our hue and the color of our moral character, from those who are around us.
~ John Locke

Most of us are chameleons, and we live with several layers, in several worlds each day. We are one person with our lovers, another person with each family member, another person with each of our coworkers and often even a different person with each stranger we pass by during the day.

It seems sages and crazies on the street are less chameleon-like, and often it is only followers who decide a person is a sage or a crazy (not that I think crazy is the proper word). For instance, take someone like Chogyam Trumpa Rimpoche: many who met him became followers, and many walked away thinking he was crazy.

Always, in each moment, we see in others what our own minds need, at that very moment, to help guide us forward. If we don't get it, we may step backwards for a moment but like the universe, all beings are evolving forward. Of course, the Buddhist would say that this is on a relative plane; in absolute reality, there are no beings.

May I always be just a little crazy!

Best Wishes for Peace Profound
Love for All
Dony Hia

There You Are…

And remember, no matter where you go, there you are.
~ Confucius

    How many times have people moved, trying to get away from a problem, only to find the same problem pops up in this new area? It is obvious if the same problem keeps reoccurring, it is not an external move that will help; it is an internal move that is needed. We can do internal shifts that change how we relate to the world, and thus how the world relates to us.

Best Wishes for Peace Profound
Love for All
Dony Hia

Spirit and Flesh...

The Paradox of Meditation.
The meditation experience is interesting because on one hand it is about completely letting go of everything, and on the other hand, it is about paying more attention. It's a paradox. Let go of everything and have the courage and faith and conviction to keep letting go, fearlessly, no matter what arises. But don't let go of consciousness, don't let go of attention, don't let go of awareness. Meditation is the paradox between those two positions.
~ Andrew Cohen

It seems to me when we really let go of everything, and are still very conscious of our surroundings, the world becomes almost surreal. We start to notice our whole environment is a dance of energy. The world seems to appear very electric and vibrant. We can live in the world but not of it. At this point, we are as much, or more, spirit than flesh.

Best Wishes for Peace Profound
Love for All
Dony Hia

Dream Beings…

All human beings are also dream beings. Dreaming ties all mankind together.
~ Jack Kerouac

When we are asleep and dreaming, we are half way between this world and the spirit world. During sleep, for most of us, we are more connected to the super consciousness than when we are when we are awake. When we are in deep, deep sleep, with no dreaming, we are connected to the source. In light REM sleep we are often working things out that our waking mind cannot fathom. In deep sleep we are connected to the One, and it is here where our core is recharged. Through energy work we can merge dream time and waking time. Of course, many mystics believe we are but dreaming our lives.

Best Wishes for Peace Profound
Love for All
Dony Hia

Cleaning Potatoes…

Only in relationship can you know yourself, not in abstraction and certainly not in isolation. The movement of behavior is the sure guide to yourself. It's the mirror of your consciousness: this mirror will reveal its content, the images, the attachments, the fears, the loneliness, the joy and sorrow. Poverty lies in running away from this, either in its sublimations or its identities.
~ Jiddu Krishnamurti.

Around 1980, a Buddhist lady friend of mine spoke of how they would clean potatoes in Japan. She said the potatoes would be put into a drum with water and then rotated. As the potatoes rubbed up against one another, they would clean one another. She used this metaphor to show how we, as people, rub up against one another to clean our karma and evolve. She would also say, "What we don't like in others is what we don't like in ourselves, and what we do like in others we like in ourselves." We could expand this to what we don't like in our world we don't like in ourselves, what we do like in our world we like in ourselves. Simply put our world mirrors our minds.

There have been a few times when I was out and about and I only saw Buddhas, and the world looked like Nirvana.

Best Wishes for Peace Profound
Love for All
Dony Hia

Joy and Happiness...

Joy is a net of love by which you can catch souls.
~ Mother Teresa

The purpose of our lives is to be happy.
~ 14th Dalai Lama

Joy and happiness are a human birth right. I believe most humans enter a womb with joy and happiness. Even in the womb, some people seem to start to lose joy and happiness. Others seem to lose them through struggles in childhood. The nice thing is, with anyone they are never really lost, joy and happiness can only be misplaced; one can always find them again. It just takes effort to find things we misplace.

Happy Birthday Michelle... Love Ya, Dad...

Best Wishes for Peace Profound
Love for All
Dony Hia

Brain waves:

Gamma waves 30-70 Hz

Beta waves 13-30 Hz like normal waking

Alpha waves 7-13 Hz like normal meditation

Theta waves 4-7 Hz like hypnosis

Delta Waves 1-4 Hz like Samadhi

It seems to me the lower the Hz the easier it is to tune to the waves of Joy and Happiness.

Stumbling into Our Bliss...

If you do follow your bliss you put yourself on a kind of track that has been there all the while, waiting for you, and the life that you ought to be living is the one you are living. Follow your bliss and don't be afraid, and doors will open where you didn't know they were going to be.
~ Joseph Campbell

Whether you follow your bliss or not, you have put yourself on a track that has been there all the while.

I can't say that I have followed my bliss. I think by just working on healing my fears for forty-plus years I have just stumbled into bliss. In this past year of marriage to Luyu I feel I have managed to have fifty years of happiness in one year, my most blissful year to date.

Last night, as I was carving and sanding on a couple of walking sticks, I thought about how I get into such a peaceful blissful state when I create artful projects. Had I had more courage as a very young man, my career might have been one of art; then again, if I had taken that path, I might not be as at peace as I am today. Who knows, with a different path I might not even be here today.

Then again, how could I feel more bliss than I do now? I like the way I have stumbled ;-).

Even with my present joy, I have a feeling that a miracle is moving towards me within a couple of months, one that will bring joy to me and others. Maybe it will be artful.

May everyone stumble or bravely walk into their bliss.

Best Wishes for Peace Profound
Love for All
Dony Hia

Removing Mask…

The privilege of a lifetime is being who you are.
~ Joseph Campbell

At a very young age, we start to place our masks over who we really are and what we really feel. For instance, we are angry and our parents tell us we should not be angry. We may have placed a happy mask over our anger at that moment in order not to disappoint our parents. Or maybe at a time when we were very young, we made a mistake and our parents, or someone else called us stupid. What do we do, we create a stupid mask hiding our brilliance.

Much of our youth is creating masks, and suppressing our true identities. If we are lucky, there comes a time, and teachings, that shows us how to safely remove our mask and let our inner light shine through. We all have a very bright light at our core.

Best Wishes for Peace Profound
Love for All
Dony Hia

A few Thoughts on Karma...

Once you know the nature of anger and joy is empty and you let them go, you free yourself from karma.
~ Bodhidharma

Bodhidharma was an Indian monk who is considered by many the founder of Zen Buddhism. He took Buddhism from India to China in the 5th or 6th century.

Contrary to popular misconception, karma has nothing to do with punishment and reward. It exists as part of our holographic universe's binary or dualistic operating system only to teach us responsibility for our creations—and all things we experience are our creations.
~ Sol Luckman

Sol Luckman, modern artist and author.

You must acknowledge and experience this part of the universe. Karma is intricate, too vast. You would, with your limited human senses, consider it too unfair. But you have tools to really, truly love. Loving the children is very important. But love everyone as you would love your children.
~ Kuan Yin

Kuan Yin, Avolokitesvara in Sanskrit. Avolokitesvara is in masculine form, and Kuan Yin is feminine form. I like the translation of Avolokitesvara as "hearer of cries of the world." In either form, they are known as Lord of Compassion. So it was a human who wrote and attributed the above quote to Kuan Yin.

Of all physical beings on the planet, probably only humans concern themselves with karma. All other beings probably just live moment to moment until they die. They seem to be more Zen like.

Best Wishes for Peace Profound
Love for All
Dony Hia

Goethe...

In the human spirit, as in the universe, nothing is higher or lower; everything has equal rights to a common center which manifest its hidden existence precisely through the harmonic relationship between every part and itself.
~ Goethe

Humans, and probably all beings in the universe, have a core, and I feel this connects all with One and one with All. In this sense we all are connected to the center of the universe. We all help the One evolve, and we are all helped by the One.

Best Wishes for Peace Profound
Love for All
Dony Hia

Our Own Frequencies...

The physical Universe is an aggregate of frequencies.
~ Buckminster Fuller

In other words, Buckminster Fuller is saying the entire universe is none other than vibrating energy.

The reason our bodies are able to hold together is because each of our cells, each of the atoms which make up the cells, each of the vibrating strings which make up the atoms, vibrates at the same frequency.

While many of us will have a frequency, a vibration, which is close to others, each human, each being actually has his or her own frequencies. In one of energy class, the teacher actually amplified each of our frequencies. It was amazing to experience. You could sense, feel, experience, each person's frequency.

When the teacher amplified one person's frequency, almost everyone would have the same sense of that frequency, such as high, low, or middle range. You would also get a sense of sharp, dull or other feelings. Some of the comments made on mine were, middle to low frequency, metallic edgy and the one I like the most: several said they sensed a childlike energy in my frequency.

Best Wishes for Peace Profound
Love for All
Dony Hia

Perfection…

As long as our orientation is towards perfection or success, we will never learn about unconditional friendship with ourselves, nor will we find compassion.
~ Pema Chodron

    For much of my life, I was worried about perfection to the point of being agoraphobic. Now I just try to take each moment for what it is. I understand each moment is perfect as it is, as long and I don't try to interject my opinion of good, bad or indifferent. Each moment just is!

Best Wishes for Peace Profound
Love for All
Dony Hia

A Core Full of Wealth...

We already have everything we need. There is no need for self-improvement. All these trips that we lay on ourselves—the heavy-duty fearing that we're bad and hoping that we're good, the identities that we so dearly cling to, the rage, the jealousy and the addictions of all kinds—never touch our basic wealth. They are like clouds that temporarily block the sun. But all the time our warmth and brilliance are right here. This is who we really are. We are one blink of an eye away from being fully awake.
~ Pema Chodron, *Start Where You Are: A Guide to Compassionate Living*

We may tend to think that our world comes from the outside in; it is more accurate to say our world flows from the inside out. How each of us sees, each of our worlds starts on the inside. Things appearing to come from the outside are really drawn to us from the inside; much like a magnet draws iron ore. Our basic wealth lies in each of our cores. The more we can live from our core, the more wealth, happiness and bliss we will materialize in our seemingly outer world.

Best Wishes for Peace Profound
Love for All
Dony Hia

Many, Many Minds...

The human body contains a great many biological oscillators, all hooked together in the organism we know as ourselves. The three most powerful are the heart, gastrointestinal tract, and brain.
The internal energy fields we sense within us, coming from all our biological oscillators (from cells to organs to the combined, whole organism), contain certain kinds of information about our internal world.
We feel that information as certain kinds or groupings of emotions. These emotions give us informational, sensory cues about what is going on within us. If we only pay attention.
~ Stephen Harrod Buhner, *Secret Teachings of Plants*

Each oscillator in our body, and there are thousands, is in its own way a mind. I would say the chakras are also oscillators; they certainly are minds.

We have all heard, "He lives from his heart," or "She is in touch with her heart." Another saying is, "He goes by his gut." I personally make many decisions from my gut.

None of the minds in our body work independently of the others. Some minds, or chakras, may have more an influence on us than others; I tend to live a lot from my second and sixth chakras. All the chakras influence who we are and how we react to and see our worlds. Science did us a disfavor when it tends to say our minds are in our brains. Our minds are throughout our body, and many exist even outside our bodies. While most traditions work with seven chakras, in energy class, we work with an eighth chakra, eighteen inches below our feet, and a ninth chakra, eighteen inches above our heads. These two chakras help sustain our auric field. The more balanced our chakras (minds), the more equally we live from all of them, and I would guess, the more bliss we experience within and share without.

Best Wishes for Peace Profound
Love for All
Dony Hia

Small Child or Children...

I don't grow up. In me is the small child of my early days.
~ M.C. Escher

There is a small child, more correctly there are small children in all of us. This small child, or children, is ourselves. If these children are happy, we are probably happy; if they are not happy for some reason, then we struggle for happiness ourselves. If the child or children are not happy, it is usually because of trauma the child felt in some past moment. The child may have felt trauma and no one but the child noticed; each child handles things differently. The amazing thing I have discovered is just about anyone can go back and rescue their inner child, or children. One can rewrite the memories of the children, and thus rescue them, removing their fears and bringing them happiness; there is no time in mind. Think what the world might be like if everyone was able to do this. I am sure most of the fear and anger in the world is from small children frozen in time. And these children are "driving the bus," as Alison would say.

Best Wishes for Peace Profound
Love for All
Dony Hia

Communicating with the World...

The mystery of life isn't a problem to solve but a reality to experience.
~ Frank Herbert

We feel the touch upon us, and those millions of unique touches hold within them specific meanings sent to us from the heart of the world and from the heart of the living beings with which we inhabit the world. This interchange changes the quality of our lives and reminds us that we are never alone. We are one organism among many, one en-souled form among a multitude.
~ Stephen Harrod Buhner

We tend to believe it is our brain that communicates with the world; in reality, our whole body is continually sending messages into, and receiving messages from the world around us. This nonverbal communication explains why when we meet someone new, before we even exchange any words, we may feel that we like or dislike them. Our heart, our gut and all our other minds are constantly communicating with our brain. When we think our brain has made a decision it may be that our heart, gut or some other chakra really had the lead on the decision made. Our bodies send out and receive vibrations constantly, just like ripples on water. Our bodies often decide whether they like or dislike these vibrations before our brain even has time to make a decision.

Best Wishes for Peace Profound
Love for All
Dony Hia

One with...

*Though the gods have the power of speech
more often they choose a flower or a plant:
elder leaves pressed on a blotter,
or spring buds emerging from a winter stem.*

*These messages they send—
so ordinary we usually miss them:
an easy laughter and lightness,
or legs casually crossed and touching.*

*The way a serpentine dike blends seamlessly into bedrock
or the way two possible lovers move,
starting and stopping passing and pausing,
on an April trail.*

*The subtlest oracles are always the most obvious—
seeing what is clearly in front of us the most difficult:
a butterfly hatching from a ruptured dream,
or a splintered tree rooting in the soil where it fell.*
~ Dale Pendell

    For some reason I really enjoy this poem. I think it is because each line reminds me of a picture in my mind of when I see something similar and time stops for a moment. With fall rains coming, I know I will start spending time in a cool moist forest, and to some extent I will become one with the plants, and especially fungus, in the places I wonder.

    I think if I could spend a year in a forest, I would gain more enlightenment than from all the books I have read.

    Being here now is all the enlightenment one ever needs.

Best Wishes for Peace Profound
Love for All
Dony Hia

Running on All Cylinders…

And now here is my secret, a very simple secret; it is only with the heart that one can see rightly; what is essential is invisible to the eye.
~ Antoine de Saint-Exupery

    While the heart is an essential part of seeing (knowing) correctly, I would guess a complete balanced system is needed to live fully. Trying to see with only the heart would be like trying to run on just one cylinder. All the organs, all the chakras, and our auric fields are all part of one complete system. The smoother each part functions the smoother the entire vehicle, in this case a human vehicle, runs.

    Each of us, each being, is also part of a larger vehicle…

Best Wishes for Peace Profound
Love for All
Don Hughes

Expressions...

All the things and events we usually consider as irreconcilable, such as cause and effect, past and future, subject and object, are actually just like the crest and trough of a single wave, a single vibration. For a wave, although itself a single event, only expresses itself through the opposites of crest and trough, high point and low point. For that very reason, the reality is not found in the crest nor the trough alone, but in their unity.
~ Ken Wilber

    As humans, we can only express ourselves through other humans. As a being we can only express ourselves through other beings. As a vibration we express ourselves with all other vibrations. Since the entire universe is a dance of vibrating energy, and we are vibrating energy, we are expressed in the entire universe; more amazingly, the entire universe is expressed in us.

Best Wishes for Peace Profound
Love for All
Don Hughes

Poison to Medicine...

Every sweet has its sour; every evil its good.
~ Ralph Waldo Emerson

There is a Buddhist saying: One man's poison is another man's medicine. Most medicines are made from poison, and in large doses, almost everything becomes poison, even water. This is the way karma often works. While Hurricane Sandy caused a lot of destruction, she also created a lot of work opportunities for a lot of people; things will be rebuilt. In each of our lives things happen which seem like poison at the time. Only later do we understand it was not poison, but medicine.

Best Wishes for Peace Profound
Love for All
Dony Hia

The Heart, and Other Areas of Consciousness…

The heart is the primary organ of perception; the brain supplies a supportive, secondary—though essential—role.
~ Stephen Harrod Buhner

The intellect is powerless to express thought without the aid of the heart.
~ Henry David Thoreau

We have been taught thought only comes from the brain and this is why most of us feel consciousness in our head. For most of my life, I have also felt thought in my gut. While I have felt thought in my heart, when I was young I began trying to shut this organ of cognition down; I used my gut for intuition not the heart. As an addition to my practices, I try to spend a few moments, a few times a day, in which I place my consciousness in my heart, not my head or gut.

When we place our awareness on different organs, or different chakras, if we pay attention, we can see how we relate to our world a little differently depending on which organ or chakra we are paying attention to. As mentioned, the more we can balance and live through all of them, the more balanced our life will be.

Best Wishes for Peace Profound
Love for All
Dony Hia

Finding Heart...

Each of us in our own way can try to spread compassion into people's hearts. Western civilizations these days place great importance on filling the human 'brain' with knowledge, but no one seems to care about filling the human 'heart' with compassion. This is what the real role of religion is.
~ 14th Dalai Lama

Maybe if more of us spent time in our hearts, and other chakras, and less time in just our heads the world would be filled with more compassion and, yes, understanding.

In yesterday's *Fresh Morning Breath* I mentioned I am trying to spend more moments in my heart. Late this morning, I saw a worker breaking a rule he had been warned not to break before. I told my GF we need to fire him because of this, and we got his check. In the afternoon, when he received his check, he came to me with the job steward and asked, pleaded actually, for one more chance, promising he would never do it again. At first I said no, he had been warned several times and written up before. When he asked one more time that he not be fired, I felt myself drop into my heart, knowing this young man is a hard worker. When I dropped to my heart I told him, "One chance, and you are to take a three-day suspension!"

I think this heart decision will turn out good for the company and just as importantly, for this young man. I think he will come back Friday with a less arrogant attitude. Hope it works out well.

Best Wishes for Peace Profound
Love for All
Dony Hia

Finding Love...

Love is of all passions the strongest, for it attacks simultaneously the head, the heart and the senses.
~ Lao Tzu

The only word I would change in Lao Tzu's quote is "attacks." I would change that word to "nourishes."

Let's see how it reads if we change that one word: Love is of all passions the strongest, for it nourishes simultaneously the head, the heart and the senses.

Love is probably the most potent medicine in the universe and it seems to heal whether you receive love or give love.

Best Wishes for Peace Profound
Love for All
Dony Hia

Sharing Light…

Thousands of candles can be lit from a single candle, and the life of the candle will not be shortened. Happiness never decreases by being shared.
~ Buddha

Luyu and I spent four days in Mendocino. Mother Nature was kind; she only gave us one light rain while we were in her forest. Yet it seemed to rain heavy when we were driving between spots.

On Saturday, I led a foray of about twenty people, and while Luyu and I were very pleased with our finds, we were both more excited to see the faces on others when they found mushrooms.

When we returned to the Mendocino camp, you could see the excitement on everyone's faces, especially those who foraged for the first time. The whole camp is done by volunteers; volunteers who share both knowledge and energy. It is as if the volunteers take their light and pass it into another.

Best Wishes for Peace Profound
Love for All
Dony Hia

Finding a Path...

You must realize my friend, that the deeper we go into this, both written and spoken words of formal language become less and less adequate as a medium of expressions.
~ Manuel Cordova Rios

Enlightenment can never be given, or even shared with another, not even by a Buddha. Enlightenment has to be experienced, and once experienced, it is impossible to fully describe. Buddhas and other enlightened beings can point out a path, but they cannot walk the path for another being. And while one may start out on a path pointed out by another, the final steps have to be taken by one's self.

Each of us has to take our own final steps into enlightenment; no other being, or deity, can do if for us.

Best Wishes for Peace Profound
Love for All
Dony Hia

Form and Balance...

All true artist, whether they know it or not, create from a place of no-mind, from inner stillness.
~ Eckhart Tolle

    Now, I don't know if I have the right to call myself an artist because I have sold so few pieces over the years. What I do know is when anything artful flows through me, that is just what it really does; it comes from a place more than just me. I never start with a design, I start with a thought and an idea of what I might want to do, and then it seems to develop of itself.
In energy class we have learned a rigid pattern wants form; we recognize our world, more than other patterns, through form. I know for me, especially in art, I seem to need form and balance. It is good to know one's self. Even though the three attached photos are of different mediums I can see the form and balance I strive for in each one. I wrote 'I strive for,' yet I am sure it is an energy more than just me striving for this form and balance. The photos are of a backyard fence, Ikebana, and a dinner.

Best Wishes for
Peace Profound
Love for All
Dony Hia

You are the Sky...

You are the sky. Everything else – it's just the weather.
~ Pema Chodron

We tend to think we are our body and our mind, but this is not the case. Our body and mind are like clothes we put on with each incarnation. When we experience our core, we can get a real sense of what Pema is talking about. In energy class we are guided to experience our core. In our last class we were guided to experience our template of perfection self, which is just below our highest of high selves. I can't put words to my template of perfection self, other than it is where I can first sense movement of energy. When I do artwork, I can sense it starting to form as high as the template of perfection self; I can't feel anything higher.

One of the meditations we do, which I find very balancing and grounding, is to sense an energy, a light traveling down from our highest self, down through our template of perfection, down through our core and into earth mother. While I have no real feeling or experience of my highest self, I can still do the meditation; it just seems to gain its first weight at the template of perfection.

I think above all of our highest selves, there is only One.

Best Wishes for Peace Profound
Love for All
Dony Hia

Death and Birth…

Tell a wise person or else keep silent,
because the mass man will mock it right away.
I praise what is truly alive,
what longs to be burned to death.

In the calm water of love-nights,
where you were begotten, where you have begotten,
a strange feeling comes over you
when you see the silent candle burning.

Now you are no longer caught
in the obsession with darkness,
and a desire for higher love-making
sweeps you upward.

Distance does not make you falter,
now, arriving in magic, flying,
and, finally, insane for the light,
you are the butterfly and you are gone.

And so long as you haven't experienced
this: to die and so to grow,
you are only a troubled quest
on the dark earth.
~ Goethe

In every moment there is a death and a birth. The thing is, we usually rebirth ourselves much as we were in the last moment. Life often does throw something our way to make us rebirth in a new way; it could be a tragedy, or just a frustration of riding the same merry-go-round of day-to-day life. Whatever the cause, in order to grow, we have to let something in our consciousness die.

Best Wishes for Peace Profound
Love for All
Dony Hia

Childlike Eyes...

O human, see then the human being rightly: the human being has heaven and earth and the whole of creation in itself, and yet is a complete form, and in it everything is already present, though hidden.
~ Hildegard of Bingen

There is nothing outside of us that we need or want which is not already within us. People think we bring things from without to within, but what we really do is bring what is from within to the presence around us.

Every moment, if we are truly in the moment, has everything we need and is a perfect representation of where our mind is in that moment.

For just a moment, when you finish reading this, let go of any past thoughts, and don't let any future thoughts come to mind. Close your eyes for just a moment as you do this. Then, whenever you open your eyes, look around with childlike eyes. If you are not a little amazed at everything you see in your presence, you probably did not clear your thoughts and did see with childlike eyes.

Best Wishes for Peace Profound
Love for All
Dony Hia

Search the Bag…

When we are one or two years old, we had what we might visualize as 360-degree personality. Energy radiated out from all parts of our body and all parts of our psyche. A child running is a living globe of energy. We had a ball of energy, all right; but one day we noticed our parents didn't like a certain parts of that ball.
~ Robert Bly

I believe Bly is correct, for the most part, but in many cases the energy is actually dimmed in the womb. Some children, unfortunately, notice in the womb that their parents do not really want them, or like them.

Behind us, we have an invisible bag and the parts of us our parents don't like, we, to keep our parents' love, put in the bag. By the time we go to school, our bag is quite large. Then our teachers have their say, and then we do a lot of bag-stuffing in high school. This time, it's no longer the evil grownups that pressure us, but people our own age.
~ Robert Bly

The bag is our subconscious mind, and often because of what others think, we stuff some of our best parts into the bag we carry. In order to be whole beings, we need to look back into the bag and recover hidden parts. We lose a lot of energy every time we try to suppress our true nature. Even the parts of ourselves we might not like, we need to look at and ask why.

Best Wishes for Peace Profound
Love for All
Dony Hia

Extending our Identity...

Once we have... "fallen in love outwards," once we have experienced the fierce joy of life that attends extending our identity into nature, once we realize that the nature within and the nature without are continuous, then we too may share and manifest the exquisite beauty and effortless grace associated with the natural world.
~ John Seed

    The natural world outside us is neither happy nor sad, ugly nor beautiful. We choose to make the outside fit the inside, not the other way around. If we feel joy inside, we see joy on the outside, if we feel sad on the inside we see sadness on the outside. For the most part, I feel magical and mystical on the inside.

Best Wishes for Peace Profound
Love for All
Dony Hia

Foundation for All Abundance...

Acknowledging the good that you already have in your life is the foundation for all abundance.
~ Eckhart Tolle

When you acknowledge the good in yourself, you naturally start to acknowledge it in those around you.

Seems when I acknowledge the good in the design of nature, nature supplies me with abundance. For me, abundance is not just my physical needs being met. Abundance is also the great joy I find seeing the good in others. I feel blessed my frequency is tuned such that I am surrounded with so many great people.

I see the abundance in all the beings in nature such as the attached mushrooms. I felt honored that they chose to come home with and nurture Luyu and me.

Best Wishes for Peace Profound
Love for All
Dony Hia

It is All Still There, Maybe Even Haunting Us...

I died as a mineral and became a plant,
I died as a plant and rose to animal,
I died as an animal and I was Man.
Why should I fear? When was I less by dying?
~ Rumi

The further we are from our origin, the less we remember it. Most of us don't remember much or anything from four years or younger. It is a rare being that remembers a past life. Yet, I feel and believe Rumi is correct; we have all been evolving for a long time.

Rosicrucians, Buddhists, American Indians and followers of many other traditions believe all matter is imbued with spirit, thus life.

In energy class, one of the matrixes we build is the children's twenty count, based on an Indian tradition. The first five energies we call on are as follows: Grandfather Sun, Grandmother Earth, Sacred Plants, Sacred Animals and Sacred Humans. This follows what Rumi states; *one is built up upon the other.*

It is said that in our reptilian brain and our subconscious mind, everything we have evolved through is still there. A lot of the way we respond to life is from these past life experiences still stored within our being. Our next life will be laid upon this one.

Best Wishes for Peace Profound
Love for All
Dony Hia

A Couple Thoughts from Eckhart…

Anything that you resent and strongly react to in another is also in you.
~ Eckhart Tolle

Sometimes letting things go is an act of far greater power than defending or hanging on.
~ Eckhart Tolle

I remember thirty-two years ago, when I started practicing Buddhism, a lady would say, "What we don't like in others, we don't like in ourselves."

At that time, it seemed there were people I did not like very much. These days though, there are not many people I don't like. If I start to think I don't like someone, I try to understand why in my own mind, not theirs, I feel I don't like them.

We all have patterns, and I know the pattern is not the person. People often block energy movement within, when holding on to or defending something that might be better let go of. Blocked energy creates stress and often creates illness.

Best Wishes for Peace Profound
Love for All
Dony Hia

So Little Time, So Many Miracles…

There are only two ways to live your life. One is as though nothing is a miracle. The other is as though everything is a miracle.
~ Albert Einstein

This morning after looking Tilo in the eyes, patting him on the head, looking into the eyes of my beautiful warm-hearted wife, hugging her, and kissing her smooth soft cheek, I headed out the door to work.

When I stepped onto the front porch, looking straight out ahead, I saw the moon. While you could see the outline of the entire moon, there was only a sliver of yellow light, forming a glowing crescent on the bottom. Above the moon and slightly to the left, the planet Venus shined in all her glory. This sight caused me to pause, look up at the dark sky and see several bright stars twinkling in the cool, crisp early morning sky. After my pause, I proceeded to slowly walk down the stairs, still glancing up every few steps.

As I took in all this beauty, my mind said, "How many more beautiful mornings will you have?" The Buddhist in me reminded me how impermanent everything is and how we need to appreciate fully with our whole heart, every time we are given these beautiful moments.

Everything is a miracle!

Best Wishes for Peace Profound
Love for All
Dony Hia

Fresh Eyes…

You have uttered the right word, however," Merlin went on. "Transformation. But it is yourself that must constantly be Transforming. You cannot bring the same stale self to the world and expect the world to be new for you.
~ Deepak Chopra, *The Way of the Wizard*

    I had someone a few years ago ask me how Tilo and I can walk the same path to the lake and back every evening. The thing is while we may walk the same route we never walk the same path, each walk is new and fresh. While Tilo naturally is always living in the moment, I manage through a little effort to do the same.

    Fresh eyes see a fresh world each moment.

Best Wishes for Peace Profound
Love for All
Dony Hia

Creating Ourselves…

The most creative act you will ever undertake is the act of creating yourself.
~ Deepak Chopra, *The Way of the Wizard*

I like this quote! I consider myself artistic and creative, and to think I have had a large part of creating myself is intriguing. The greatest thing about creating ourselves is that it is an endless project.

We recreate ourselves each moment. And if we don't like who we are, or where our life is at any given moment, we can start right there to create ourselves a new.

I look at my family and friends and I think, "Ahhh, they are all talented and creative at their creations."

Best Wishes for Peace Profound
Love for All
Dony Hia

Hard Light...

Molecules form and dissolve, returning to the primordial soup of atoms. But consciousness survives the death of the molecules on which it rides. What was once a bundle of energy in a sunbeam turns into a leaf, only to fall and change again into soil. The change of state crosses many boundaries. A sunbeam is invisible, whereas leaves and soil are visible. A leaf is alive and growing, whereas sunbeams aren't. The colors of light, leaf, and soil are different, and so on. But all these transformations exist as constructs of the mind. The actual energy present in the sunbeam experiences no change at all.
~ Deepak Chopra, *The Way of the Wizard*

    I don't know how long ago the first time I, half kiddingly, said I think of people and all manifestations as being hard light; I know it was many years back. Today when I say this, there is no *half kidding*. All is of the same source, and this source is energy, and this energy is light. For thirty-three-plus years, I have been reading philosophy, and/or religious, especially Buddhist, literature. Probably since at least four years old, I've been trying to figure out life and what it means. While knowledge does help us understand the world we live in, it is only experience which can touch our depths. These days I no longer feel a need to understand life, probably because I am spending so much time just living and loving life as it is. I am starting to experience things as true which in the past I only thought of as partially true.

Best Wishes for Peace Profound
Love for All
Dony Hia

Softening No…

The Problem is that words carry psychological meanings too. It is through words that parents make children feel good or bad, right or wrong. The most powerful expressions anyone can use are yes and no. The effect of these two syllables is to build boundaries or break them down. Everything you think you can do has a yes buried somewhere inside it, usually uttered by a parent or teacher in the distant past. Everything you think you cannot do has a no buried in it, from the same sources.
~ Deepak Chopra

When my daughters, Michelle and Jaime, were young, I too was young, not much more than a child. Both of these young ladies have turned out great, as I see it. I hope in a small way my influence around them was a part of this. By the time DeShaun, my grandson came along, I was just a little bit wiser, I think. I think I make a pretty good grandpa, and a better father these days.

My wife Luyu, left yesterday for China. On January 16th she should return with Yizi, her (our) daughter. Yizi is very bright, often at the top of her class. For me I can see the wisdom of eyes in her pictures, and I look forward to being a part of helping, and watching her, as she grows. As with Michelle, Jaime and DeShaun, I am sure Yizi will aid in my own wisdom development.

Best Wishes for Peace Profound
Love for All
Dony Hia

Transformation...

There is a wellspring of life within you where you can go for cleansing and transformation.
~ Deepak Chopra, *The Way of the Wizard*

In energy class, we are taught where our core is located, and if you can draw yourself into this core, you can get an understanding of what Deepak Chopra is speaking of. When I went into my core in class, I felt if I could go in deeper and out on the other side I would shake hands with the One. This is the location where we can connect with the divine in ourselves.

Our bodies are layers of dancing energy and most of the struggles we have are blocked energy. It can be our own energy or other people's energy blocked in our energy field. We can unblock and balance our own energies, and we can remove energies which are not our own. By freeing and having natural flows of energy, we can transform our lives to be more like heaven on earth. Earth will not change. Only how we relate to it changes.

If you want to find out more about the chakras and core, you can go on the web and type in Human Energy Field.

Best Wishes for Peace Profound
Love for All
Dony Hia

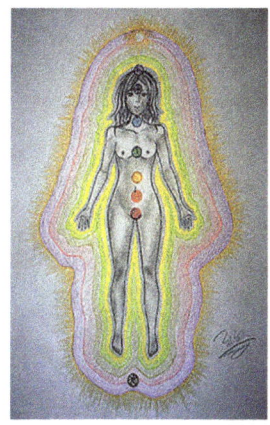
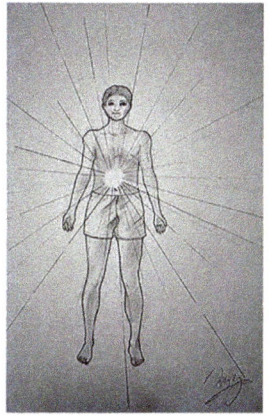

Enjoy the Vibration...

We live as ripples of energy in the vast ocean of energy.
~ Deepak Chopra

It is kind of mind boggling to think the entire universe is made up of the same basic building blocks; vibrating strings of energy. Then again, if one thinks about it, it only makes sense. If the universe wasn't built up from a single basic energy, materializing out of the void only to return again, the universe would be static and dead. If matter were solid, the big bang would have been a big poof.

This same beautiful design, of nothing being solid and nothing being permanent, is the design that gives us the ability to grow and blossom into whatever we believe we can be. The only thing that ever holds us back is that we don't believe.

While I am not sure what direction the future will take me, I do know I believe more, and have more confidence about the future, than I ever have before.

Sit in silence for a moment and sense the vibrations, ripples of energy. If you can sense it, there are several layers of vibrations. The environments around you have several different vibrations. There is even one very, very deep vibration which is the vibration of the universe—shall we say, the breath of the universe. Then if you can, try and feel the vibration of your own being. If you can do this, realize no one else has quite the same vibration as you. It is like no two snowflakes are the same; no other being in the entire universe has the exact same vibration as you.

I know I am not the first one to tell you, YOU ARE SPECIAL!

Best Wishes for Peace Profound
Love for All
Dony Hia

Little "m", Big "M"…

The capital 'm' Mind, or Mind as such, is the empty or spatial quality of our being. This; is the primordially present and un-originated condition, in which the small 'm' is a fluctuating manifestation. If that seems a little difficult to follow—consider an ocean and its waves. The movement of the waves; the currents beneath the waves; the white spray that animates the surface of the ocean—these are all small 'm' mind. The body of the ocean itself is the capital 'm' Mind.
~ Ngakpa Chogyam, *Wearing the Body of Visons*

The fluctuations (the vibrations) are the strings of the string theory which manifest all phenomena, including us and our minds. The ocean, the capital 'M', is like the void where all vibrations emanate from and return to.

Unlike material manifestations, thoughts come from, and return to, the capital 'M' very rapidly.

This is where it becomes interesting and tricky for me. If the thoughts come from and return to the One Mind, they are really not ours. They really belong to the One Mind, and we just borrow our thoughts as we do our body. If this is the case, where does free will come into play, and how do we ever change which thoughts come to us?

Buddhists and mystics say if we want to change which thoughts we receive, we change our own vibration. Changing our vibration is like changing the dial on a radio. Having worked with this concept for thirty-plus years now, and especially in the last couple of years of energy work, I know Buddhists and mystics are correct. For me, these days, I do feel life is more free will than it is a destiny.

Best Wishes for Peace Profound
Love for All
Dony Hia

Magic of Our Ancestors…

It is, as we will see, a general fact that the conscious elements of one stage tend to become the unconscious elements of the next, continually, stage by stratified stage. Thus, the primitive typhonic men and women apparently experienced even while "awake" a magical level that is retained in us moderns preeminently in dreams. So it is that each night, as we sink back into the sphere of the dream, we each and all are converted into sorcerers, soaring above the ground in magical flight and transforming the world at whim. And each night, in the dream, we meet face to face with our ancestors, and even converse occasionally, I daresay, with the Sorcerer of Trois Freres.
~ Ken Wilber, *Up From Eden*

Our subconscious mind does not just contain elements of our human ancestors. It contains elements of our reptilian and all other ancestors right back to the first single-cell life created in an ocean 3.6 billion years ago. Being one who remembers so many dreams, I certainly understand what Wilber speaks of. Seems now is the perfect time to be reading *Up From Eden* by Ken Wilber, which my daughter gave me some time ago.

It also seems a lot of the mystical work we are doing in energy class is reconnecting with the magic of the ancestors Wilber speaks of.

Best Wishes for Peace Profound
Love for All
Dony Hia

Fear of Waking Up...

When you realize it's a dream you can afford to play. The same thing happens when you realize that ordinary life is a dream, just a movie, just a play. You don't become more cautious, more timid, more reserved. You start jumping up and down and doing flips, precisely because it's all a dream, it's all pure Emptiness. You don't feel less, you feel more - because you can afford to. You are no longer afraid of dying, and therefore you are not afraid of living. You become radical and wild, intense and vivid, shocking and silly. You let it all come pouring through, because it's all your dream. Life then assumes its true intensity, its vivid luminosity, its radical effervescence.
~ Ken Wilber

All logic has told me for years and years life is a dream; as the Buddha said, "Foam on surface of the Sea."

My own nightly dreams have hinted to me life is but a dream since I was a young boy. Of course believing life is a dream is not the same as realizing life is a dream. In order to realize it, one has to experience it with body and mind. I think it is only fear that keeps me from taking the next step. It is not easy to let go of one's life as you know it, then step into another life you don't know. Then again, I have done this so many times in a semi-sleeping state.

Best Wishes for Peace Profound
Love for All
Dony Hia

A Few Thoughts on Impermanence...

A warrior chooses a path with heart, any path with heart, and follows it; and then he rejoices and laughs. He knows because he sees that his life will be over altogether too soon. He sees that nothing is more important than anything else.
~ Carlos Castaneda

This existence of ours is as transient as autumn clouds, to watch the birth and death of beings is like looking at the movements of a dance. A lifetime is like a flash of lightning in the sky, rushing by, like a torrent down a steep mountain.
~ Buddha

We are like the spider. We weave our life and then move along in it. We are like the dreamer who dreams and then lives in the dream. This is true for the entire universe.
~ The Upanishads

Come on sweetheart let's adore one another before there is no more of you and me.
~ Rumi

These days I am reminded of impermanence.

If Zack at work was my right hand, Jim certainly was my left. For over a year Jim and I were the first ones in the office, we would talk work but we also talked life. I miss those mornings.

Nabil, a very intelligent, good looking, young man, like me (ha-ha), just informed us he is leaving the company. I have so enjoyed watching the three young men in our job site office mature in their own right here at work. When they first started, the general contractor acted like they were too young to be in the positions they were placed in. Now Zack, Nick and Nabil have the respect of all their piers...

Lately things *be a changing*. Recently, a few friends I knew as couples are no longer couples.

My daughter told me her grandfather, who in my mind is a great man, is in intensive care.

As my wife is away, I think of how I miss her grounding presence.

So this morning, as I am writing, I love the sorrow I feel in my heart as I think of impermanence. I love this sorrow because it reminds me that I do have Heart; I don't always remember this.

So as Rumi would say, let's enjoy one another with our whole hearts, for to soon we will be gone.

Best Wishes for Peace Profound
Love for All
Dony Hia

Hidden Thoughts...

Most thinking, in fact, is done in sub-vocal talking, with a flurry of quiet voices, and frequently as part of a dialogue between Child, Adult, and Parent ego states. Take, for example, the following from Berne: There are four dialogs possible between simple ego states: three dialogues (P-A, P-C, A-C), and one triologue (P-A-C). If the Parental voice splits up into Father and Mother, as it usually does, and if other Parental figures chime in, the situation is more complicated. Each voice may be accompanied by its own set of "gestures" expressed by a chosen set of muscles or a special part of the body.
~ Ken Wilber, *Up From Eden*

We tend to think all our thoughts are stored in our head, but as Eric Berne showed, and most alternative healers know, we don't only bury thoughts in the caverns of our brain we store thoughts in every part of our body, sometimes even in our auric field outside our body. When I finally released the energy that held me agoraphobic for forty-five-plus years, I felt it dissipate six inches up, and 6 inches back, outside the right side of my head.

A lot of the energy causing people to spin the same troubled thoughts over and over again is stored in muscles, organs and even bones. I know through my own work releasing locked energy, not only did my thoughts shift, all of the muscles in my body, which had been tense as long as I could remember, relaxed.

Best Wishes for Peace Profound
Love for All
Dony Hia

No Separate Self...

There is no holy life. There is no war between good and evil. There is no sin and no redemption. None of these things matter to the real you. But they all matter hugely to the false you, the one who believes in the separate self. You have tried to take your separate self, with all its loneliness and anxiety and pride, to the door of enlightenment. But it will never go through, because it is a ghost.
~ Deepak Chopra, *Buddha: A Story of Enlightenment*

    I think Buddhism, and especially Tantric Buddhism, teaches more than any other philosophy, or religion, that good and evil are byproducts of the human mind. This is a very hard teaching to understand if one believes our body and human mind are who we truly are. We truly are much more than this body and this mind, which are with us for one lifetime only. We wrap ourselves in a new body and a new mind with each new incarnation until we remember what and who we truly are. What we truly are is spirit!

    From what I understand, we never find enlightenment. We only remember what we have always been all along.

Best Wishes for Peace Profound
Love for All
Dony Hia

Flowing with the River...

Don't try to steer the river.
~ Deepak Chopra

    If you use the metaphor life is like a river, for the most part it is fine to just flow with the currents. There are times, though, when one might want to divert some of the water of the river to nourish the croplands.

    Many dream therapists say that dreaming of water means one is going into one's subconscious mind. I wish I had a dollar for every time I have dreamed I am in a river, lake or ocean for the last fifty plus years.

Best Wishes for Peace Profound
Love for All
Dony Hia

Taste of Heaven...

Every parting is a form of death, as every reunion is a type of heaven.
~ Tryon Edwards

Before leaving home this morning I gave Tilo a few extra treats and told him we are in for a little taste of heaven today. Of course, he just cocked his head and looked at me. I could see him thinking, there goes dad again, blah blah blah.

Not being human and not being able to communicate future things, little does he know that he will probably be peeing all over himself when he sees Luyu has come home. Hell, after twenty-six days, I hope I don't do that at the airport. Then again, that would surely show Luyu how much I missed her.

I am not only excited to see her, I am also very excited to see the face of our daughter, Yizi, when she arrives in America. I also am looking forward to tonight when she sees the universe I painted on her bedroom ceiling. I painted thousands of stars, a moon, a few planets, and a few comets in glow-in-the-dark paint on her curved ceiling. Since she was born under the sign of Pisces, I also painted the Pisces constellation.

The nice thing about my practice is that I grasp at none of this; I will dance with the energy, let it go, and then dance with the next energy wave.

Best Wishes for Peace Profound
Lover for All
Dony Hia

Come Together, Then Fall Apart...

We think the point is to pass the test, or to overcome the problem, but the truth is that things don't really get solved. They come together and they fall apart.
~ Pema Chodron

    As Chogyam Trungpa Rimpoche would say, "The path is the goal." If you look for a pot of gold at the end of the rainbow, you miss the beauty of the rainbow. Of course, we need to plan for the future, but if our mind gets too caught up in some future goal, we will miss the beauty of life in each moment. Plan and dream but be very flexible with the outcome of these plans and dreams; they too are impermanent.

Best Wishes for Peace Profound
Love for All
Dony Hia

Passing Forward...

Bear in mind that the wonderful things you learn in your schools are the work of many generations. All this is put in your hands as your inheritance in order that you may receive it, honor it, add to it, and one day faithfully hand it on to your children.
~ Albert Einstein

A lot of what I have learned, and want to pass on to my family and others, unfortunately is not taught in schools. My favorite teachings in life can only be learned by studying the sages, prophets and mystics. Through working with a few mystics in the last three or so years, I feel I've learned more valuable things than I learned from years of sitting in a structured class room.

Yizi moved in on Wednesday and I feel, like with Luyu, I have known her energy for lifetimes. I feel for the three of us, as with Michelle and DeShaun, this is not the first lifetime we have met. If this is the case, I feel blessed that the universe has brought us together again.

Best Wishes for Peace Profound
Love for All
Dony Hia

A Few Thoughts from Lincoln...

It has been my experience that folks who have no vices have very few virtues.
~ Abraham Lincoln

And in the end it is not the years in your life that count, it's the life in your years.
~ Abraham Lincoln

When you reach the end of your rope, tie a knot and hang on.
~ Abraham Lincoln

When I awoke early this morning from a night of pleasant dreams, my first thought was I should use Abraham Lincoln quotes for today's *Fresh Morning Breath* thoughts. I have no idea why he was floating around in my mind, and wondered how spiritual he could be. Turns out there are many Lincoln quotes I could use. I could really relate to those I shared.

I certainly have my vices and have come to know a few of my virtues. Some are born good; others, like myself, have had to work hard to be good.

I look back and I see my life in the years. I have been blessed in that my life has been quite difficult at times. My life has made me spiritual and also made for a few good stories. I still see a lot of life in the years ahead.

Looking at Lincoln's third quote above, I think there has been quite a few times in the last fifty-nine years I have tied that knot and held on with white knuckles. It seems it has paid off in ways I could not have even imagined just a few years ago.

Best Wishes for Peace Profound
Love for All
Dony Hia

Intelligent Gifts...

Human beings have a variety of intelligences, such as cognitive intelligence, emotional intelligence, musical intelligence, kinesthetic intelligence, and so on. Most people excel in one or two of those, but do poorly in the others. This is not necessarily or even usually a bad thing; part of Integral wisdom is finding where one excels and thus where one can best offer the world one's deepest gifts.
~ Ken Wilber

Each one of us has gifts which we are meant to share with the world. For some, these gifts just naturally arise, for others, like me, we may have to search these gifts out. In my life, I think people in general are a gift.

These days I so enjoy learning about people, and learning where they are at in their lives. I truly hope that one of my gifts is touching people in a way that brings them joy, and at the same time teaches them different ways in which they can look at their world.

Best Wishes for Peace Profound
Love for All
Dony Hia

Funny Thing, This Ego...

What is it in you that brings you to a spiritual teacher in the first place? It's not the spirit in you, since that is already enlightened, and has no need to seek. No, it is the ego in you that brings you to a teacher.
~ Ken Wilber

Funny thing, this ego. On one hand it fights for existence, and on another it seeks ways to annihilate itself. I believe as long as one has a teacher, the ego is still driving the bus. All true sages recognize something inside themselves that none of their teachers could show them. All sages have teachers up to a point, then something wakes up their own inner teacher. This is when they find their own truth, which no teacher on the outside could impart to them. At this point, while sages still have egos, a higher vibration than the ego is driving the bus.

Best Wishes for Peace Profound
Love for All
Dony Hia

You are in Charge After All…

It is important to realize that there is nobody else who can wake us up and save us from samsara. There is no such thing in Buddhism. That may be Buddhism's biggest drawback, and at the same time its greatest advantage. This view shows us that there is nobody else in control of our lives, our experiences, our freedom or our bondage. Who is responsible? Who is in control? It is us. We are in control. We can bind ourselves further in samsara or we can free ourselves from it right now. It is all up to us. We are the ones who have to keep looking at our thoughts, looking for the nature of our mind. There is no guru, deity, Buddha or bodhisattva out there to look for it for us. Although they would happily do this, it would not help us; it would only help them. We have to do it for ourselves. That is the Key Point.
~ Dzogchen Ponlop Rinpoche.

The oldest surviving Buddhist texts are Pali texts, which was a middle-Indian language and may have been the language of Siddhartha Gautama Buddha himself. I have translations of these oldest texts and have read parts of them. For me the reading was dry, but there was one thing I really liked. I liked how there were little or no miracles. I felt more as if I was reading thoughts from a psychologist on how to live one's life, rather than thoughts of a religious teacher. Even these texts were written hundreds of years after Gautama's death, so we don't know how true they are to Buddha's teachings. What they do teach is, as Ponlop teaches, one is very much in charge of one's own life: no god to thank, no devil to curse.

Best Wishes for Peace Profound
Love for All
Dony Hia

A Few Subconscious Thoughts…

Our subconscious minds have no sense of humor, play no jokes and cannot tell the difference between reality and an imagined thought or image. What we continually think about eventually will manifest in our lives.
~ Robert Collier

The conscious mind may be compared to a fountain playing in the sun and falling back into the great subterranean pool of subconscious from which it rises.
~ Sigmund Freud

Whatever we plant in our subconscious mind and nourish with repetition and emotion will one day become a reality.
~ Earl Nightingale

I enjoy the subconscious mind and started to become friends with my own when I was very young. I am sure it was a survival instinct. At around four years of age, maybe even earlier, my dreams started being as vivid as my waking hours.

Some say when we dream of water, we are going deep into our subconscious mind. Last night, two of the three dreams I had were in water. We are also, all aspects of our dreams, mineral, vegetable and animal. We have passed through all of these on our evolution to being human.

In the first dream last night, I was diving and gathering up piles of jewels and pearls from the ocean floor. Next, I took another man to where I was diving to give him the treasure. He said that he did not want to take it now. I told him he should, before someone else discovers the jewels and pearls. I awoke feeling I have riches inside.

The second dream was not in water, but I felt water was close by. In this dream I would see people and was able to determine what colors they should put on to show their essence color. With one lady, it was green earrings. With a young man, it was that he should wear a blue shirt or paint his cheeks blue. There were others, but I don't see them clearly now. When I awoke from this dream, I felt the energy class I am taking is awakening something that is opening my senses in me.

In the third dream Max, my daughter's step-grandpa was going underwater, and there were others going underwater also. I swam across the water with the end of a rope in my hand and the other end tied to a dock. As I swam, I let the center of the rope sink, hoping to get under the people in the water below. As I pulled the rope, one lady rose and was able to climb into a boat. I thought I was going to be able to bring Max to the surface, but he did not want to rise. He wanted to slowly sink deeper into the water. When I did pull the rope tight, it rose a few feet above the water. I looked down the rope and I saw Jean, Michelle's mother, my first wife, standing on the rope. She was very happy and thanked me for what I had done. When I awoke from this dream, I felt that Jean, who has already passed, will meet Max when he soon passes.

Best Wishes for Peace Profound
Love for All
Dony Hia

Dream of a House with Many Rooms…

Who looks outside, dreams; who looks inside, wakes.
~ Carl Jung

Carl Jung talked about recurring dreams he had in which he would discover parts of his house that he didn't know existed. In his dream, the house represented his personality and the new things he discovered in the house related to new developments in his work.

While any dream is working with our subconscious mind, when I dream of houses with rooms, I feel I am working more with my conscious mind. For me the rooms in the house are where I compartmentalize my thoughts.

Last night I dreamed I went into this house that a lady in her sixties had remodeled. She had her family there and also rented out rooms. As I walked through the rooms, I saw the textures and different colors of each room. I entered the house on the first level and started to climb stairs. As I walked up from the first floor, there was a lady getting dressed in a doorway. She had not put a top on and her breasts were reflecting the light of the room. She looked slightly embarrassed, and so did I. I turned away to not embarrass her further.

Next I headed off into another room to check out work the remodeler had done. I looked into several rooms and studied the craftsman's work. In some cases I thought the work was great. In other cases I thought I could have done a better job.

At first I thought it was only a two-story Victorian house, then I saw another staircase. When I walked up this staircase, I found an attic loft turned into a somewhat long rectangular room. When I walked into the room, I could see where someone had draped and attached a blue flower-patterned sheet to the ceiling. There was a lady in this room, and I sensed she was renting it. I looked at her, and told her, if I had done the remodel work, I would have built a nice molding around the top of the walls.

At this point, I was going to leave the house but could not find my shoes, which I had left on one of the lower staircases. As I was looking for my shoes, I looked out one of the windows of the house and saw a heavy rain had started to fall. I thought I was not prepared to go out into the rain, especially since it seemed so sunny inside the house. It was at this point in the dream that I awakened.

I am starting a new project for our company and am taking over for someone who has been involved for nearly a year. I have been saying I need to get my head wrapped around this project, and other than the women in the dream, I believe the dream mainly represents trying to do this. Not finding my shoes lets me know I am a little stressed. If I had no pants on, it would tell me I was more stressed. If, as in the past, I dreamed I was naked in a classroom, I would know that I was very, very stressed.

I love how my mind (minds) talk to themselves in dreams.

Best Wishes for Peace Profound
Love for All
Dony Hia

Mind's Nature...

The mind's own basic nature is ultimately neutral. It can be influenced by negative as well as by positive emotions. Take, for instance, those who have a short temper. When I was young I was quite short-tempered. However, the mood never lasted for twenty-four hours. If negative emotions are in the very nature of our mind, then as long as the mind is functioning the anger must remain. That, however is not the case. Similarly, positive emotions are also not in the nature of the mind. The mind is something neutral, reflecting all sorts of different experiences or phenomena.
~ 14th Dalai Lama

I will take the Dalai Lama's thought one Buddhist step further. Individual mind, subject object, is an illusion we created when we separated from the One. In between any two thoughts, there is a gap, and in this gap there is no separation from the One. When we are aware of the gap, we are the witness of a mind, but we are not this mind. Witness the gap; don't mind the gap because the mind misses the gap.

The moment you become aware of the functioning of your mind you are not the mind. The very awareness means that you are beyond: aloof, a witness. And the more aware you become, the more you will be able to see the gaps between the experiences. Gaps are there, but you are so unaware that they are never seen. Between two thoughts, experiences, there is always a gap, however imperceptible, however small.
~Osho

Yes, if you can see a mind, you are not this mind, you are the witness. Our witness is much closer to the One than our normal human mind is.

Best Wishes for Peace Profound
Love for All
Dony Hia

Dancing Currents...

Evolution does not isolate us from the rest of the Cosmos, it unites us with the rest of the Cosmos: the same currents that produced birds from dust and poetry from rocks produce egos from ids and sages from egos.
~ Ken Wilber, *Integral Psychology*

Nobody is smart enough to be wrong all the time.
~ Ken Wilber

Wilber's comments on currents have meaning for me this morning. As I laid awake early this morning, Luyu's leg thrown over mine, enjoying her snoring, thinking how blessed I feel in the moment; for just a flash, I felt myself as only dancing energy. This is about the third time I have had this experience and it is quite intriguing. The picture in my mind, and I believe I may have written this the last time it happened, is a drop of water rising out of a pond when a pebble is dropped into the water. Drops will rise from the water only to fall back a moment later. Of course, I don't know if, as a drop, I am still rising or falling back into the source. Mystics would say it is only an illusion that we ever left the source. In the moment, this morning, I was one with the source, simply a dancing current.

Isn't this a great saying: "Nobody is smart enough to be wrong all the time." For some reason it reminds me of something I have often said throughout my life: We can learn something from everyone we meet; we just have to pay attention.

Best Wishes for Peace Profound
Love for All
Dony Hia

Emotional Awareness...

The first step is just simply to observe it. Simply recognize the emotion and then watch it as it grows or as it continues. Just simply watch it. In the beginning, just to have an idea that [the emotion] is coming is very important and effective. In the Vajrayana [Tantric] sense, the way to watch these emotions is without stopping them. If we recognize the emotion and say, "Yes, it is passion," and then try to stop it, that's a problem. Rejection our emotions is a problem in Vajrayana.
~ Dzogchen Ponlop Rinpoche

If we can watch, and be aware of our emotions, happy, sad or mad, we are in control of that moment. If we lose awareness of the emotion, then the moment is in control of us. Any emotion we are in full awareness of is the correct emotion for that moment. Even with anger, if we know and can watch our anger, it will be something constructive; if we are unaware of our anger, it will become destructive. This is the same with all of our emotions.

Best Wishes for Peace Profound
Love for All
Dony Hia

Wisdom...

True wisdom is free of the dramas of culture or religion and should bring us only a sense of peace and happiness.
~ Dzogchen Ponlop Rinpoche, *Rebel Buddha: On the Road to Freedom*

Where most religions fail is that they don't keep up with the times. They hold to dogmas which may have been the perfect thing one, two or three thousand years ago, but not for today's wisdom and understanding. I have to agree with Ponlop: wisdom is beyond religion and culture; where ones religion or culture works for some situations, True Wisdom works in all situations.

Best Wishes for Peace Profound
Love for All
Dony Hia

Like Fluffy Clouds Floating By…

There is nothing which is not an intermediate state between being and nothing.
~ Hegel

    Thoughts arise, enter the mind, and then subside back to where they originate from. If we don't react to the thoughts, they pass like fluffy clouds through a clear sky. One simple way towards happiness is knowing which thoughts to build upon and which simply to let slip back to whence they came. I believe meditation is one of the best ways to learn how to watch our thoughts and learn to "know when to hold them, and when to fold them," as Kenny Rogers sings.

Best Wishes for Peace Profound
Love for All
Dony Hia

For Michelle…

Mostly it is loss which teaches us about the worth of things.
~ Arthur Schopenhauer

I have read a lot of people think of Buddhism as pessimistic because so much of the philosophy revolves around impermanence and constantly reminds us how short our lives really are. The underlying teaching is really to teach us how precious our human life is, and not to waste even a single moment.

If not for the short-lived life of flowers, we would take them for granted. It is because we know how fleeting a flower is that we stop, take a moment and enjoy its beauty.

In universal time, we are more fleeting than a flower, and thus we should, as often as we can, stop and smell the roses.

Max, you added to this world, and the seeds you planted in others will surly sprout and blossom in their own time. I can feel the hearts reaching out to you, and I can feel you touching them as you move on to your next journey. Travel well!

Best Wishes for Peace Profound
Love for All
Dony Hia

Come know me...

Seeking happiness outside ourselves is like waiting for sunshine in a cave facing north.
~ Tibetan Saying

I wrote the story below in 1979 while going through a divorce and first being introduced to a Buddhist practice.

It wasn't too long ago that I felt very insignificant. I felt as though I were swimming in a timeless sea, not even noticeable amongst the crowds. Then a change started to happen. There was a swirling twisting in my existence, and I was whirled up and away from everyone else. I was caught in my own circle of life, not knowing where I was going, yet enjoying the changes in me. As I was morphing, I found my personality somewhat flat; still, I tried to glimmer.

Winds of faith began to blow against me, and changes were happening rapidly. I found myself shaping up, becoming well rounded. A few times I struggled to hold back, fearful of expanding too far. Each time I resisted, these winds of faith would blow harder and harder. Soon I found myself unable to hold back and decided to relax my resistance. When I relaxed, I found my very substance was enlarging; I felt in a moment I would be totally transformed.

After the transformation took place, I realized I was complete. I was no longer bound by the circle of life that had dislodged me from the multitudes. I felt free to choose my own way, live my own life.

Just as quickly as the winds started, they faded away. I made a conscious decision just to float along on the currents of life, letting them guide me where they would. I was just floating along and glistening in the brilliant light the day.

In my heart I knew that I couldn't just float along on life's current forever; time would eventually run out. So I made the decision to make the very best of whatever time I had left; I would shine right till the end.

In what seemed to be a blink of an eye, it started. I was descending on life's last breath. Not one to be discouraged, I said I would hold myself together right until the end.

My essence has burst from what I once was, and I look back and reflect.

I realize for many that I was only a soap bubble created by a small child. Yet in my own heart I know the truth: I was the only bubble who could have filled and fulfilled the space I had. Because of me the child smiled!

Best Wishes for Peace Profound
Love for All
Dony Hia

Good Vibrations...

Nothing rest; everything moves; everything vibrates.
~ The Kybalion

The mystics, since at least the time of Hermes some 4,000 years ago, have known this, and taught that we can change our own vibrations. As we change to a higher vibration, we become more spirit; if we change to a lower scale, we become more like matter. Ken Wilber, and probably most philosophers, believe that most humans are at level four. Of course, some are still at level three and below and many are entering or have entered level five. Beings like Jesus, Buddha, Babaji and such were, or are, vibrating at levels seven or eight. I believe above these vibrations one would not take on a body in the flesh.

Kundalini, Tantra and other yoga's which use the chakra system work with the same vibration scale as mentioned in the Kybalion. While they often only mention seven chakras many work with more when students get to higher levels.

In Lynda's class, we work with nine chakras. I wish more people had the opportunity to work with these systems. I certainly believe one of the reasons I feel so young inside is because of the vibrations within my system.

My daughter, Michelle, emailed me this: "Dad, it seems like just yesterday when I gave you the joke gift of a woman's private part (I rephrased Michelle's wording) for your fifty-seventh birthday. I can hardly believe it's now your sixtieth! You've got the spirit of a twenty-five-year-old and the wisdom of a sage. I am so proud to call you Dad! And am excited you're starting sixty with a beautiful, young family. I love you. Michelle! HAPPY 60th BIRTHDAY!"

Michelle, thank you, and I am so happy to see you traveling your own path, which is similar, yet different to the one I have traveled. The fruition of my path has really ripened in the last few years. I have confidence your own fruition will come earlier in life than mine has. With the family and friends I have these days, I feel I have and eat my cake too most moments. Love You, Dad.

Best Wishes for Peace Profound
Love for All
Dony Hia

Change Your Mood… Change Your Vibration…

To change your mood or mental state—change your vibration.
~ The Kybalion

There are many ways we can temporarily change our vibrations. For instance if one feels a little sad, a walk in nature can lift the spirits. The reason the spirits are lifted in nature is that nature, without all of the hustle and bustle of city life, tends to vibrate on a higher frequency. Often though, when we leave nature, we go back to our regular vibration.

If one wants to permanently raise one's vibration, there are many ways that work: mantras, prayers, affirmations, and one of my favorites, meditation. When we raise our vibration, we actually start to live on a higher plane. It does not take much to look around and see that not everyone on the planet is living on the same plane.

As above, so below; as below, so above.
~ The Kybalion

As above, so below… I felt a little of above came down to our dining room when I saw the sixty roses Luyu had purchased for me. We both liked the box they came in. Reading the packaging, we saw the roses were from Tibet, and when she purchased Purple, (more lavender), because she knows I believe this is my spirit color, the flowers were called soul mate.

I love the vibrations in our house…

Best Wishes for Peace Profound
Love for All
Dony Hia

Dream Teachers...

Go confidently in the direction of your dreams! Live the life you've imagined. As you simplify your life, the laws of the universe will be simpler.
~ Henry David Thoreau

The mystics say we dream our life, and before each birth we choose which lessons we want to learn in the life we are taking on. Sometimes, if we don't feel rested we take on a fairly easy life, with few lessons to learn. If we are rested and feel courageous, we may take on a life with many challenges, so our souls can evolve a lot in just one lifetime. With this in mind, I am not sure I am ready for the simpler life that Thoreau speaks of.

In energy class when we build a twenty-count matrix, at number seven in the southwest we call on the sacred dream. Then again at number seventeen, we call on the dream teachers. These are my favorite numbers, and places, in the twenty count.

Last night, I dreamed that an IOR inspector said the foundation of our house needed repair. I went under the house and saw the inspector, Chris, had painted three areas that needed repair. I thought I could do the repair myself. This upset the inspector because he wanted to make money doing the repair. I asked for a quote and was handed an itemized quote broken down by areas. I added up the bill and it came to over nine thousand dollars. At that time, I decided I could do the work myself. When I awoke, I thought, yes, there are a couple of areas I could firm up the foundations of my life.

Thank you, dream teachers.

Best Wishes for Peace Profound
Love for All
Dony Hia

In the Silence…

Learn to get in touch with the silence within yourself and know that everything in this life has a purpose.
~ Elisabeth Kubler-Ross

In each moment, there is something to wake us up. The more we can quiet our minds and actually be in the moment, the better chance we have to recognize the wisdom in each and every moment. Even the silence itself can be a lesson. The silence in our world is masculine, which holds space where we can rest, recharge and dream our worlds; the feminine is active where we bring dreams and ideas into manifestations.

Best Wishes for Peace Profound
Love for All
Dony Hia

The Eyes See in the Dark…

In a dark time, the eye begins to see.
~ Theodore Roethke

Easy times are times for souls to rest; dark times are times for souls to grow, and grow they must. Buddhists and many mystics say we are evolving our way back home to the One. Buddhists and many mystics say all beings eventually succeed, we all find our way back home; no beings are left behind, and no beings are lost to eternal hells. Even if we step back for a lifetime, or even a few lifetimes, we again start to ascend Jacob's ladder.

Well, it is the Mystic Kabbala that mentions Jacob's ladder, but it is the same thing. Even early Christianity wrote of reincarnation, especially in the Gnostic tradition.

Best Wishes for Peace Profound
Love for All
Dony Hia

Bank Account of Life...

The cost of a thing is the amount of what I call life which is required to be exchanged for it, immediately or in the long run.
~ Henry David Thoreau

    I understand what Thoreau is saying. When I started my career years ago, I thought it took so much time away from what I thought I wanted to do: Art. It seemed like I was using up a lot of life just for a paycheck. It turns out forty years later, if I look back, I can see my career has given me a lot of life for very little cost. The career did not kill the artist inside; it may just be what developed the artist in me. The work itself, and the people I have known over the past forty years, have in many ways been art for me.

    Often, by looking at people, one can get an idea if they are paying too much for life, with too little return.

    Luyu and I were sitting on the couch last night, and at one point she turned to me, and said, "How much happiness we have, and how few wants." There is a large bank account for life in that statement.

Best Wishes for Peace Profound
Love for All
Dony Hia

Calm Rising…

The creation of something new is not accomplished by the intellect but by the play instinct acting from necessity. The creative mind plays with the object it loves.
~ Carl Jung

The conscious mind is much like the surface of an algae filled pond—one can see what's on the surface, and maybe the first few inches, but not all of the action going on below. While one might see a few frogs just showing their eyes, maybe a turtle on a rock, and a few water bugs walking on the surface, often in water, the majority of the life is below the surface and out of sight.

It is the subconscious mind that supports, and in many ways controls, the surface life we experience. There is only a creative conscious mind because it is supported by a more creative subconscious mind. All habits, and patterns we have, are contained in the subconscious mind. If one wants to change a behavior, one needs to reprogram the subconscious mind first. One of the most successful ways of reprograming the subconscious mind is through affirmations.

If one wants to be creative, a great way to do this is to calm the surface mind until it's as calm as resting water. We have all seen a body of water so calm the surface looks like a mirror. Once the conscious mind is this calm, it is easier for creativity from below to rise to the surface, from the subconscious mind to the conscious mind.

Best Wishes for Peace Profound
Love for All
Dony Hia

State of Mind...

From a Buddhist point of view, the actual experience of death is very important. Although how or where we will be reborn is generally dependent on karmic forces, our state of mind at the time of death can influence the quality of our next rebirth. So at the moment of death, in spite of the great variety of karmas we have accumulated, if we make a special effort to generate a virtuous state of mind, we may strengthen and activate a virtuous karma, and so bring about a happy rebirth.
~ 14th Dalai Lama

Health is merely the slowest possible rate at which one can die.
~ Unknown

    Yesterday I received a call from one of my sisters that Mom had a severe stroke; the outlook does not look good for Mom. Her name is Ida, and may I ask that those of you receiving today's *Fresh Morning Breath* send wishes that her mind is at peace, no matter what the outcome is.

    Yesterday I told Luyu, after we received the call, that Mom's personality is as soft as a rose. Last night as I finally started to fall asleep, I kept seeing yellow rose petals rolling out of thoughts from Mom.

Best Wishes for Peace Profound
Love for All
Dony Hia

Dealing with Suffering...

In dealing with those who are undergoing great suffering, if you feel "burnout" setting in, if you feel demoralized and exhausted, it is best, for the sake of everyone, to withdraw and restore yourself, the point is to have a long-term perspective.
~ 14th Dalai Lama

Yesterday, I followed the Dalai Lama's advice. After spending Monday in Sacramento at the hospital, seeing my mom suffer, myself suffering with the flu and a fever, I woke up Tuesday with my body feeling like it had been hit by a truck. Still, as always I got out of bed and came to work. After a couple of hours, I made the decision to treat myself kind and headed back home and went to bed. Then I asked Luyu to go to Chinatown and pick up a package of flu herbs. She gave me a cup of the tea at three o'clock and by four o'clock I was feeling 100% better.

It seems that Mom is going die with a very good attitude. She knows she is dying and seems to have no complaints. My sister said that yesterday Mom had whispered, "Hurt, hurt." Then the hospice nurse gave her morphine and a moment later Raynell heard her giggle and say, "Good."

In Buddhism, it is said that if we can die well, we will have a good rebirth. I am sure Mom believes she is going to heaven. I, on the other hand, believe Mom is going to have a good rebirth—not in a heaven, either on this planet or maybe somewhere else she is needed in the universe.

Best Wishes for Peace Profound
Love for All
Dony Hia

Only Through Experience Can We Know…

You cannot teach a man anything; you can only help him discover it in himself.
~ Galileo Galilei

All truths are easy to understand once they are discovered; the point is to discover them.
~ Galileo Galilei

I could describe a flower to you, but unless you have experienced a flower, you would not understand what I was speaking of. And yes, of course you have experienced a flower, and the way you experience a flower is different than how I experience a flower. It is the same with a spiritual or mystical path: unless one travels the road oneself, one will never know the terrain.

I am amazed at the things we experience in the safety of the matrix built in energy class. Yesterday we were guided to create energy boundaries and to feel others' energy boundaries. When I walked towards the boundary set by one person I was working with, it felt like I had walked into a force field that stopped me in my tracks. I could even feel with my hands as I pushed against it; it felt like pushing against a balloon, the more I pushed the more it resisted. Everyone in the class was able to experience somewhat the same effect as we all worked with different partners.

Best Wishes for Peace Profound
Love for All
Dony Hia

Growing One Step at a Time...

Every man takes the limits of his own field of vision for the limits of the world.
~ Arthur Schopenhauer

Since I started Tantric, and then energy work a few years ago, my own field of vision has grown; it has grown enough where I realize how small it still is. Yet, I have experienced things recently which, just a few years ago if people had told me they experienced such things, I would have thought it was just their imagination. I also know there are things around me, us, at every moment which at this time I cannot see. I have no doubt our teacher of the energy class can see energy fields; she has been able to help us experience them.

Since starting this work I have seen people's auric colors on their hands. I am also convinced one of my friends in the class, Don, can see souls or spirits when they are out of a body. While I cannot see things, I believe others are able to. I no longer limit my beliefs to just what I am experiencing in any given moment.

My world has expanded in ways I did not know, or believe, would happen in this incarnation.

Best Wishes for Peace Profound
Love for All
Dony Hia

A Little Chaos is Good for Us...

You need chaos in your soul to give birth to a dancing star.
~ Friedrich Nietzsche

    It is our trials and tribulations that build our characters. In times of joy, it is best not to get too swept away, because joy and sorrow are like two opposite sides of a wheel—they both keep coming around.

    If we conserve some of our energy when we are on top of the world, we will have plenty to pull ourselves back up when feel we are on the bottom.

Best Wishes for Peace Profound
Love for All
Dony Hia

What Man is…

What a man is contributes much more to his happiness than what he has or how he is regarded by others. ~ Arthur Schopenhauer

When I was young, I was much like a chameleon, changing my personality to meet others' expectations.

These days pretty much what you see is what you get; I much prefer trying to be authentic to who I am.

There is a joy in just relaxing into who we are, and it takes a lot less energy.

Best Wishes for Peace Profound
Love for All
Dony Hia

All about Love...

People say I make strange choices, but they're not strange for me. My sickness is that I'm fascinated by human behavior, by what's underneath the surface, by the worlds inside people.
~ Johnny Depp

True love stories never have endings.
~ Richard Bach

Yesterday, I saw our neighbor Ben for the first time in months. I asked him if he could show Yizi, the dollhouse and castle he has been working on. Years ago Jeanne and I had a cat named Milly that abandoned us when I brought a third cat home. Milly chose to live with Ben, and Ben grew to love Milly, who he thought we called Muni, and so Muni became her name.

Ben first started building a small wooden castle, which looks like a 10,000-dollar dollhouse to me. Next, about seven years ago, Ben started building Muni a castle in his back yard. Muni died about four years ago, but the love for Muni continues on as Ben continues to work on the castle. He is just starting to put on small tiles, which will look like granite stones.

Ben is a very talented artist both in sculpture and painting; I have attached one of his paintings of a mermaid, which seems to be a theme he likes.

I asked Ben where he had been for several months and he said in China and Viet Nam looking for a wife. Unfortunately, he said, he'd had no luck.

I see what Ben has done for the love of Muni; I can only imagine what he might build for a wife. I feel fortunate to know Ben, and his innocent love for Muni (Milly) touches me.

Best Wishes for Peace Profound
Love for All
Dony Hia

Filling Spaces in Our Minds...

The way to overcome negative thoughts and destructive emotions is to develop opposing, positive emotions that are stronger and more powerful.
~ 14th Dalai Lama

    We cannot pull a vacuum in our minds and just say I want no negative thoughts. Just in saying that, one puts out a postulate that one's mind has a tendency for negative thoughts. On the other hand, if one starts to fill one's mind with positive thoughts these thoughts will take up space and leave less, or no space for negative thoughts. This is why positive affirmations work so well, they remove space for negativity.

Best Wishes for Peace Profound
Love for All
Dony Hia

Be the Witness...

Everything changes once we identify with being the witness to the story, instead of the actor in it.
~ Ram Dass

I know what Ram Dass speaks of. When one starts being the witness instead of just being the actor, the world takes on kind a surreal nature and one is not thrown by suffering or sucked in by bliss. One comes to realize, like everything else, suffering and bliss are as impermanent as day and night or light and dark.

The day my mom had her stroke, my body came down with the flu and it was only after the funeral, three weeks later, that my body stopped hurting. As always I tried to be the witness to all that was going on, not my body and not my mind. In doing so, while my body ached and my heart was heavy at the core, the witness was not suffering, nor even hurting. If we can find the witness we really are, we realize this witness is never born and never dies. This witness is either our highest of high selves or the One above that. And above the one there is none; this One is All.

Best Wishes for Peace Profound
Love for All
Dony Hia

Journeys and Mushrooms...

The spiritual journey is individual, highly personal. It can't be organized or regulated. It isn't true that everyone should follow one path. Listen to your own truth.
~ Ram Dass

Everyone is alone on his or her journey. Not only do we not know another's path, we really do not know one another. How we see each other is for the largest part a reflection of our own minds.

We can look at how people see us and come to realize this. Each of us has people who think we are sinners and others who think we are saints; of course, we are neither. Through my own spiritual studies, I have come to realize each of us are mirrors reflecting back to others what they need to see in us for their own growth on their own life's journey.

I've got to find the porcini mushrooms for the festival and I've looked everywhere. Anyone know where they are?
~ Unknown

For some reason mushrooms have become part of my mystical, and to some extent spiritual, journey. It seems to be a contagious path in our home. While I can't really know how deep mushrooms have earned their way into Luyu's and Yizi's consciousness, I do know they have become part of their lives.

Yesterday, Yizi and I picked pink oysters and shitakes out of one of our mushroom patches in our back yard. Later after dinner and enjoying our harvest, Luyu, Yizi and I were talking. As we talked, Yizi was drawing something on her little electronic device. When she finished, she said she drew one of the mushrooms on my shirt. When I looked at her drawing, it took me to a mystical place where mushrooms live. I hope you enjoy her happy mushroom as much as I did.

Best Wishes for Peace Profound
Love for All
Dony Hia

No Desires in This Moment...

As long as you have certain desires about how it ought to be you can't see how it is.
~ Ram Dass

If we are having desires about how something should be, we are not living in the moment. If we are truly living in the moment, we do not have desires about how things should be; we see they really are. If we can catch ourselves having desires about how it ought to be, we can come right back to the moment and accept what is.

Yesterday when I got home from work, I saw Luyu had had an accident with the Jeep. For a brief moment I started to go into pattern; I caught myself thinking, I hope it was not with another car. Then I caught myself again and said, "It is what it is." When I walked into the house, I saw Luyu looking quite distressed. Luyu said someone had helped her park, and she parked so close to a wall that when she backed up she hit the wall. I looked at her, smiled, and said that I was glad it was not another car. While I was fine, Luyu was stressed and started to redirect her stress towards Yizi. I let Luyu know what she was doing and it was not fair.

Soon the energy in the house was back to its pleasant vibration.

Best Wishes for Peace Profound
Love for All
Dony Hia

Namaste...

Treat everyone you meet like God in drag.
~ Ram Dass

To me this short sentence is a great way to say Namaste. One good translation for Namaste is this: The Divine in me recognizes the Divine in you. This says to me, no matter what your outwardly appearance, I still can see the God in you. For the most part, I try to do this with all things, big and small.

Best Wishes for Peace Profound
Love for All
Dony Hia

A Balanced Middle Path…

Existence is paradoxical; paradox is its very core. It exists through opposites; it is a balance in the opposites. And one who learns how to balance becomes capable of knowing what life is, what existence is, what God is. The secret key is balance.
~ Osho

There is a path in Buddhism called the Middle Path. It is like a string instrument. If the strings on a violin are too loose, there will be no sound. If the strings on a violin are too tight, not only will the sound not be right, the string will probably break. Our lives should be like the proper strings on a violin, not too tight not too loose.

It is said that Gautama had gotten down to trying to live on one grain of rice a day before he almost died. As the story goes, a young girl found him lying on the sand next to the Ganges River. She fed him rice milk and helped him gain back his strength. Gautama realized he could not reach enlightenment without a body. With his strength back, he made the decision to sit under the Bodhi Tree and not move until he reached enlightenment. Once Gautama became enlightened, he did not become too loose. He had learned balance between not too tight and not too loose.

This is the core of Buddha's teachings on balance. As we go through life, we should not be too hard on ourselves, or too soft with ourselves.

Best Wishes for Peace Profound
Love for All
Dony Hia

Conscious Living...

Consciousness means living with a witness; unconsciousness means living without a witness. When you are walking on the road, you can walk consciously — that's what Buddha says one should do — you are alert, deep down you are aware that you are walking; you are conscious of each movement. You are conscious of the birds singing in the trees, the early morning sun coming through the trees, the rays touching you, the warmth, the fresh air, the fragrance of newly opening flowers. A dog starts barking, a train passes by, you are breathing . . . you are watching everything. You are not excluding anything out of your alertness; you are taking everything in. The breath goes in, the breath goes out . . . you are watching everything that is happening.
~ Osho

When we mention meditation, most people think of someone sitting in meditation. Meditation is actually nothing more than awareness, and the more we can be aware of the moment during the day, the more we are in a state of meditation.

I think for the masters, it may be there is very little time during the day that they are not aware of, and not living in, the moment.

Best Wishes for Peace Profound
Love for All
Dony Hia

Everyone's Got It...

Hide not your talents. They for use were made. What's a sundial in the shade?
~ Benjamin Franklin

I believe that every person is born with talent.
~ Maya Angelou

Use what talents you possess; the woods would be very silent if no birds sang there except those that sang best.
~ Henry Van Dyke

I too believe everyone is born with talent and our top talent, if developed, is also our life's purpose.

We don't always reach our life's purpose in the life we choose. If we do though, when we live out this chosen purpose, it appears effortless.

I do not yet know what my life's purpose is, but I have seen many of my talents blossom in the last few years. I would like to think, if I could develop it, my life's purpose would be to touch people's minds and hearts and maybe, just maybe, help guide them into opening both; as I have been opening mine over time.

There seems to be a lot of talent in our house with Luyu, Yizi, Tilo and, yes, me. These are two of Yizi's art works, two Ikebana arrangements I did, and a collage of some of my artwork from the past.

Best Wishes for Peace Profound
Love for All
Dony Hia

Costumes and Masks…

In most of our human relationships, we spend much of our time reassuring one another that our costumes of identity are on straight.
~ Ram Dass

Not only do we spend time reassuring one another that our costume of identity is on straight, we spend a lot of time convincing ourselves that the masks we wear are correct.

Not many humans know, and fewer would be willing to show their authentic selves. It is not only fear but a lack of knowledge of our authentic selves that keeps us wearing a mask. The only way we can find our authentic selves is to remove our costumes and masks. We have to do this one at a time.

I, like most, do not yet know my authentic self. Yet having spent a fair amount of time the last few years removing my mask, I am starting to hear a voice deep inside saying, "I live here and everywhere."

As I've mentioned before, deep inside I saw a very young Dony with long curly blond hair which Mom loved. I remember her saying many times, she cried when your dad took you to the barber and had it cut. The curls never came back. I smiled when one of the last times I saw her healthy she said, "Your hair is getting long and it looks really nice." It is because of the energy class and Mom saying how good she thought my hair looked that I continue letting it grow; the hair is authentic.

There are probably many sages and mystics who wear little masks and who are also authentic. Then again, there are many who claim to be sages or mystics but are not; they are wearing masks.

Best Wishes for Peace Profound
Love for All
Dony Hia

Between Extremes...

Experience life in all possible ways -- good-bad, bitter-sweet, dark-light, summer-winter. Experience all the dualities. Don't be afraid of experience, because the more experience you have, the more mature you become.
~ Osho

Osho is correct in that if we did not step into hell once in a while, we would not seek growth.

Many religions speak of dying and going to heaven or going to hell. Buddhist thought is don't think of these places as in the future; heaven, hell and all in between are here.

When I was young, the Baptist church we were taken to tried to teach us to long for heaven, and with all our mind, fear hell. When I was very young, it worked but by the time, I was in my early teens I wasn't buying their message and started looking for something which made a little more sense to me. I am not saying Baptist belief is wrong; it was just wrong for me.

After about thirty-five years of reading different religions and philosophies, I am not excited about the thought of heaven, and not fearful about the thought of hell. I spend most of my time dancing somewhere in between the two extremes. I like this world I have been creating.

Best Wishes for Peace Profound
Love for All
Dony Hia

Enough is Enough...

Our whole spiritual transformation brings us to the point where we realize that in our own being, we are enough.
~ Ram Dass

As we evolve, it seems the easier part is to realize we are enough for others; not so easy, we are enough for ourselves.

We can stop being thrown by what others think of us and what we think of them. We can even stop thinking about how they may treat us.

We often tend to be gentler with others than we are to ourselves. Many times, we place far too many expectations on ourselves that we would not place on others.

These days, I am much gentler with myself than I was in the past.

Best Wishes for Peace Profound
Love for All
Dony Hia

Between Real and Unreal...

It's all real and it's all illusory: that's Awareness!
~ Ram Dass

Buddhists and followers of many other traditions claim we are dreaming our lives. Granted it is a very substantial dream, still I agree it is a dream. If we live our lives as if the dream is real, we are off the point. If we live our lives as if the dream is not real, we are off the point. Our body comes into existence and then fades out of existence, but the dreamer is neither born nor dies.

There were a couple sayings quoted in the energy class yesterday which I really like:

"Worries are prayers we don't want" (Abraham Hicks). When we worry, we are actually dreaming these things into existence.

"Have a nice day; unless you have made other plans" (A friend of the teacher). If we are not having a nice day, we have already dreamed we were not going to have a nice day.

The nice thing about dreaming our lives is that it is a lot like lucid dreaming one does while sleeping. In lucid dreaming, one realizes in the dream, one is dreaming. Once one realizes this, one can often change the dream to what one wants to dream about. Once we realize we are dreaming this life, we can also change it to what we want, even overcoming past Karma, which is also a dream.

Best Wishes for Peace Profound
Love for All
Dony Hia

Learning, Understanding and Experiencing...

Learning never exhausts the mind.
~ Leonardo da Vinci

    Learning, for me is pleasure; understanding what I learned is a greater pleasure. Experiencing what I have learned and grown to understand is even a greater pleasure.

    There are mystical things I have learned and think I understand, but have not experienced yet. Maybe if I keep working, I will experience them.

Best Wishes for Peace Profound
Love for All
Dony Hia

Thoughts from Gauguin the Savage…

Oh yes! He loved yellow, this good Vincent, this painter from Holland – those glimmers of sunlight rekindled his soul that abhorred the fog that needed the warmth.
~ Paul Gauguin

We all have our yellow, whatever that might be, which gives our souls warmth. I am fortunate to have many yellows, philosophy, hard work, and most important: wine, women and song.

Life is hardly more than a fraction of a second. Such a little time to prepare oneself for eternity!
~ Paul Gauguin

When I forget I am not prepared, when I remember I am as prepared as I ever need, I am in the moment where eternity lives.

In art, one idea is as good as another. If one takes the idea of trembling, for instance, all of a sudden most art starts to tremble. Michelangelo starts to tremble. El Greco starts to tremble. All of the
Impressionists start to tremble.
~ Paul Gauguin

The thought of enlightenment makes me tremble. Instead of letting this trembling pull me forward, I use it to hold me back in my comfort zone.

Best Wishes for Peace Profound
Love for All
Dony Hia

Nature is Everywhere...

Climb the mountains and get their good tidings. Nature's peace will flow into you as sunshine flows into trees. The winds will blow their own freshness into you and the storms their energy, while cares will drop away from you like the leaves of autumn.
~ John Muir

This last weekend, I had the chance to take Muir's advice, and even better, share the experience with family and friends. While the mountains did share the freshness of the air, and the beauty of the scenery, I tried to remember that I can find beautiful nature in the city as well.

If I slow myself down and look around, I remember even the buildings are nature, or at least from nature. The glass, the wood and the steel all come from the earth and will eventually return to the earth. In between coming and going, these items bring their own beauty and in their own way, nature's peace.

Best Wishes for Peace Profound
Love for All
Dony Hia

A Few Thoughts on Happiness…

The summit of happiness is reached when a person is ready to be what he is.
~ Desiderius Erasmus

What is the meaning of life? To be happy and useful.
~ 14th Dalai Lama

I caught the happiness virus last night when I was out singing beneath the stars.
~ Hafiz

Happy people seem to know happiness is a personal choice; unhappy people tend to think happiness depends on others.

I love the saying I caught the happiness virus. This is a virus I wish everyone could catch, and I wish it could spread like a plague!

Best Wishes for Peace Profound
Love for All
Dony Hia

Removing Barriers...

Your task is not to seek for love, but merely to seek and find all the barriers within yourself that you have built against it.
~ Rumi

We tend to think we are solid but physics and mystics remind us otherwise. Like everything else in the universe, we truly are a dance of energy. If things are not going the way we would like, it is because of an energy block. The easiest way to block energy is by harboring negative thoughts. The easiest way to get energy flowing again is through positive thoughts. If all blocks were removed, we would be pure love and not even take on a body. If you don't believe this, ask God if he has a body.

Best Wishes for Peace Profound
Love for All
Dony Hia

Spirit in all Directions...

There is nothing but God, nothing but the Goddess, nothing but Spirit in all directions, and not a grain of sand, not a speck of dust, is more or less Spirit than any other.
~ Ken Wilber

God is the masculine in everything, Goddess is the feminine in everything, and Spirit is the motion in everything. Spirit is neither masculine nor feminine. It is the dance of energy which expresses the God and Goddess in all manifestations.

Best Wishes for Peace Profound
Love for All
Dony Hia

A Few Quotes and Thoughts on Dreaming...

Those who have compared our life to a dream were right, we sleeping wake, and waking sleep.
~ Michel de Montaigne

Dreams are illustrations . . . from the book your soul is writing about you.
~ Marsha Norman

Dreaming permits each and every one of us to be quietly and safely insane every night of our lives.
~ William Dement

A dream which is not interpreted is like a letter which is not read.
~ The Talmud

Dreaming is one of the riches in life. I also think that to the extent I am sane, it is because of dream release. I say *dream release* because for me, stress gathered through the day is released through dreaming. I know my brain builds up electricity during the day and is released at night through dreaming. I know this because I have awakened, and while still dreaming watched the dream go from recognizable images to being more like sparks of electrical discharge.

Yesterday my coworker and friend, Zack, asked if I was going to stop by his job and do lunch with him this week. That question turned into one of my dreams last night. I have also been handed one of the toughest jobs of my forty-year career. These too items made for a fun and interesting dream.

In the dream, I went to meet Zack for lunch. Instead of going to one of the restaurants we normally go to, we were going to eat from a gourmet lunch wagon. As I ordered the food, I noticed some ladies off to our left flirting with us. The thing I noticed most about the ladies was one blond lady's vibrant purple pants. The dream changed and I realized there was nowhere for us to sit. Next, I realize that I am laying on a rug under a big rig. I look to my left and see the ladies sitting and eating. I wondered how am I going to eat laying down, the big rig started to move. My first thought was that I hope I am not crushed. My second thought was if I don't move, the truck won't run over me. Then I see the truck is pulling a trailer rig, which would crush me. I thought the trailer might stay. Sure enough, the big rig pulled away and the trailer stayed. With the big rig gone, I got up to grab food and one of my pots on the truck. I reached to grab the food and I knocked over a pot of goulash. As I do this, I see the pot is green and mine was cast iron. I saved the goulash that did not hit the ground, and then I awakened from this dream.

Events and images from the day that went into the night's dream:

1. Zack asked me to meet him for lunch.

2. Yesterday, I had to be careful walking into the basement of the job because of trucks and backhoes.

3. I have cast iron camping pots and pans on our counter, which Luyu and I have been talking about taking to the basement since we returned from camping.

4. The ladies, ladies are always floating around in my mind somewhere.

I know the part of the dream of not letting the truck run over me is not letting the job overwhelm me.

I woke up refreshed and rich after such a vivid dream.

Best Wishes for Peace Profound
Love for All
Dony Hia

A Few More Thoughts on Happiness...

Precisely the least, the softest, lightest, a lizard's rustling, a breath, a flash, a moment - a little makes the way of the best happiness.
~ Friedrich Nietzsche

Let us be grateful to people who make us happy, they are the charming gardeners who make our souls blossom.
~ Marcel Proust

Those who can laugh without cause have either found the true meaning of happiness or have gone stark raving mad.
~ Norm Papernick

Doing cartwheels in the green grass of happiness and skipping high towards the blue heavenly skies of joy!
~ Terri Guillemets

    Last month in energy class, we were told of a Buddhist monk whose daily practice is to get on a train, sit down and start laughing. His laugh is so contagious, first another is laughing, then another, and finally everyone in his car is laughing. When everyone is laughing, he goes to another car and starts again. What a great practice, even if some might think it is a little crazy.

    I am looking forward to today's energy class. We will be working with the light side of the fight or flight pattern of those who tend to leave their body when they feel danger.

    These people tend to be artist, psychics, writers and other professions where being on the outer wave lengths, might be very beneficial. Each of the five fight-or-flight patterns has a dark side, which inhibits our growth, and a light side, which accelerates our growth.

Best Wishes for Peace Profound
Love for All
Dony Hia

Not Hurting…

The meaning of good and bad, of better and worse, is simply helping or hurting.
~ Ralph Waldo Emerson

In one sutra it is written that when Buddha was giving a talk, someone asked, "How do we know if a path is good or not?" His answer was, "If it helps you but hurts others, it is not a good path. If it helps others but hurts you it is not a good path. But if it helps you and it helps others it is a good path." Sounds like simple advice, and the richness is in its simplicity.

One thing we must remember: we do not always know if we are helping or hurting another anymore than we always know if we are hurting or helping ourselves. I like the thought of not hurting ourselves or others.

Best Wishes for Peace Profound
Love for All
Dony Hia

Imagination...

Imagination is more important than knowledge. Knowledge is limited.
~ Albert Einstein

    Unless aliens planted knowledge in our head, all knowledge was first imagination. Imagination is creativity, and it is imagination which keeps the universe evolving, not knowledge.

Best Wishes for Peace Profound
Love for All
Dony Hia

Gifts...

The greatest gift is to give people your enlightenment, to share it.
~ Buddha

Everyone we meet is a teacher and has a gift for us. Some, like family, are teaches we may require being around a long time. Others may be just strangers who we look in the eye as we pass on the street or a walk in a park. I would venture even one step further to say everything in our environment is a teaching. In every moment, there is something very near to us in our environment that is there to wake us up. The teachings are always there. It is often, as students, that we miss the lesson.

Take a moment, look around. "Ah, there it is! See it?"

Best Wishes for Peace Profound
Love for All
Dony Hia

Nobody Else…

It is all up to us. We are the only ones who have to keep looking at our thoughts, looking for the nature of our mind. There is nobody else in control of our lives, our experiences, our freedom or our bondage.
~ Dzogchen Ponlop Rinpoche

Dang, I wanted someone, or some deity to do if for me, just slap me upside the head, and then I would wake up. There are Zen stories about teachers whacking students with a stick at just the right moment and the students would have an awakening.

Well I guess that just isn't going to happen, so I will keep dreaming my own life and maybe wake up when the time is right.

Best Wishes for Peace Profound
Love for All
Dony Hia

Good and Evil...

"I do not believe in the God of theology who rewards good and punishes evil."
~ Albert Einstein

Good and evil are human concepts. Probably no other animals on the planet conceives of good and evil. In our lives, we dream, our souls probably use the concepts of good and evil to help us evolve as we climb Jacob's Ladder on our way back home.

Best Wishes for Peace Profound
Love for All
Dony Hia

No Difference…

There is no difference between this moment and enlightenment.
~ Dzogchen Ponlop Rinpoche

With so much destruction in the world, it is hard to think of each moment as enlightenment, but I believe it is true. If we look at the universe from a relative perspective we see things such as good or bad, warm or cold, light or dark, samsara or nirvana and so on. If we see the universe from an absolute perspective we see the entire universe is no more, and no less, than a dance of energy.
Since the Big Bang, no energy has been added to the universe and no energy has been removed. I heard this from a teacher in the fourth grade and a light went on in my mind. I thought, I run on energy (I did not think of my whole being as energy back then) so in one way or another, I have been forever and will be forever. After fifty or so years and a fair amount of reading on the subject, I see the entire universe as a brilliant, radiant dance of enlightened energy.

Of course, this understanding won't buy me a cup of coffee at the local coffee shop, but it does bring me a certain peace of mind that . . . I am eternal.

Best Wishes for Peace Profound
Love for All
Dony Hia

Till You Reach the End…

Begin at the beginning and go on till you come to the end; then stop.
~ Lewis Carrol, *Alice in Wonderland*

There is a certain wisdom in this short quote. We naturally do it every day.

We wake up in the morning, go to the end of the day, and usually know when it is time to stop. We also do this with so many things in our lives.

I did this with schooling; there was a time to stop and start to work.
We have all done this in relationships; there was a time to stop.
The thing which throws a lot of us, is it is easy to begin and
often hard to know when to stop. I just saw this with a
friend who was retiring; it seemed to make him sad
that a new end had arrived and he would have
to stop. Some people seem to know, when
dying, it is time to stop and go peacefully,
others go kicking and scratching. Hope
I am one who will be able to stop
without too much resistance.
There is a saying: art is
Knowing when to
to stop. Guess
it is time to
Stop.

Best Wishes for Peace
Profound. Love for
All. Dony
Hia

On this Plane...

Do what you can on this plane to relieve suffering by constantly working on yourself to be an instrument for the cessation of suffering. To me, that's what the emerging game is all about.
~ Ram Dass

What hits me most about Ram Dass's quote is the words "plane" and "emerging game." Choosing to be born on this planet as a human is one plane, but within this plane there are many other planes. On this planet, at this moment, there are people who are still living in jungles as they have for thousands of years, and there are also enlightened masters. While each lives on the same planet, as humans, their worlds (planes) are far apart.

I believe the emerging game is that we all have the ability to evolve and live on higher planes. I would say the highest plane we can exist on is the one on which we return to the One.

Best Wishes for Peace Profound
Love for All
Dony Hia

All about Balance…

Sadness gives depth. Happiness gives height. Sadness gives roots. Happiness gives branches. Happiness is like a tree going into the sky, and sadness is like the roots going down into the womb of the earth. Both are needed, and the higher a tree goes, the deeper it goes, simultaneously. The bigger the tree, the bigger will be its roots. In fact, it is always in proportion. That's its balance.
~ Osho

I remember when Bhagwan Shree Rajneesh (later known as Osho) was run out of the US. It wasn't too long after I saw a picture in the paper of several of his followers driving Rolls Royces in a line in a small town in Oregon. At the time, I thought, what a crazy person! Today, thirty-plus years later, I think he was a sage. I believe he was correct when he wrote "its balance."

In one of the meditations taught in energy class, we connect our core upward through our template of perfection to our highest self. Then we also connect it down through our roots to the center of earth.

The upward movement is our masculine connection and downward is our feminine connection. Ikebana represents this well. It is a connection of heaven and earth through man. We are most alive when we are in balance.

Best Wishes for Peace Profound
Love for All
Dony Hia

Below the Voice...

Listen to your being. It is continuously giving you hints; it is a still, small voice. It does not shout at you that is true. And if you are a little silent you will start feeling your way. Be the person you are...
~ Osho

If you can silence yourself, you may hear the voice Osho spoke of. If you silence yourself even more, you may touch the silence behind the voice, behind all.

A meditation taught in energy class is the *I Am* meditation. We were told it is a very old meditation. All you do in this meditation is very slowly repeat, "I Am." As you do this, even if your mind still has some chatter, you will start to sense a silence in your core. Your core is located in the center of your body at or just below your solar plexus.

For me, this meditation has given me a sense of the silence where I am connected and come forth from the One.

Actually, since I have done this meditation several times, I find it easier to go into this silence.

Even just typing about it in this *Fresh Morning Breath,* I am experiencing the silence in my core.

Best Wishes for Peace Profound
Love for All
Dony Hia

Right Where You Are…

The next message you need is always right where you are.
~ Ram Dass

    It is easy to forget the message above when we have a bad day at work, our child does something we disapprove of, or our partner says that we don't like them and so on. Yet, these disturbances are exactly what we need in the moment for a chance of growth.

    Instead of looking at the opportunity, we, more often than not try and push the moment away. And when we are not living in the moment, we are not truly living.

Best Wishes for Peace Profound
Love for All
Dony Hia

Finding Wings…

It's only when caterpillarness is done that one becomes a butterfly. That again is part of this paradox. You cannot rip away caterpillarness. The whole trip occurs in an unfolding process of which we have no Control.
~ Ram Dass

In Shambhala, Chogyam Trungpa Rimpoche used to say, "We wrap ourselves in a cocoon where we hide our true selves from everyone else." I believe, according to him, most of us never break our way out of our cocoon.

I might rephrase this to say, "How many of us die, still wrapped up in our beautiful self-spun silk, still contemplating who we really are?"

My "caterpillarness" seemed hard when I was young, yet I could always see the butterfly inside. This is the carrot that pulls me forward.

Am I out of my own cocoon? I think maybe I am just pulling out wings still curled up and wet. I can picture my wings though, bright with blues, yellows, greens and gold, ready to carry my soul to heights untold.

Best Wishes for Peace Profound
Love for All
Dony Hia

Ah, My Friend the Ego...

The Ego is an exquisite instrument. Enjoy it, use it--just don't get lost in it.
~ Ram Dass

Often we read where someone says get rid of the ego, or overcome the ego. We can never get rid of our egos. It is a package deal: life-ego, ego-life.

Ego is *me and other, other and me*. We can have glimpses of *no me* and *other*, but we cannot live that way.

It is actually our egos that make us special, or at least different from one another. Could you imagine an artist without an ego? I think not!

Tibetans might say, "Saddle up and ride the ego, instead of letting the ego saddle up and ride you."

There is the term, "Wind Horse," which before Buddhism adopted it, represented the soul. It seems to me that in Buddhism, it represents being able to ride your life, your ego, instead of letting life ride you.

If you are Wind Horse, you are dancing with the energy you are and the energy around you.

Best Wishes for Peace Profound
Love for All
Dony Hia

Merely Steps...

It is important to expect nothing, to take every experience, including the negative ones, as merely steps on the path, and to proceed.
~ Ram Dass

Yes we need to take everything as merely steps on the path in each moment, but we also need to remember in each moment that we can change our path.

Each moment we experience is an accumulation of the karma we have accumulated over eons of time. Even with all this conditioning, any moment we can say, "Ah, I am changing my path."

For instance, I have been handed a very difficult project that seems to have implanted in it a lot of negative energy, making almost every step more difficult than it should be. So in each moment I say, "Ah, this is my karma."

Also in many moments I put out to the universe, am I here because I can bring a lot of positive energy to the project, or am I here for a sign that it is time to make a change on my path. Until I hear a loud voice in my being saying otherwise, I will continue to try and bring on as much positive energy as I can.

After all, all is just a dance of energy (light). Smiling as I type.

Best Wishes for Peace Profound
Love for All
Dony Hia

Wakan Tanka...

Wakan Tanka/Great Sprit/The Everything/The Great Mystery. Wakan Tanka translates to our inner Great Spirit of self beyond personhood and personality, beyond identity into soul consciousness. As a consciousness of mind, we are dreaming ourselves awake in a physical body. As a cell of the Great Sprit's body, we are in its thought of its Self. We are one with the Great Spirit in pure orgiastic light, love, and awareness. For it is completion.
~ Thunder Strikes with Jan Orsi, *Song of the Deer, The Great Sundance Journey of the Soul*

In energy class, we build a matrix in which to do our work. The one we use is a twenty-count matrix from the Southern Tradition, which some tribes of Indians used as far back as they can remember. When we build a matrix, we open a portal and call on the energy of each of the twenty. My favorite is Number 17, Kachina-Hey, the dream teachers who teach us how to dream our lives.

The reason I shared Number 20 (Wakan Tanka) instead is that when I read this one, it reminded me of something that came up when I was having a conversation with my sister Virginia (Ginny) when we were young; I believe around fourth-grade.

We were discussing God and the universe and it came up that maybe we are like cells on a larger body. I don't remember if she said it or if I did, but it is something that I have always felt is true.

In Buddhist thought, there is only one and everything is just part of the One; self and other are an illusion.

Best Wishes for Peace Profound
Love for All
Dony Hia

The Sacred Dream...

Symbols of the Dream: This is our life experiences, the playing out of our personal and sacred dreams fueled by our desire to live life fully awake, aware, and alert to reality in the Now. It is how we experience life through the process and symbol. This is also the place of dreams of the collective of humanity and their and their impact on Grandmother Earth's dream of her life experience and evolutionary excellence.
~ Thunder Strikes

When we build a matrix for our energy work my cells always seem to light up when we get to Number 7: Sacred Dream, and Number 17: Dream Teachers.

I consider my ability to dream so vividly, and to remember them as clearly as I remember my waking hours, one of the riches of my life.

For me, to travel to so many places and experience so many things while asleep makes me feel as if I get to live and learn both while awake and while asleep.

Of course, the dream teachers remind us we are dreaming this life even when we think we are awake.

Working with the energy of the dream teachers I am starting to get a slight taste of this.

Pinch me, I think I am dreaming!

Best Wishes for Peace Profound
Love for All
Dony Hia

Much More...

There's much more in any given moment than we usually perceive, and that we ourselves are much more than we usually perceive. When you know that, part of you can stand outside the drama of your life.
~ Ram Dass

If our minds did not filter out most of what is going on around us in any given moment we literally could not handle it. We can though, through practice, expand our awareness to help us maneuver through each moment. We can learn to let our energy dance with the energy around us instead of fighting with the energy around us. After all, it's all just energy.

Best Wishes for Peace Profound
Love for All
Dony Hia

The Other 99 Percent...

What I give form to in the daylight is only 1% of what I see in the Darkness.
~ M. C. Escher

I don't grow up. In me is the small child of my early days.
~ M.C. Escher

    Escher's first quote above makes perfect sense to me since our conscious mind only scratches the surface of who we really are. I have often thought that if we could turn ourselves inside out, the planet would not be large enough to hold us. Inside each of us, we have layers and layers that go all the way back to the beginning: to the One.

    In dreaming, I get a sense of just how many layers we have. In imagination, I get another sense of how many layers we have.

    In me, there are several children who refuse to grow old.

Best Wishes for Peace Profound
Love for All
Dony Hia

We Choose…

Our choice of parents intentionally sets us up for challenges and adversity, a mold that will provide the greatest opportunity for us to learn our karmic lessons and to develop excellence in our character. You may have experienced a childhood that seemed happy and devoid of adversity, with parents who were loving and supportive. Nonetheless, your spirit personality still had to deal with these challenges on a spiritual level.

~ Thunder Strikes

Buddhists say it is our karma which determines our next birth.

Schopenhauer believed it was the will of the unborn child that draws parents together. Many mystics actually believe we pick our parents.

Last night, when I was reading the above passage a thought came to mind; how big were your balls when you chose your parents? For the women reading this, in some lifetimes you were born the male of the species, so maybe you can relate.

When I was working with Alison, she took me back to before I was born during one session. She had me see my spirit circling the planet and asked what color my spirit was. I saw it as purple. Then she asked me to see my parents embraced and asked me the color of their spirits. I saw my mom as a cool calming blue. I saw my father as a bright, energetic, enticing red.

Then she had me start to enter the womb. As I started to do this I saw my father's bright red be covered over with a black cloud and his energy became more like a volcano ready to erupt.

At that point, I actually found myself trying to turn around and fly away but it was too late. It was as if my spirit was caught in a force field drawing me down and in.

Was this all imagination? Maybe, still in my soul there is a sense that this is how it happened. Knowing where I started this incarnation's journey and where I feel I am now, I am glad I was not able to pull away.

Best Wishes for Peace Profound
Love for All
Dony Hia

Life in the Second Chakra...

Our sexual catalyst energy is our soul force, and it functions in two very important ways. Through this prime mover energy, we exercise our free will in order to be truly determinate humans. We use it to increase our orgasticness to insure good health, vitality, and longevity.
~ Thunder Strikes

When I was working with Alison, she mentioned one time our second chakra is where we get our life.

This makes sense to me in that our first chakra is earth. Our second chakra, which is animal and also our sexual chakra, is where life starts for us.

Alison also mentioned she could see my second was too open, which can limit our ability to set boundaries.

In energy class we were taught a method for opening and closing our 2nd chakra.

A few times walking around Lake Merritt, I have closed my second chakra down and each time I am amazed at how my awareness shifts. When my second chakra is wide open, as it normally is, my awareness is mainly on the people and animals around the lake. When I close down the second chakra, my awareness expands to the sky, buildings and hills further out from the lake. I become much more aware of my senses and environment.

With my second chakra wide open I seem to be energized by the people and animals around me. Some more than others! Yet there is the risk of actually taking in others' energy, which would not be good.

Best Wishes for Peace Profound
Love for All
Dony Hia

Endless Tomorrows...

I believe we are reincarnated; you, I, we reincarnate over and over. We live many lives, and store up much experience. Some are older souls than others and so they know more. It seems to be an intuitive "gift." It is really hard-won experience.
~ Henry Ford

Reincarnation answered questions for me, which the Baptist religion I was born into could not. The question the Baptists could not give me an acceptable answer to was this: Why are some children in the world born into a world of suffering and others into luxury?

I did not, and do not, buy it when a preacher says it is God's will. To me this would mean there was, shall we say, a kind of sadistic god in charge of our world.

I believe that Gnostics believe the god in charge of our universe is a less than perfect god conceived by Sophia, mother god, without the help of a father god. While that would explain a lot, it is not a philosophy in line with my thinking.

Reincarnation, on the other hand, does explain why someone might be born suffering and another born seemingly well off. In reincarnation, not only do we have a hand in how this life goes, we have a hand in how our next life will go. Reincarnation also says our karma determined how we came into this life.

Best Wishes for Peace Profound
Love for All
Dony Hia

A Few Thoughts on Energy…

Passion is energy. Feel the power that comes from focusing on what excites you.
~ Oprah Winfrey

The more you lose yourself in something bigger than yourself, the more energy you will have.
~ Norman Vincent Peale

Love is a sacred reserve of energy; it is like the blood of spiritual evolution.
~ Pierre Teilhard de Chardin

In absolute reality, we are no more and no less than a dance of pure energy.

In the relative reality we dream for ourselves on this plane of existence; how our energy flows through us determines our quality of life.

From a mystical standpoint, Pure Love vibrates at the highest frequency and is the most subtle form of energy. Thus, energy flows best through love.

At this time, I feel more love flowing through me than I ever have, and at the same time feel more love around me. There are moments when it seems as if every cell, every molecule, every atom within is dancing.

This incarnation has been quite a ride and interesting work for me. And yet, I also feel in a way that my best journey is just beginning.

Best Wishes for Peace Profound
Love for All
Dony Hia

No Wisdom-Tree, No Flaws...

One day the Fifth Patriarch told his monks to express their wisdom in a poem. Whoever had true realization of his original nature (Buddha Nature) would be ordained the Sixth Patriarch. The head monk, Shen Hsiu, was the most learned, and wrote the following:

The body is the wisdom-tree
The mind is a bright mirror in a stand;
Take care to wipe it all the time,
And allow no dust to cling.

The poem was praised, but the Fifth Patriarch knew that Shen Hsiu had not yet found his original nature, on the other hand, Hui Neng couldn't even write, so someone had to write down his poem, which read:

Fundamentally no wisdom-tree exist,
Nor the stand of a mirror bright.
Since all is empty from the beginning,
Where can the dust alight.
~ Hui-neng, the 6th Patriarch of Zen

    Hui-neng was the sixth and last Patriarch of the Chan Buddhism. Zen Buddhism developed from Chan.

    This weekend, Luyu, Yizi and I were in a friend's coffee shop, and I saw on Bob's Wisdom Board a quote. I cannot remember exactly how it read but the thought went something like this: "Love is not using another's flaws as weapons against them."

    After reading it, at one point, I smiled at my friend and said, "You know there really are no flaws."

    Since the weekend, the sixth Patriarch's poem has come to mind several times. I thought I would share it.

You can search throughout the entire universe for someone who is more deserving of your love and affection than you are yourself, and that person is not to be found anywhere. You, yourself, as much as anybody in the entire universe deserve your love and affection. ~ Buddha

Best Wishes for Peace Profound
Love for All
Dony Hia

Beautiful Garden…

A family is a place where minds come in contact with one another. If these minds love one another, the home will be as beautiful as a flower garden. But if these minds get out of harmony with one another it is like a storm that plays havoc with the garden.
~ Buddha

It's amazing to me how beautiful our home, inside and out, has become in the last couple of years.

Yesterday after work, I went out to our garden to pick some cucumbers for dinner. Near the cucumbers is one of our mushroom patches. It seems the oysters have liked the two days of rain; two days ago I only saw pink specks in the patch.

A little olive oil, just a touch of soy sauce, salt and pepper; what a great taste!

I have to say, I believe Luyu and Yizi brought the beauty deities with them when they moved in.

As Forest would say: And that is all I have to say about that!

Best Wishes for Peace Profound
Love for All
Dony Hia

The Thought...

The thought manifest as the word. The word manifest as the deed. The deed develops into habit. And the habit hardens into character. So watch the thought and its ways with care. And let it spring from love, born out of concern for all beings.
~ Buddha

The Bible says first there was the word, of course before the word there was a thought. If the mystics are correct, before the Big Bang there was The Thought. All that is comes out of that first thought.

There is one thing even before our thoughts and that is our karma. Does this create a catch 22?

On one hand, the thoughts we pull in may be because of our karma. On the other hand, it is said how we react to a thought creates future karma. Can we step off the karma loop, or are we predestined from the time of the Big Bang?

The Buddha said, "Watch the thought." He also said, "In order to learn how to watch the thought, watch the breath." In his statement of watching the thought, the Buddha is saying, to me, that we have a choice. First we have the choice to watch a thought. Then we have the choice of whether we act upon the thought or not. How we react to a thought in a present moment will, at least partially, determine what the next moment will be. With this line of thought, and again I may be wrong, I believe we can step off the Karma loop and our lives are not predestined.

I don't even think the universe is predestined. Scientists can't agree whether the Big Bang will continue on as an ever-expanding universe or will become the Big Crunch upon itself. There are arguments for both sides.

Just a thought to ponder...

Best Wishes for Peace Profound
Love for All
Dony Hia

Open Minds...

Believe nothing, no matter where you read it, or who said it, no matter if I have said it, unless it agrees with your own reason and your own common sense.
~ Buddha

    The above quote is a good one about believing nothing, no matter where you read it unless it agrees with your reason.
    I have seen a similar quote many times over the years, but it did not have the part *where you read it.* The reason I feel someone added to an earlier quote is that Buddhism was an oral tradition for the first 200 years. The way the Buddhist community first remembered the teachings was through verses and songs.
    So, since the Buddhist community in Gautama's time had no writing, I find it hard to believe he said "no matter where you read it."
    Think about it though, if the Buddha did say, believe nothing I say unless it agrees with your wisdom, what a peaceful philosophy he shared.
    There are so many supposedly religious people out there these days who not only expect you to believe what they say, they are willing to kill those who don't.
    When I share the *Fresh Morning Breath* thoughts it is as the Buddha taught, take what might help or bring a little joy and toss anything that doesn't resonate.

Best Wishes for Peace Profound
Love for All
Dony Hia

Killing the Buddha...

We are attached to the perceptions of others to guide us, and we look to them for our empowerment. This is an illusion. "When you see the Buddha on the road, kill him," goes the saying. Following the Buddha's perception (that is, attachment to the perceptions of others) will only give you an illusionary empowerment. You must experience your own perception within Sacred law.
~ Thunder Strikes

Some twenty-plus years ago, I read the book, *If you Meet the Buddha on the Road, Kill Him! The Pilgrimage of Psychotherapy Patients* by Sheldon B. Kopp.

I don't remember too much about the book other, than Kopp was a psychologist who had worked in psychiatric hospitals and prisons.

One story in the book I do remember is what he said about a Jewish mother; he was Jewish himself, if my memory serves me.

The story went something like this: A Jewish man kills his mother, maybe there was a girlfriend or wife involved, I can't remember. I do remember that he cut out his mother's heart and was running with it in his hands. As he headed out the back door and down some stairs, he heard his mother's heart say, be careful not to fall. My thought after reading the story was: Talk about Love.

I used to be Buddhist, but I killed that part of me. . . Well, not 100 percent.

Best Wishes for Peace Profound
Love for All
Dony Hia

Emptiness...

If you use your mind to try and understand reality, you will understand neither your mind nor reality. If you try and understand reality without using your mind, you will understand both your mind and reality. ~ Bodhidharma

Bodhidharma is credited with taking Ch'an (Zen) Buddhism into China.

Some stories have him coming from India and other stories have him coming from Persia. Most accounts have him as an ill-tempered monk.

It seems a lot of the Buddhist monks were ill tempered. Marpa, one of the early Tibetans to go into India and bring back Kagyu Buddhism, was said to be a drunk who beat his students.

It is said he tortured Milarepa (one of my favorite characters in Buddhism) for years before sharing with him his highest teachings. For some reason, I think of my own father as being Marpa like.

I think what Bodhidharma was alluding to was this: Reality is emptiness, thus you cannot find emptiness by filling your mind with thoughts and conceptions. You can only experience reality (emptiness) by emptying all thoughts and conceptions. The Heart Sutra is all about emptiness.

Best Wishes for Peace Profound
Love for All
Dony Hia

Middle Path...

Wisdom says we are nothing. Love says we are everything. Between these two our life flows.
~ Jack Kornfield

This is the Middle Path of Buddhism. While the Middle Path is attributed to Gautama Buddha, it was Nagarjuna, who lived in India (also home to Buddha), who founded Madhyamaka (middle path) Buddhism. He is also famous for his contribution of Sunyata (emptiness).

It is said that when the Buddha taught the Middle Path, he said our lives should be like the strings on a violin, not too tight, not too loose. If the strings are too slack there is either no music or poor music. If the strings are too tight, the music is not right or the string snaps and again there is no music. Life is all about balance: The Middle Path.

Best Wishes for Peace Profound
Love for All
Dony Hia

Right Now...

You can't stop the waves, but you can learn to surf.
~ Jack Kornfield

I think a lot of people, if not most, dream of a time when life will be easier. I used to do it a lot myself. The thing is, life will never be better than it is right now. Because life is perfect in the Now, the universe does not get it wrong.

Only our human mind creates things that appear to be wrong; they are not. Even if you are suffering at this moment, think of it as perfect.

Think of it as an opportunity to learn to grow. Think of suffering and challenges as the fertilizer to help you blossom into the beautiful flower I know you are.

I even have to remind myself of these thoughts now and again.

Best Wishes for Peace Profound
Love for All
Dony Hia

Transforming Difficulties…

To undertake genuine spiritual path is not to avoid difficulties but to learn the art of making mistakes wakefully, to bring to them the transformative power of our heart.
~ Jack Kornfield

How often we try to pull away from difficulties or pains of the heart.

I found a few years ago if, instead of trying to pull away from difficulties or pains of the heart, I could dive into the depths of my heart where I felt the pain, I could find a deep joy and compassion for myself. When I could find this, the heart changed from pain to warmth and joy.

There have been times I have thought: One can only know, and be good, to the extent that one has known, and been, bad. Some days I think I can be damn good.

Now I am going to walk out of my office and onto this very, very difficult project.

Since we create our own realities, have a great day, unless you have made other plans.

Best Wishes for Peace Profound
Love for All
Dony Hia

Charging and Discharging...

Think of yourself as a battery. Energy is put into the battery from one direction, thus charging it. It discharges as it sends energy to the starter, the clock, the radio, or other parts of the car, while the running engine continues to recharge it. If the charge and discharge are not balanced, the battery will become overcharged or undercharged and malfunction. Our body is no different. Much of our energetic dysfunction, in all aspects of ourselves, is an imbalance of our body charge and discharge. When you hold and transform energy properly in your body, you are utilizing energy for good health.

~ Thunder Strikes, *Song of the Dear*

    Most problems we have are improper energy movement or even frozen energy in our body. I would go as far to say that most phobias are frozen energy. My own agoraphobia, which I carried for many years, I found later in life resulted from locked energy from a torturous father in the first nine years of my childhood.

    When I worked with Ipsalu Tantra, I released bundles of frozen energy, then released even more working with Alison. The energy class teaches us how to have proper flow of energy in and through our bodies. I feel so blessed to be able to do this energetic work. I truly wish everyone could do this type of energy work. I think the world would be a better place.

    On another note! I remember when my daughter, Michelle, asked me, at around age four what happens when we die. From Buddhist thought, I told her that we leave for a while and then are reborn. She did not understand this. Then I told her we are like batteries in her toys. We come into this life with a certain amount of energy, and when we use up that energy, we have to go get recharged and come back as a new battery. I remember her smiling and accepting this analogy.

I would say that energy work is my favorite work of date and something I will be working with until this battery has to go be recharged.

Best Wishes for Peace Profound
Love for All
Dony Hia

Energy Manners...

Our life is vast. It does not stop at the limits of what we personally experience. It is not something concrete or bounded. I do not think it is valid to view our life as limited to just ourselves—as if our human life extended only as far as our own body. Rather, we can see that a life extends out in all directions, like a net. We throw a net, and it expands outward. Just like that, our life extends to touch many other lives. Our life can reach out and become a pervasive part of everyone's life.
~ 17th Karmapa

Our lives can extend out and become pervasive or invasive to other beings. Also, other beings energy can become invasive to our energy field. In our energy class, one of the things we are taught is to have "manners" with our energy. We are told we should not have anyone else's energy within our bodies and we should not leave our energy in others.

Most of us though, have others' energy in us: parents, friends, lovers and even pets. This energy may be in the form of words, which play in our heads, or it can even be anger locked in muscles. We also leave our energy in others bodies or auric fields.

In the class, we are taught a meditation, *Me Not Me*, where we remove the energy of others and bring home energy we have left with others.

During one session working with Alison, who works in much the same way as we are taught in the energy class, I had energy within my body, where I held pain, which seemed not to be of this earth. When I released that pain, it was almost like blob heading back out into space.

Best Wishes for Peace Profound
Love for All
Dony Hia

Ebb and Flow...

Even a happy life cannot be without a measure of darkness, and the word happy would lose its meaning if it were not balanced by sadness. It is far better to take things as they come along with patience and equanimity.
~ Carl Jung

The entire universe is but an ebb and flow. Things recede then they return to us, both good and bad.

When things seem bad, one needs to realize this is impermanent, and good things will flow back into existence. This thought a lone can remove sadness.

On the other side, when things seem really good, one needs also to remember this too is impermanent and hard times will return. This thought should keep one humble.

The universe is also a living breathing being. With every in-breath there is new life and with every out-breath there is a death. It is the same for us: every in-breath is birth of a new moment and every out-breath is a death of that moment.

Best Wishes for Peace Profound
Love for All
Dony Hia

Souls Shedding Skin…

We must be willing to get rid of the life we've planned so as to have the life that is waiting for us. The old skin has to be shed before the new one can come.
~ Joseph Campbell

Many mystics believe that before we take on an incarnation, we view what our life might be. There is not just one script but several, and depending on the choices we make, at each step, our lives take turns for better or for worse. An interesting and fun book on this subject is *Journey of Souls* by Michael Newton. Of course, we don't really know what lies ahead when we move on. Still, this book was an enjoyable read for me.

In a few moments, I will be heading off to our energy class. I sure enjoy these classes. There is only one more class after this one for our second year. Then I start the third-year class with two new teachers.

In *Journey of Souls*, Dr. Newton narrates and comments upon the progressive "travel log" of twenty-nine of his clients who movingly describe what happened to them between their former reincarnations on earth. They revealed graphic details about how it feels to die, who meets us right after death, what the spirit world is really like, where we go and what we do as souls, and why we choose to come back in certain bodies.

Best Wishes for Peace Profound
Love for All
Dony Hia

Where to Find the Way…

The Way is not in the Sky. The Way is in the Heart.
~ Buddha

    In tantric Buddhism, and in mystical schools that work with the chakras, it is only in the fourth (heart) chakra that we truly start becoming compassionate humans.

    We have the heart, the mechanical pump moving life-giving blood through our system; and then we have the heart chakra, which is a mind. Also it is said: until the masculine and feminine are truly balanced in the heart chakra, one cannot reach enlightenment. I would think, if one were to reach enlightenment, all chakras would need to be balanced, and some schools say the heart chakra can only be balanced after the others are.

    Last evening while cooking dinner, I was touched by something Luyu said to me. She looked at me, gave me a kiss, and said, "One of the things I love about you is you have such a young heart." I smiled and thought, an old soul with a young heart.

Best Wishes for Peace Profound
Love for All
Dony Hia

Reintegrate the Children...

But it is not what I am saying that is hurting you; it is that you have wounds that I touch by what I have said. You are hurting yourself. There is no way I can take this personally.
~ Miguel Ruiz

We all have a wounded child, or wounded children, inside of us. When something in our environment reminds the wounded child of the original wound, the child takes over driving the bus. The wounded child is frozen in time until we find a way to rewrite the story, rescue the child and reintegrate the child back into our heart.

When the child starts driving the bus, we are in our fight of flight pattern.

Working with Alison I rescued and reintegrated many a frozen little child. With so many rescued children reintegrated into my heart, my heart feels very young and fresh these days.

In our energy class, one learns methods to avoid going into pattern, and how to quickly come out of pattern if one catches oneself slipping into pattern.

Both Saturday and Sunday morning when I walked around the lake, I saw my environment with childlike wonder. Everything, animal, plant and mineral seemed so electric, vibrant, and magical. I wondered if this is how the saints and sages see the world all the time.

Best Wishes for Peace Profound
Love for All
Dony Hia

Wearing and Removing Mask...

Without wearing any mask we are conscious of, we have a special face for each friend.
~ Oliver Wendell Holmes

The most important kind of freedom is to be what you really are. You trade in your reality for a role. ...You give up your ability to feel, and in exchange, put on a mask.
~ Jim Morrison

The privilege of a lifetime is being who you are.
~ Joseph Campbell

We all wear several masks to protect ourselves from both real and imaginary fearful situations.

A large part of healing work is to remove our unnecessary masks. Very few, in one lifetime, can remove all masks. It may not be a good idea to remove all masks; we need not remove those we really need for our safety and wellbeing. I hope to remove as many as I can in the time I have left, but I am sure I will need to keep several.

I would like, at some time, to see the shiny silvery Dony, I got a glimpse of hiding in the bowels of my first chakra. I saw him there while doing a healing retreat in Kentucky. I would like to see him show a little more of himself. But alas he still has fears of coming into the light.

Best Wishes for Peace Profound
Love for All
Dony Hia

Your Soul Will Not be Denied…

Whether you like it or not, your soul will not be denied, for its sole purpose for being here as a spirit personality in physical form is to grow and evolve. It is not here to build a bigger house, become a president of the corporation, own a summer cottage, bask at Club med or retire at 60. The sacred dream of your soul is not your career, how much money you make, or even contributions you make for the good of the collective. These may satisfy your desires and bring you the fulfillment and joy of accomplishment and pleasure, but they should not be the defining meaning and purpose of your life. They do not define who you are. They are adventures and rewards on your journey, not your destination.
~ Thunder Strikes

Yesterday after working in my backyard, I read the paragraph above. At that moment, I felt it would be a good *Fresh Morning Breath*.

Last night I received a call that a friend had passed, and I thought maybe I should write something else. Then I thought, it is very appropriate as I evolve into my own purpose for choosing this incarnation.

I think of my young friend whose father passed, who may feel he has the weight of the world placed on his shoulders now. I find I am I trying to draw up every ounce of positive energy I can to send his way.

It is often only when our hearts ach that we truly understand how capable of love we humans can be.

Best Wishes for Peace Profound
Love for All
Dony Hia

Don't Beat Up the Ego...

Two people have been living in you all your life. One is the ego, garrulous, demanding, hysterical, calculating; the other is the hidden spiritual being, whose still voice of wisdom you have only rarely heard or attended to.
~ Sogyal Rinpoche

I think Sogyal is a little to unnecessarily rough on our friend the ego. First of all we would not be here if not for our ego. It is the ego that believes itself to be a separate self.

It was our ego that chose us to be born in the first place. That lazy spiritual being would have been contented with just hanging around as a part of the One; day in and day out, just being part of that Big Bang-Old One. The ego, on the other hand, says, "I am separate; I am alive; I am going to dance in the energy field and web of life."

In the Middle Path we train the ego as we might a wild horse. When the ego serves us, we do not serve the ego. Then the spiritual being can say, "Yes, you go out and dance. I am going to stay here at home and watch just like I am watching a moving." Thus the spiritual being and the ego become best friends in their own unique dance.

Best Wishes for Peace Profound
Love for All
Dony Hia

Walk the Walk…

One thing: you have to walk, and create the way by your walking; you will not find a ready-made path. It is not so cheap, to reach to the ultimate realization of truth. You will have to create the path by walking yourself; the path is not ready-made, lying there and waiting for you. It is just like the sky: the birds fly, but they don't leave any footprints. You cannot follow them; there are no footprints left behind.
~ Osho

As a child, and through much of my adult life, I was both agoraphobic and insecure, which I guess go hand in hand. To scratch my way out of these fears, I spent at least 40 years reading how others, saints and sages walked their paths. And sure enough, as Osho said, there were no footprints.

My boss, and in the last few years, friend, when work got really tough, would call it our *baptism by fire*. In some ways, much of my own life has been baptism by fire. This has created in me not only my own path with my own steps, but it has also encouraged me to find ways to share with others that they have to walk their own path, to walk the walk.

This last week, two dear friends of mine have been thrown into their own newest *baptisms by fire*. While I know both of these people will walk through the fire unharmed, my heart goes out to them as they go through the process. I reach down deep inside, to my core, draw up all the positive energy that I can muster, and send it to my friends to support them as they walk their own walk.

Best Wishes for Peace Profound
Love for All
Dony Hia

Open Heart...

Humankind has not woven the web of life.
We are but one thread within it.
Whatever we do to the web, we do to ourselves.
All things are bound together.
All things connect.
~ Chief Seattle.

Yesterday, I was in the last class of the first two years. At lunch, I went off by myself to eat. I went to a Nepalese & Indian restaurant. Under the glass covering the table was a story and at the bottom of the story was the Chief Seattle quote above. At the moment, it seemed to resonate with me but I did not know why.

Today was my first day back at work after vacation, and in some ways I feel I have walked into a hornet's nest. Two of the men who I admire the most seem to be at each other's throats. Each is such strong a force and at the top of his field. Yet, they are so much alike, they are like trying to put two positive sides of a magnet together.

Standing on the outside, I see nothing but an opportunity for growth in all of us. In life, sometimes we get to be the positive side of the magnet, and other times we get to be the negative side. If we think that we have to be one side, or the other, we might fight this. If we can think *we get to be*, instead of *have to be*, we can find joy in experiencing both roles.

This project needs both of these strong personalities. I hope good communication lets both of them enjoy both roles, the positive and the negative sides of the magnet.

Sometimes in these morning thoughts, I get to open my heart. This is one of those times; I have a lot of respect and love for both of the men I wrote about today.

Best Wishes for Peace Profound
Love for All
Dony Hia

Instructions for Life...

Take into account that great Love and great achievements involve great risk. When you lose, don't lose the lesson.
Follow the three R's:
- Respect for self.
- Respect for others.
- Responsibility for all your actions.

Remember that not getting what you want is sometimes a wonderful stroke of luck.
Learn the rules so you know how to break them properly.
Don't let a little dispute injure a great relationship.
When you realize you've made a mistake, take immediate steps to correct it.
Spend some time alone every day.
Open your arms to change, but don't let go of your values.
Remember that silence is sometimes the best answer.
Live a good, honorable life. Then when you get older and think back, you'll be able to enjoy it a second time.
A loving atmosphere in your home is the foundation for your life.
In disagreements with loved ones, deal only with the current situation. Don't bring up the past.
Share your knowledge. It is a way to achieve immortality.
Be gentle with the earth.
Once a year, go someplace you've never been before.
*Remember that the best relationship is one in which your **love** for each other exceeds your need for each other.*
Judge your success by what you had to give up in order to get it.
Approach love and cooking with reckless abandon.
~ 14th Dalai Lama, Instructions for Life

Luyu and I have decided to go, at least a once a year, to someplace we've never been before for vacation. This time it is Toronto. Being here, I find Toronto the cleanest large city I have ever been to.

So far in all our travels in Toronto, we have only seen a couple of pieces of trash. Even some of the poorer places we have walked through, are spotless. It certainly must be a different mindset than back home in Oakland.

If it is true, as the saying goes, that cleanliness is next to Godliness, God must be close by.

Even with all this beauty, half my heart is home in California supporting the friend whose father passed. I am somewhat troubled that my body is not there also.

Best Wishes for Peace Profound
Love for All
Dony Hia

Pieces of the One...

The problem in Western society is that you don't look at life and death as a whole. You isolate death. That's why there's so much fear.
~ Sogyal Rinpoche

Quoting Dudjom Rinpoche on the Buddha-nature No words can describe it, no example can point to it. Samsara does not make it worse, nirvana does not make it better. It has never been born, it has never ceased. It has never been liberated, it has never been deluded. It has never existed, it has never been Nonexistent. It has no limits at all, it does not fall into any kind of category.
~ Sogyal Rinpoche

Sogyal Rinpoche is the author of the book, *The Tibetan Book of Living and Dying*. It is a great book for anyone facing death and for anyone facing life, for that matter.

Life and death are kind of like the seasons: one keeps rolling into the other endlessly.

In Tibetan Buddhism, there are many bardos, life is a bardo, death is a bardo, dreaming is a bardo. There are also bardos in between life and death and dreaming and waking.

The thing is, the Buddha-nature, or whatever term you chose, is never born and never dies. It just keeps rolling from one bardo to the next, evolving back to the One. At the same time, it is only through the many that the One can experience itself.

We are all pieces of the One. And if you still your mind, you can experience this Oneness.

Best Wishes for Peace Profound
Love for All
Dony Hia

Love That environment...

As a student I learned from wonderful teachers and ever since then I've thought everyone is a Teacher.
~ Bill Moyers

Moyers' quote rings so true for me; everyone is a teacher. Even more than that, however we perceive others, both human and nonhuman beings, is a reflection of our own mind. So not only is everyone a teacher, everything is a teacher; everything is a guru.

You want to know the state of your mind, take a look at how you see the world around you. I know for myself that I love this magical dance of energy appearing to be both real and surreal at the same time. And oh, is it so filled with love.

I think the pains I feel in my chest sometimes might just be my fourth chakra opening wide.

Best Wishes for Peace Profound
Love for All
Dony Hia

Men are from Mars...

If we are to feel the positive feelings of love, happiness, trust, and gratitude, we periodically also have to feel anger, sadness, fear, and sorrow.
~ John Gray, *Men Are from Mars, Women Are from Venus*

We may all be Martians. Evidence is building that Earth life originated on Mars and was brought to this planet aboard a meteorite, said biochemist Steven Benner of the Wertheimer Institute for Science and Technology in Florida. An oxidized form of the element molybdenum, which may have been crucial to the origin of life, was likely available on the Red Planet's surface long ago but unavailable on Earth.

When I read the above article on the web, I thought maybe John Gray was Right. So I thought I would use one of his quotes from his book, *Men Are from Mars, Women Are from Venus*.

While these days I don't often feel much anger, sadness, fear or sorrow, I have certainly felt my share of these emotions in the past.

If not for these, what we often wrongly think of as negative emotions, we probably would not appreciate love, happiness, trust and gratitude as much as we do.

Often during the day the thought *I am blessed* comes to mind.

Best Wishes for Peace Profound
Love for All
Dony Hia

The Way of White Clouds…

Life has no meaning in itself, but only in the meaning we give it. Like the clay in the artist's hands, we may convert it into a divine form or merely into a vessel of temporary utility.
~ Lama Anagarika Govinda

Lama Govinda (1898-1985) wrote a book called *The Way of White Clouds*.

For me it was one of the most beautiful books I had read about Tibet; some of his descriptions painted such mystical images in my mind. Years later when I was able to go to Tibet, our group went to areas as beautiful as Govinda had described in the book.

I truly understand what Govinda was speaking of when he says life has no meaning other than what we give it.

In the beginning I may have started with mud, didn't, and couldn't even afford clay.

In the last few years I feel I have been working with precious metal as I form a mystical life for myself.

I am beginning to experience things in this life that I had believed I would have to wait for another life to experience.

The thing is, as one evolves and finds a more mystical life, one cannot give this to anyone else. One can only point the way for others to become their own artists and art. Even a Buddha cannot enlighten another being; much less can an ordinary unenlightened being enlighten another being.

Each being has to enlighten themselves, finding their own way into the light.

Best Wishes for Peace Profound
Love for All
Dony Hia

Dialing in on Good Thoughts...

Feelings and thoughts do not define who we are; they are just part of the weather of our inner world.
~ John Daishin Buksbazen

Even more than thoughts do not define who we are, we don't even own our thoughts. We own the action of following, or not following our thoughts, but we don't own the thoughts. If you think you own your thoughts, have a thought come to mind and try and hold on to it. It won't be long before you realize the thought you were trying to hold onto has come and gone, and another thought has entered your mind. Thoughts belong to the void from which they arise and return.

If one wants to change which thoughts enter the mind, one has to change the receiver. Yes, we are all receivers tuned to the thoughts that continually fill the airwaves from the void. We all, to some extent, change the receiver as we grow older. We as adults, for the most part do not receive the same thoughts as we did as small children. Even enlightenment is a matter of tuning and receiving thoughts of enlightenment.

In energy class we were taught a couple of simple ways of opening up the receiver when we are caught in tunnel vision, where a thought keeps circling in our mind. When we are in tunnel vision, the thought keeps popping up into our minds, behind the spot between our eyebrows. To change this, one can try to think from the edges of our mind, sort of trying to think from the outer edge of our sculls.

Another method is to take our right hand and place it over the area of our heart.

I have tried both of these methods and both have worked for me. I do find trying to think from the outer edges of my brain works faster and is more powerful. Try either one of these, the next time you find a thought from the past, circling in your mind and you rather it not be there.

Best Wishes for Peace Profound
Love for All
Dony Hia

One Watching...

Once you become aware of your own body and its movements, you will be surprised that you are not your body. This is something of a basic principle, that if you can watch something then you are not it. You are the watcher, not the watched. You are the observer, not the observed. How can you be both?
~ Osho

We can carry yesterday's *Fresh Morning Breath* into today. If you observe your thoughts, you can realize you are not your thoughts, you do not own them. In a real sense, you do not even own your body. Your body is just earth, wind, fire, water and prana drawn up from mother earth with the support of Father Sun.

Your body is on loan for this one life only. Next life the watcher will borrow another body, much like we might borrow a coat.

The watcher is never born and never dies. I believe if one can get a taste of the watcher, one realizes the watcher is part of and an extension of the One.

Best Wishes for Peace Profound
Love for All
Dony Hia

Accept...

Lu-tsu says, `Accept the situation you are in. It must be the right situation for you; that's why you are in it. `Existence cares for you. It is given to you not without any reason. It is not accidental: nothing is accidental. Whatsoever is your need is given to you. If it were your need to be in the Himalayas, you would have been in the Himalayas. And when the need arises, you will find that either you go to the Himalayas or the Himalayas come to you. It happens . . . when the disciple is ready, the Master arrives. And when your inner silence is ready, God arrives. And whatsoever is needed on the path is always supplied.
~ Osho

   I agree with the statement, nothing is accidental. One cannot truly believe in Karma, and then also think there are things which are accidental.
   Some people have a hard time even accepting that they deserve things when things are going great. When things are going great, they look over their shoulders expecting something bad to happen. In doing this, sure enough, they create the trouble they believe is coming. I know this because for many, many years, I had done this. No more though; things just seem to keep getting better and better, and I joyfully accept this.
   Then there are those who, when things are going bad, don't accept things as they should be. They think they don't disserve the bad, and if they don't blame another person, they blame a devil or non-caring god.
   I look back, and I can't see a time I thought my troubles were because of another person, being, or deity. Even as a small child, and even though I did not know about karma, I always felt somehow responsible for my own life's conditions.
   When people accept that their lives are their own making, they seem to start working towards the life they want.

Best Wishes for Peace Profound
Love for All
Dony Hia

Our Golden Cord…

Enlightenment is the Journey from the head back to the heart, from words back to silence.
~ Jock Brocas

I think enlightenment is the journey back to our core. The journey may have to pass back from the head to the heart, but then it needs to continue to the core. The heart is never fully silent, only deep in our core is there true silence.

Our core is in the center of our body, and if you could see it, you would see it actually extends above and below. It extends down to the center of the earth and above through our template of perfection on up to our highest of high selves. From our highest of high selves, it extends back to the One.

In tracing my own golden light cord back, I only start to sense the silence as I near the template of perfection. I have not been able to experience my highest of high selves yet. I am sure if at some point I do, there will be a silence as I have never experienced and which no words can describe.

Best Wishes for Peace Profound
Love for All
Dony Hia

Inviting in Fear...

The only way to ease our fear and be truly happy is to acknowledge our fear and look deeply at its source. Instead of trying to escape from our fear, we can invite it up to our awareness and look at it clearly and deeply.
~ Thich Nhat Hanh

Have you ever noticed when you face and overcome a fear that particular fear never rises again?

If I think way back, it seems I can remember a time I was afraid to sleep with the light off. No, not yesterday: further back.

I can also look back and see a time I was afraid to lose love from someone. There was a time I was afraid of being in charge of a big job. There was a time I was afraid of divorce, before I mastered it.

These days, I don't have so many fears. I do have a fear of heights but only when I am in a high place near an edge.

One thing I did realize at a fairly young age was that if I have fears, others must also have fears. This created a certain compassion for others that I would not have had if I had not had my own fears.

I think deep inside there is another fear. I think this fear is of having an awakening, reaching a state of enlightenment. I think fear holds many of us back in this one area. I think we are afraid if we have an awakening our whole world we have created for our self might shift. Our ego says we might lose who we are!

I guess when I was young I had more fears than joys; these days I certainly feel full of joys.

Best Wishes for Peace Profound
Love for All
Dony Hia

The Other 84.5 Percent...

And silence, like darkness, can be kind; it too is a language.
~ Hanif Kureishi

In one sense, I think it is silence that holds it all together. Everything comes from silence and returns to silence.

When you are listening to someone talk, try and see where the sound comes from. Our first thought would be the sound comes from the vocal cords but if you can really sense it, like all sound, it comes from the silence on the other side. The sound comes from and returns to the same place our thoughts come from. Even planets and stars come from and return to this silence, often called the void.

Scientists say the universe is about 84.5 percent dark matter. They don't understand the dark matter and only know it exists because it has a gravitational pull. They say this dark matter doesn't absorb or emanate light. Measuring the dark matter with the best instruments of today, it appears totally silent. Maybe, just maybe, this dark matter is the void from which everything emanates and then returns to.

I think the best way for someone to experience the silence from which everything emanates and returns to is meditation. If one really wants to experience the silence, I suggest going into a forest where no one else is around, no mechanical noises exist, and sit and meditate on the silence there.

Best Wishes for Peace Profound
Love for All
Dony Hia

Another's World...

I realize that maybe you can't change the world by your actions alone, but you can change yourself. And when you did, the world around you might also change in the very act of attempting to understand you, just as we all try to understand each other.
~ John Francis

To the extent we change, our individual worlds change. We tend to think there is one world, but this is not the case. There are billions of worlds.

A cat may cross your path but the cat cannot know your world, and you cannot know the cat's. Our worlds are too different and difficult for one being to understand the other's. It is actually the same with people; people cross our paths, but we can never truly know another person's world.

Even those people closest to us, wives, husbands, family and lovers, only cross our paths; we can never truly know another's world. No matter how close we are to another, in all actuality, we are seeing their world through our own eyes, our own thoughts. On top of this, almost all people wear masks they project out to the world.

I would say welcome to my world, but I know you can never know my world any more than I can know yours. I can say I like the reflection of my world I get when I am around you.

Thanks for the reflections!

Best Wishes for Peace Profound
Love for All
Dony Hia

We Create Our Own Worlds...

Just as a picture is drawn by an artist, surroundings are created by the activities of the mind.
~ Buddha

For me this is one of the Buddha's most important teachings, and one which is very hard for most of us to wrap our minds around. From a psychological point of view, the way we see the world is created by our own minds. This seems easy to understand.

From a mystical view, on the other hand it may not be so easy to accept. In mysticism, we are taught that we actually create the physical world around us. In my heart, I feel this to be true. We do this by the karma we create, which draws thoughts in or blocks thoughts from our consciousness. Our consciousness then manifests these thoughts in our physical world. Of course, there is a lot more to it, and I have over simplified the subject. I do, however, feel this to be true: we each create our own worlds.

At birth, we start creating the worlds we will experience in this life. At death, it all dissolves as if our world were just an evaporating mist.

A great, and I think fun, book on this subject is *The Tibetan Book of the Dead*. It reads like a Stephen King novel.

Best Wishes for Peace Profound
Love for All
Dony Hia

Go through the open window...

Play your part in the comedy, but don't identify yourself with your role.
~ Wei Wu Wei

As long as there is a "you" doing or not-doing, thinking or not-thinking, "meditating" or "not-meditating", you are no closer to home than the day you were born.
~ Wei Wu Wei

Are we not wasps who spend all day in a fruitless attempt to traverse a window-pane – while the other half of the window is wide open?
~ Wei Wu Wei

What Wei is pointing out is, the "I" we think we are is an illusion. Behind this "I" there is a watcher, which is not an illusion. This watcher is "awareness," and this awareness is not an "I" or an illusion. It is our trueness, which is never born and never dies.

Maybe Wei's remark of being like wasp implies that we seek ourselves, our identities, outside in a world which we think of as real, which is an illusion and we miss the mark. It is by heading in that direction we can find the ONE reality, the ONE we truly are.

Best Wishes for Peace Profound
Love for All
Dony Hia

Perfect fit...

Whenever you find yourself on the side of the majority, it is time to pause and reflect.
~ Mark Twain

    Of course, in many ways I live like the majority, work hard, pay bills, eat, sleep and play. Inside though, I don't think I have ever sided with the majority. Growing up, I didn't quite fit in with the rest of the family, nor did I at school. Later when I started work, I also found that I didn't fit with the majority, even if I did work well with them. Hell, for much of my life, I probably felt that I didn't fit with myself. These days though, I really like the fit of almost every moment; in the present moment there is always a perfect fit.

Best Wishes for Peace Profound
Love for All
Dony Hia

Beautiful Aloneness…

And meditation is nothing but enjoying your beautiful aloneness. Celebrating yourself; that's what meditation is all about.
~ Osho

On a relative reality basis, what Osho says above is correct. In absolute reality, in meditation, and outside meditation, there is no *yourself* or any other *self,* and I believe Osho knew this. Meditation is taught as a method to experience no self. Once this is truly experienced, even meditation is not necessary any more. There is a quote credited to Buddha which goes like this: "It is as if when one reaches the other shore he still carries a raft."

In the few times, I have truly experienced no self, like last Saturday walking Lake Merritt; I am always without other human contact. I have experienced this feeling while driving alone and while walking alone in a forest. When one experiences this oneness, at least for me, there are no desire left unfulfilled; in emptiness there is a fullness, which tingles the body with bliss. I have experienced this, in my whole life, fewer than ten times. Only once have I experienced this in meditation and this was while sitting in my backyard in Vacaville years ago.

These days, I can experience a beautiful aloneness even in a crowd.

No self is another story; very seldom do I get to experience this.

Best Wishes for Peace Profound
Love for All
Dony Hia

Ah, That Dance of Energy...

There are many ways to calm a negative energy without suppressing or fighting it. You recognize it, you smile to it, and you invite something nicer to come up and replace it; you read some inspiring words, you listen to a piece of beautiful music, you go somewhere in nature, or you do some walking meditation.
~ Thich Nhat Hanh

Everything around us is a dance of energy, even if it is something as solid as a block wall. Also, other than electrical polarity, positive and negative energy is a human concept, a duality of mind. I don't believe there is another animal on the planet that thinks of something as being positive or negative. They just experience what is; they truly live in the moment.

Today is the first class of the third year of energy class. I must say that I am excited and a little nervous at the same time. The third & fourth years are not taught by the same person as the first two years, they are taught by a man and woman team, and I am not sure what to expect yet. I do know we will be working with and playing with the energy in and around us.

Best Wishes for Peace Profound
Love for All
Dony Hia

Any Moment...

You can make any human activity into meditation simply by being completely with it and doing it just to do it.
~ Alan Watts

Every moment we are here now, we are meditating. If we are not here now, we are not meditating even if we are sitting on our zafu or gomdem (meditation cushion). After thirty years of spending a lot of time, most days, sitting on a zafu or gomdem, I have stopped this practice.

For me now most of my days are spent in meditation, no matter what I am doing. A couple of my favorite meditations are walking Lake Merritt with Tilo and also cooking. Work can be a great meditation, and one performs better when one is here now. I know when I walk a job, and I am here now, I see so much; I catch a lot of things, long before they become a problem. I also get a real feeling of how most workers are doing.

Lovemaking is also a very rewarding mediation if one is here now, not just for one's self but for one's partner also, unless of course one is by one's self.

As you can see, anything, and everything, in any moment can be a meditation just by being here Now.

Best Wishes for Peace Profound
Love for All
Dony Hia

Water vs. Fire…

Water does not resist. Water flows. When you plunge your hand into it, all you feel is a caress. Water is not a solid wall, it will not stop you. But water always goes where it wants to go, and nothing in the end can stand against it. Water is patient. Dripping water wears away a stone. Remember that, my child. Remember you are half water. If you can't go through an obstacle, go around it. Water does.
~ Margaret Atwood

I remember in 1979, when first starting my Buddhist practice, a lady said to me, "Your practice should be like water, not like fire." She added, "A fire is strong, but it burns itself out quickly, where water takes time to build force; once it does, it is unstoppable." Being Pieces and Water Snake, it seemed natural to me, thirty-four years later, my practice, while not just Buddhist, is still gaining momentum.

In around 2005, another friend, from Shambhala, did my astrology per my time and location of my birth. While I can't read the symbols she said, per the risings, whatever that means, I have a lot of fire in my sign. Ann's next comment was, "That explains a lot!" Not quite sure what she meant.

Best Wishes for Peace Profound
Love for All
Dony Hia

Who Knew…

The Buddha realized, a person is not a finished, unchanging entity but a process flowing from moment to moment. There is no real 'being,' merely an ongoing flow, a continuous process of becoming.
~ William Hart

In Buddhism there is no soul but there is a watcher. The watcher, the one which is aware, is unchanging and moves with us from life to life. This watcher may be our highest of high selves, the one projecting this life.

According to the Deer Tribe, Highest of High selves reflect as many as eight beings at one time, on different planes; true or not, it is still a nice thought.

Today at noon, Luyu and I are heading to Tahoe for our second anniversary weekend. I must say I like this flowing moment-to-moment business. Who knew I would love life more at sixty than I did at fifty, or any previous decade!

Oh yeah, the watcher probably knew.

Best Wishes for Peace Profound
Love for All
Dony Hia

Compassion…

Simplicity, patience, compassion, these three are your greatest treasures. Simple in actions and thoughts, you return to the source of being. Patient with both friends and enemies, you accord with the way things are. Compassionate toward yourself, you reconcile all beings in the world.
~ Lao Tzu

I am fairly good with simplicity, and very good with patience, but compassion is something I constantly need to remind myself of. Compassion is a tricky one for me. One side of me, because of my beliefs in karma, says one needs to take care of one's self on the long road home; then the other side says you can help point the way. So for me, compassion is more just pointing the way. It goes back to the old saying: you can give someone a fish or you can teach them how to fish. I lean towards the side of teaching how to fish. But once in a while, I am also willing to hand out a fish or two.

Best Wishes for Peace Profound
Love for All
Dony Hia

Hidden Inside...

The Creator gathered all of Creation and said,

"I want to hide something from the humans until they are ready for it. It is the realization that they create their own reality.

*The eagle said, "Give it to me. I will take it to the moon."
The Creator said, "No one day they will go there and find it."*

*The salmon said, "I will bury it on the bottom of the ocean."
The Creator said, "No. They will go there too."*

*The buffalo said, "I will bury it on the Great Plains."
The Creator said, "They will cut into the skin of the earth and find it even there."*

Grandmother Mole, who lives in the breast of Mother Earth, and who has no physical eyes but sees with spiritual eyes, said, "Put it inside them."

*And the Creator said,
"It is done."*
~ A Sioux and Hopi Creation Story

The energy class I am taking is based on several traditions, from East, West, North and South.

There are books out there showing the amazing similarities between the Hopi and Tibetan peoples; not only in their art but they have several similar words in their languages. Both are also of red skin. This makes me wonder if Tibetan's, of the Bon faith, walked across the Barron Straights 10,000 years ago. Both have taught for at least a few thousand years that we create our own reality, and both have nature-based beliefs.

By the way, it is only from inside that we can realize we create our own realities.

Best Wishes for Peace Profound
Love for All
Dony Hia

Going; and Coming Back…

Maybe you are searching among the branches, for what only appears in the roots.
~ Rumi

I believe the enlightenment of the sages is in the roots, the deep roots extending to the other side of the subconscious mind. You have to go to the other side of the darkness, of the subconscious mind, to find the clear light.
The story of Jonah in the belly of the whale, in the Bible, is really a metaphor of getting lost in the subconscious and then coming back. I would say just about every prophet and sage goes through the same process, Buddha did, Jesus did and modern sages like Eckhart Tolle did. The thing is, if they come back with the wisdom they touched upon, they are sages. If one goes into the deep roots and doesn't come back, one just ends up crazy.

In Tantric Buddhism, one is taken deep into the roots and hopefully brought back. This is why one is warned not to do a lot of the practices without a guru; they emphasize one can get lost in the subconscious and not return.

Best Wishes for Peace Profound
Love for All
Dony Hia

Break the Chains that Bind...

Hurt people hurt people. That's how pain patterns get passed on, generation after generation after generation. Break the chain today. Meet anger with sympathy, contempt with compassion, cruelty with kindness. Greet grimaces with smiles. Forgive and forget about finding fault. Love is the weapon of the future.
~ Yehuda Berg

Without the right tools, breaking patterns is not that easy. When people hurt other people, it is because they are in a fight or flight pattern

Patterns are really locked energy, which is often locked not only in the mind, but also in the body.

People more often than not go into fight of flight pattern for something that happened in the past, not what is really going on in the moment. The present moment is usually over-blown because there is some kind of similarity to a past time when fight or flight was really necessary. People with PTSD (post-traumatic stress disorder) are to some extent always in pattern. I myself had PTSD from childhood. Alison helped me work through most the locked energy and worked with me to heal the PTSD for the most part. This is also the work of the energy classes. I am sure I still have locked energy and as time ripens, I will be able to let go of more frozen energy.

I truly wish this work could be done in schools because I believe it breaks the chains that bind.

Best Wishes for Peace Profound
Love for All
Dony Hia

Little Cracks...

A true friend is someone who thinks that you are a good egg even though he knows that you are slightly cracked.
~ Bernard Meltzer

Maybe, just maybe, it is our little cracks that let the light in.

Knowing and accepting my own cracks not only makes my own life more pleasant, it also makes me very accepting of others' little cracks.

I would even carry it a step further and say it is our little cracks which makes each of us special.

Best Wishes for Peace Profound
Love for All
Dony Hia

Connecting to the Fields...

One way to access the field is through the daily practice of silence, meditation, and non-judgment. Spending time in nature will also give you access to the qualities inherent in the field: infinite creativity, freedom, and bliss.
~ Deepak Chopra

If one reads Chopra's quote above one might think there is one field. There are endless fields (energy matrixes).

In our energy class, we do a twenty-count which means we connect with twenty different energy fields. A few we connect with are Sacred Animals, Sacred Plants, Spiritual Ancestors, and Book of Life.

There is a Catholic field, a Baptist field, A Zen field, A Kagyu field, a Rosicrucian field, a Jewish Kabala field, and on and on. We all connect to and draw energy from different fields even though most people are not conscious they are connected to different energy fields.

While in absolute reality I don't believe there are good or bad fields, in relative reality there are. In relative reality, we can unconsciously, or consciously, connect to negative fields as easily as we can to what we would think of as positive fields.

At any given moment, we are connected to, and operating from layer upon layers of different energy fields.

Most mystics and I also believe Love is the most powerful field in the universe.

Best Wishes for Peace Profound
Love for All
Dony Hia

Calm Abiding...

Some of the ancient Rishis held that each man's life is dependent upon karmic fixed number of breathings, and that if the duration of time required for on inhalation and expiration to be prolonged by practice of yoga, the man's life itself would be prolonged correspondingly.
~ Evans Wentz

The above is from a footnote from the book *Tibetan Yoga and Secret Doctrines*, which I first read in 1985. I am rereading the book now and when I came across it again last night I liked it as much as I did twenty-eight years ago.

If we get angry or excited our breathings increase in number and we do not extract all the oxygen we should. In either situation, our body is stressed and is not as healthy as it is if we are breathing calmly.

In several Tibetan practices it is said that one should have fifteen breaths per minute, 21,600 per day.

Once, when I was to time a twenty-minute meditation session I forgot to grab the clock. Knowing that I do breathe fifteen times per minute, I counted 300 breaths. Sure enough when we got up to do a walking meditation I saw that twenty minutes had passed. It really is a meditation just to be able to keep focused and count 300 breaths without losing track.

For me calm breathing is calm abiding.

Best Wishes for Peace Profound
Love for All
Dony Hia

Changes on the Wind...

To resist change, to try to cling to life, is therefore like holding your breath: if you persist you will kill yourself.
~ Alan Watts

Yesterday in energy class, we used the thirteen-month Mayan calendar to select our tribe name, kind of the same thing as horoscope to me. If nothing else, I found it to be fun. After that, we were able to find our tone, tone power, tone action and tone essence. With our tribe name, we also had tribe time cell, tribe action, tribe power, and tribe essence. From this we came up with our individual invocations we will be working with for the remaining two years of the class.

I must say mine really resonated with me. My name is Yellow Galactic Star.
My invocation I will be working with is "I harmonize in order to Beautify, Modeling Art. I seal the Store of Elegance with the Galactic tone of Integrity. I am guided by the power of Elegance."

These are supposedly our natural gifts that we come into life with. I really resonate with my tribe essence being art, having longed to be an artist most of my life. Maybe the Harmonizing is part of my art. On the other hand, if I brought Elegance into me with this life I buried it pretty deep, something I can work on, I guess.

As I was leaving class one of the two teachers smiled and said, "Work on that Elegance." I smiled, jumped and clicked my heals; she laughed.

Life is good and I feel changes on the wind.

Best Wishes for Peace Profound
Love for All
Dony Hia

Letting Lefty Rest...

If we listened to our intellect, we'd never have a love affair. We'd never have a friendship. We'd never go into business, because we'd be too cynical. Well, that's nonsense. You've got to jump off cliffs all the time and build your wings on the way down.
~ Annie Dillard

In our energy class, it is always discussed how our left brain is our intellectual brain and our right brain is our intuitive creative brain.

Many of the exercises we do are to teach us to use and trust the right brain more. I know for me, in many ways it is very natural because I have always relied a lot on my right brain, and also my gut brain for that matter.

I would say through the class that I am using and trusting my right brain more than I ever have.

Lately it seems there are moments when the left brain is just taking a rest, as if it knows the right brain will handle whatever comes up.

Left hand right brain.

Best Wishes for Peace Profound
Love for All
Dony Hia

Being Whole...

There is a part of every living thing that wants to become itself – the tadpole into the frog, the chrysalis into the butterfly, the damaged human being into a whole one. That is spirituality.
~ Ellen Bass

    The tadpole does not know it is a frog until it becomes a frog. The Chrysalis does not know it is a butterfly until it becomes one. And a damaged human does not realize it is whole until becoming whole.

    I'm learning to croak, flutter and be whole.

Best Wishes for Peace Profound
Love for All
Dony Hia

Healthy Spirit...

We are kept from the experience of Spirit because our inner world is cluttered with past traumas . . . As we begin to clear away this clutter, the energy of divine light and love begins to flow through our beings. ~ Father Thomas Keating

The above quote is from the book, *Frequency the Power of Personal Vibration,* by Penny Peirce. I really like that most modern energy workers are nondenominational and draw from many spiritual teachers and sources. After all, spirit is none other than a vibration of energy, of light. Whatever can help one tune to this vibration, this frequency, can and should be drawn upon.

I believe I mentioned before, one of the meditations taught us in our energy class is this: Visualizing a connection from our highest of high selves down through our template of perfection, through our core, and down to the core of the earth. If the core is open, we can draw a balance of energy from above and below; we draw masculine energy from above and feminine energy from the earth. The more balanced the flow of these two energies, the more aligned we are with the divine, and the healthier our Spirit is.

Best Wishes for Peace Profound
Love for All
Dony Hia

Keep Aiming...

An arrow can only be shot by pulling it backward. So when life is dragging you back with difficulties, it means that it's going to launch you into something great. So just Focus, and keep aiming.
~ Unknown

    Today's *Fresh Morning Breath* thought was given to me from a daughter of one of my friends on the list. Jim said his daughter has read a few of them and thought I would like this one. Well of course he was right. Not only do I like the optimism, I like the lesson it reminds me of. The reminder for me is how we are all interconnected, even with those whom we don't know. When we are able to touch someone in a good way, it can be like dropping a pebble in a pond, ripples head out in all direction. As any goodness I can share ripples through others, other's goodness ripples back to me. It is good that I am reminded to keep aiming.

Best Wishes for Peace Profound
Love for All
Dony Hia

Gift of Dreaming...

The dream world is not separate from the waking world; they are simply extensions of one another. Everything we do in the dream world is real; it's just happening at other dimensions of our awareness. It's absolutely normal for our awareness to move in and out through all the dimensions, both by day and night. What we do in our dreams, we are also doing in our waking world; the two realms are mutually supportive and co-creative.

~ Penney Peirce

I have known what Peirce is saying to be true since I was young. I feel the ability to dream vividly, and remember my sleeping dreams like I remember my waking hours, was a gift I have been given.

In the waking dream, the conscious mind separates the nighttime dream from the daytime dream. The subconscious mind and the sleeping conscious mind do not make this separation.

The subconscious mind operates in a different dimension from the conscious mind, but both dimensions are real. Dreaming is a natural way in which the conscious mind and subconscious mind speak to one another and share information back and forth through two different dimensions.

In deep sleep, which most of us have no recollection of, our conscious mind, subconscious mind, and the One Mind, or Super Consciousness meet and share information through three or more dimensions.

Mystics, and Tibetan Buddhists, say in deep sleep the One Mind recharges us.

Of course, the more we can connect with the One Mind during

the waking dream the more energy we can gather from this One Mind.

Are we dreaming the butterfly or is the butterfly dreaming us? When I wake up, I will let you know.

Best Wishes for Peace Profound
Love for All
Dony Hia

Waves of Energy Moving Towards Us...

Your past is not your potential. In any hour you can choose to liberate the future . . . Ultimately we know deeply that the other side of every fear is freedom.
~ Marilyn Ferguson

Isn't it great that at this moment, there is no future anywhere in the universe?

If there were a future in this moment, we would not have the ability to change and evolve. It is only because there is no future at this moment that we can create our futures in moments yet to come.

The future is waves of energy moving towards us, and it is up to each of us to decide how we want to ride the wave. And if the mystics are correct we can even change the wave before it arrives.

Best Wishes for Peace Profound
Love for All
Dony Hia

Silvery...

To know what you prefer, instead of humbly saying "Amen" to what the world tells you you ought to prefer, is to have kept your soul alive.
~ Robert Louis Stevenson

When I was very young, before three years old, I had to hide my soul deep, deep down in my first chakra to keep it safe.

In a retreat in Kentucky a couple of years ago, I saw a silvery little fellow sticking his head out of the darkness of the depths of this first chakra. Ever since, each day, a little more and more, I think he is climbing into the light.

Now I know this being is the light. Sometimes, I feel this being could light up a dark room.

Best Wishes for Peace Profound
Love for All
Dony Hia

Awareness of Dreaming…

We are perceivers. We are awareness; we are not objects; we have no solidity. We are boundless.
~ Carlos Castaneda

In relative reality, in which we operate daily, we do appear to have a solid body. In absolute reality the mystics believe we are pure untarnished awareness. I am in agreement with the mystics.

This last weekend my family and friends dreamed a joyful and mystical time in the forest! And I dream I am still young.

Best Wishes for Peace Profound
Love for All
Dony Hia

One Body, Many Brains…

What's in that unused 90 percent of our brain? It is no doubt intuition, imagination, and multidimensional awareness that occupy most of our consciousness. Logic is a very small part. Dreaming is the bulk of what we do, whether we're awake or asleep.
~ Penney Peirce

When one reads Peirce's quote above, one might think intuition, imagination, and multidimensional awareness are only in our brain. This is not the case. They are actually integrated throughout our entire body.

The nerves which run throughout the body are wiring for the brain, thus they are part of our brain. The nerves connect to the skin, organs and every part of the body, thus every part of the body is part of our brain. I like to think of all these connections as mind/brain. In the chakra systems every chakra in the body is sometimes thought of as individual minds that work together to sustain the entire body. The brain is nothing without the mind, or minds, which work with it.

The stomach is a mind/brain producing most of the chemicals that determine how the whole system operates. By balancing the mind/brain in the head with the mind/brain of the body, one can balance which chemicals are produced; often, this will cause a change in habits, such as diet.

Likewise, by changing the mind/brain in the stomach, the mind/brain in the head can be rewired; these two mind/brains work hand in hand. This is why and how medicines work.

So intuition, imagination and awareness can be stored, and drawn from, anywhere in the body and even in the auric field.

Best Wishes for Peace Profound
Love for All
Dony Hia

Flowering…

Even if our efforts of attention seem for years to be producing no result, one day a light that is in exact proportion to them will flood the soul.
~ Simone Weil

If we plant a seed and it does not sprout, it usually means we did not understand what the seed needed and how to prepare it.

If the seed sprouts and then dies it probably means we did not know how to care for it.

If the seed sprouts, the plant grows but it does not flower it probably means we did not know how to nourish it.

If the seed sprouts, the plant grows and a beautiful flower blooms, it probably means this plant was shown a lot of love.

All I can say is that after many, many years, I am sensing a few buds popping up within me. Thanks to all of you who have shown me so much love.

Best Wishes for Peace Profound
Love for All
Dony Hia

Being Still; Still Being...

You are never more essentially, more deeply, yourself than when you are still.
~ Eckhart Tolle

When Tolle speaks of being still, he is not talking not moving! One can be doing anything and be still; stillness of the spirit that is. Take martial arts, boxing, dancing, and other such crafts; these look most beautiful when the person doing them has a stillness of mind.

Way more often than not, the ones who perform the best are the ones whose minds and spirits are still.

Often in daily life, people let things coming at them steal their stillness away. Often this places them in one of the five fight or flight patterns. When we are in our fight-or-flight pattern, we are not our true selves; we are our patterns.

It seems doing energy work with Alison, Lynda, and now Jesse and Norma has helped me more than anything else to find this stillness. Of course, I had to travel the roads I have traveled to find this trail I am blazing now.

I would hope my own journeying can point out short cuts to others.

Best Wishes for Peace Profound
Love for All
Dony Hia

Bright Eyes...

Take care of your body with steadfast fidelity. The soul must see through these eyes alone, and if they are dim, the whole world is clouded.
~ Johann Wolfgang von Goethe

For some reason, this quote resonates with me. It might be because after the teacher leads the energy work in meditations at the end, she would always say, "Slowly bring your attention back to the room, open your eyes, touch your skin, and say I live here."

Our souls live in and around our bodies, within our own energy fields. Our bodies are just temporary housing for our souls, a place to work and learn from. We can make our bodies into a temple or a prison; it is up to each of us how we view this temporary residence.

They say the eyes are the windows to the soul. Looking into one's eyes, we can often see how the soul is evolving.

May all my friends and all those I know have bright eyes!

Best Wishes for Peace Profound
Love for All
Dony Hia

Soul's Destiny...

Since you're an individual in time and space, your body is a specific kind of lens, and you're naturally built to filter energy into the world in a certain way. Perhaps your filter shapes energy into architecture, or fine jewelry, or learning experiences for children, or complex organizations. When you do what you're built for, you experience destiny, and that precipitates an experience of unity. Your destiny, as you come fully into it, makes you feel you have been given your most cherished dream: You mean I get to do this? Problems? You soon see the hidden purpose of all problems is to correct misperception s, clear your view, and lighten you up so you can live your destiny. So if you help your soul solve its only problem, it will solve all the rest of yours. Finding your destiny solves the Soul's only "Problem."
~ Penney Peirce

    For most of my life, there has been a child in me who voiced, "When I grow up I am going to be..." Now I realize that one of the greatest gifts I have been given is the idea that a large part of me never has to grow up. Even in my daily work, there is a child inside who looks out, and this child is excited about the magical energetic world he lives in.

    At this time, my daily work no longer feels like work, it feels like playing with energies.

    I thought Dony Hia just appeared in the last few years, but he is the child sage who has always been there, probably for many lifetimes.

Best Wishes for Peace Profound
Love for All
Dony Hia

Power of Slowness...

Everything that happens in all material, living, mental, or even spiritual processes involves the transformation of energy... Every thought, every sensation, every emotion is produced by energy exchanges.
~ J. G. Bennett

Everything in the universe is energy vibration. Science shows us that in solid material atoms vibrate much faster than atoms in, say, gases. They vibrate faster but there is not as much energy in the formed molecules so the molecules do not move and are held together which forms the solid. In gases the atoms vibrate slower but have more energy, so the molecules are not held together. I think we can apply this logic to meditation.

I believe all vibrations create a weight, even if at this time we have no way of measuring it. I would think words vibrate faster than thoughts, yet have less energy. It would follow, if this is true, meditation vibrates slower than thoughts and yet has much more energy and power. I certainly have found a lot of power in meditation.

I wonder if love vibrates the slowest. Mystics certainly say it is the most powerful force in the universe.

Best Wishes for Peace Profound
Love for All
Dony Hia

Big or Small…

You are precisely as big as what you love and precisely as small as what you allow to annoy you.
~ Robert Anton Wilson

We think our world into existence moment by moment. To the extent we change our inner thoughts, our outer world changes.

Buddhists say all phenomena in the universe are reflections of the cosmic mirror. Physics say all phenomena in the universe come from and return to the zero point field. Rosicrucians, like Christian mystics, call this force spirit.

One may believe it is only our thoughts about the world that change, but our outer world does change to match our inner world. And these changing worlds are happening for every being in the universe; all are interconnected.

There are moments when I am a little contracted. There are other moments when I love the whole universe.

Best Wishes for Peace Profound
Love for All
Dony Hia

Problems or Just Evolution....

It's not that I'm so smart; it's just that I stay with the problems longer.
~ Albert Einstein

Watching my life and those of others, it seems to me we all stay with problems until they are no longer problems. This is part of our evolution, and if one believes in Karma, it is part of karma too.

If a problem comes at us in some form, and instead of solving it, we push it away, the problem will return in a similar form over and over again. It will do this until we evolve past the problem. If the Buddhists and mystics are correct, this can occur even over lifetimes.

I know one area in which this was very true for me. From the time I was a teenager until right before I met Luyu, I would always dive back into a similar relationship to the one I had left. After letting my last marriage go, I said I would not enter another relationship until I healed myself.

Through Tantric practices and energy work, I healed so many wounded little Donys that I sometimes wonder how I functioned as well as I have over the years. I am sure my Buddhist practices had a lot to do with this.

Funny, as I thought of writing today's *Fresh Morning Breath*, past memories came to mind. These memories were of being nine and ten years old, shortly after my parents divorced. I remember having problems at the time that seemed to overwhelm me.

I remember lying in bed at night, having trouble sleeping, and praying. Even back then, I didn't pray for a problem to go away, I prayed for the strength to survive and get through it. For a little guy, I guess I was given a lot of strength.

Of course, those close to me call it stubbornness.

Best Wishes for Peace Profound
Love for All
Dony Hia

Seeing the Divine…

Humanity and divinity will be identical when we recognize divinity in humanity.
~ Ernest Holmes

    One's first thought when reading the above quote might be *Not in my lifetime*. This was surely my own thinking in the past. Now it is different though, not only do I see the divinity in humanity, I see divinity in all beings and all things. There have even been a few days in the last few years in which I have only seen Buddhas. Normally, you don't see Buddhas or divinity by looking only at the surface; I find often it is my looking inward into my core where I get a glimpse of divinity.

    No matter how close I am to any being, I can never know how they see their world. Most of the time these days, I see my world as mystical and divine. Is this selfish? Not if I can share this vision.

Best Wishes for Peace Profound
Love for All
Dony Hia

Time Will Tell…

Each of us can manifest the properties of a field of consciousness that transcends space, time and linear causality.
~ Stanislav Grof

Not only can we do this, all of us manifest fields of consciousness that transcend space, time and linear causality every day. Many of our thoughts do this. It is through our thoughts that we create the future Now for ourselves. First, our mind will grasp a thought floating in the ether. Once we take in a thought and run with it, we send out energy, which then enters the Field (void). Depending on the amount of energy put into the thought, and our karma, the matching material manifestation will form out of the field.

Yesterday in our energy class, we actually worked on creating, for lack of better words, energy balls. We placed an intention into the energy and then mentally place this into the field to see if our intentions manifest.

The teachers of the energy class said pick something small. Since I don't do small well, I chose something I have wanted to manifest since I was young.

I am working on it at this very moment. Time will tell.

Best Wishes for Peace Profound
Love for All
Dony Hia

Many Consciousnesses...

Our normal waking consciousness, rational consciousness as we call it, is but one special type of consciousness, whilst all about it, parted by the filmiest of screens, there lie potential forms of consciousness entirely different.
~ William James

Scientists show our brains shift between four frequencies: Beta, Alpha, Theta and Delta. There may be more frequencies, but these are the four they have measured and seem to understand.

During normal waking hours, most of us operate in Beta frequencies. When we are relaxed, calm but not drowsy, light meditation, day dreaming, tranquil, our minds operate at Alpha frequency. When we are drowsy, in light sleep, dreaming, in deeper meditation, creative inspiration, our brains operate at Theta frequency. During deep sleep, sleep walking, sleep talking, deep trance our minds operate at Delta frequency.

As our brain waves slow down, we tend to become calmer, less worried, and even have more access to our subconscious mind.

When studying the brains of some Tibetan monks it was found that their brain frequencies are sometimes in Theta and Delta, even when they are not in deep meditation or sleep. In other studies, it has been found that our bodies, during slower frequencies create more beneficial neuropeptides and hormones, such as endorphins, serotonin, acetylcholine and vasopressin, which help release stress and pain.

Today I have my energy class, and in the class it seems to me, we work with all four of these frequencies and maybe more I haven't heard of.

I'm looking forward to the moments of the day!

Best Wishes for Peace Profound
Love for All
Dony Hia

Positive Thoughts…

Knowledge increases in proportion to its use; that is, the more we teach the more we learn.
~ Helena Blavatsky

Helena Blavatsky was one of the founders of the Theosophical Society.

I understand what Blavatsky is saying in her quote.

I started the *Fresh Morning Breath* thoughts a few years ago with a couple of Buddhist quotes, and my thoughts about them, to calm down a couple of coworkers who were about to quit at the time.

Three or so years later, I am still sharing quotes and my thoughts on them to help a few start their workdays on a positive note. The funny thing is, I feel I have learned a lot, and my own life continues to grow more positive day by day.

I want to thank everyone reading these quotes and thoughts for helping me learn and grow; all is interconnected, after all.

Best Wishes for Peace Profound
Love for All
Dony Hia

Deeper Than Sticks-and-Stones...

When we observe the world, Pribram theorized, we do so on a much deeper level than the stick-and-stones world 'out there'. Our brain primarily talks to itself and to the rest of the body not with words or images, or even bits of chemical impulses, but in the language of wave interference: the language of phase, amplitude and frequency – the 'spectral domain'. We perceive an object by 'resonating' with it, getting 'in synch' with it. To know the world is too literally to be on its wavelength.
~ Penney Peirce

    When I read the above paragraph it dawned on me how so many beings can experience so many worlds at the same time. Like crystals in cell phones, which each receive only their frequency, we all operate on different frequencies, wavelengths if you like. While some may operate on similar wavelengths, no two beings are on the exact same wavelengths.

    The field in which everything exists is so full of energy and vibration—wavelengths—if our brains and body did not have filters to block out most of it, we would all lose our minds. This makes me wonder: if those who do lose their minds first lose their filters.

    One other item came to me when I read the paragraph, a song I have enjoyed since 1978. The song is "Wavelength" by Van Morrison. To this day, every time I hear it, it charges me up. I guess for a moment that I am on Van's wavelength. It starts out saying: This is a song about your wavelength and my wavelength; you turn me on when you get me on your wavelength.

    We can get on others' wavelengths but we can never become another's wavelength, which means we can never truly know or understand another. What we think of as knowledge or understanding another is really our wavelengths understanding, not who or what the other really is. We can share parts but never our entire individual world.

Best Wishes for Peace Profound
Love for All
Dony Hia

Who's Dreaming Who...

You are the world.
~ Jiddu Krishnamurti

If you are very clear, if you are inwardly a light unto yourself, you will never follow anyone.
~ Jiddu Krishnamurti

I believe Krishnamurti is saying you are the world you live in. There is no one else who can live in this world. Many mystical schools believe we dream our lives; as does the Deer Tribe Southern tradition, which is one of the traditions our energy class works with.

The other night, I had a dream of someone who means a lot to me in the daytime world I dream. At one point the dream became lucid (I knew I was dreaming). What changed the dream to lucid dreaming was when I realized the person I was talking to had passed on to another realm. I looked at him and said, You have passed on. Am I dreaming you or are you dreaming me?

This reminded me of the ancient Chinese philosopher Zhuangzi (369BC – 286BC):

Once upon a time, I, Chuang Chou, dreamt I was a butterfly, fluttering hither and thither, a veritable butterfly, enjoying itself to the full of its bent, and not knowing it was Chuang Chou. Suddenly I awoke, and came to myself, the veritable Chuang Chou. Now I do not know whether it was then I dreamt I was a butterfly, or whether I am now a butterfly dreaming I am a man. Between me and the butterfly there must be a difference. This is an instance of transformation.

Best Wishes for Peace Profound
Love for All
Dony Hia

The Way...

But this mind isn't somewhere outside the material body of the four elements. Without this mind we can't move. The body has no awareness. Like a plant or a stone, the body has no nature. So how does it move? It's the mind that moves.

~ Bodhidharma

The true Way is sublime. It can't be expressed in Language. Of what use are scriptures? But someone who sees his own nature finds the Way, even if he can't read a word.

~ Bodhidharma

Someone who seeks the Way doesn't look beyond himself.

~ Bodhidharma

    I understand what Bodhidharma (440AD – 528AD) was saying about movement from the mind. I disagree that the mind is not also outside of the material body. The mind also extends, at least, if not more than our auric field.

    I know this from experience. I held my agoraphobia in an energy lock six inches behind the right side of my head in my own auric field. The agoraphobia was in my own mind, not outside of it. Also, the body does have awareness, as does each of the cells in the body. Each organ has its own awareness and this is why one organ can be healthy while another becomes sick.

    Yes, the Way is sublime, and while those who have found the Way can point to it through words, the Way can never be given to another, not even by a Buddha.

    Of course in the beginning, when one is seeking the Way, one will look towards others who seem to have found the Way. At some point though, if one is truly to find the Way, one has to look inward to one's own core. As in art, sports, and many other areas of life, when one truly finds their own Way they can never follow another. At this point if one is a bodhisattva one tries to point out ways for others to find their one and only Way.

Best Wishes for Peace Profound
Love for All
Dony Hia

Free from Clouds of Religiosity...

How wonderful it would be, I thought if only we could practice the teaching of the Buddha as he really taught them from his own experience – free from the clouds of religiosity that often surround them... Yet it's difficult to distinguish the tool themselves from their cultural packaging.
~ Dzogchen Ponlop Rinpoche, *Rebel Buddha: On the Road to Freedom*

I have to agree with Ponlop: Buddha was not made into a god-like figure until long after his death it appears. If one reads *The Long, The Middle or The Connected Discourses of the Buddha*, one will not find miracles as in later writings.

The discourses were translated from Pali texts, which are the oldest writings found on Buddhist teachings. As the Pali language died out and Mahayana Buddhism arose, the teachings were recorded in Sanskrit. It seems that it is in Mahayana Buddhism and Sanskrit writings in which Buddha is shown to perform miracles. I have *The Long and Middle Discourse* translations and for me they are more like reading psychology than reading religious writings.

I think if one was around in two thousand years from now, reading about Gandhi and Mandela, one would likely read they both performed miracles and maybe even walked on water.

Best Wishes for Peace Profound
Love for All
Dony Hia

My Mind Was Wandering…

One of the questions that arose from the PEAR studies was the nature of the ownership of thought. If you could influence machines, it rather begged the question of exactly where your thoughts lie. Where exactly was the human mind? The usual assumption in Western culture is that it is located in our brains. But if this is true, how could thoughts or intentions affect other people? Is it that the thought is 'out there' somewhere else? Or is there such a thing as an extended mind, a collective thought? Does what we think or dream influence anyone else?
~ Lynne McTaggart

The above paragraph discusses experiments in which people affected REG (Random Even Generators) by directing thoughts. I believe, as suggested in McTaggart's quote, that our minds are not limited to our brains.

Buddhists would go as far as to say our minds are not even our own; the idea of a separate being is an illusion. Buddhists also say if one searches for one's mind, it can never be found, within or outside of our bodies.

For me, our individual minds are just small reflections of the One Mind that Buddhists and mystics speak of.

If our minds are truly also outside of our bodies, it seems to give some truth to the statement, "my mind was wandering."

Best Wishes for Peace Profound
Love for All
Dony Hia

Yab/Yum Balance...

There was a vivid discussion of Schizophrenia, a subject dear to Jung since it was he who first took this dreadful illness from the incurable category. The main point of the lecturer was that schizophrenia can best be cured by the close relationship of the patient with a very feminine element in the therapist.
This is rarely found in any therapist of any school – and, strangely, more likely to be found in a man than a woman! I am reminded of a comment on gentleness coming from an American Indian legend. It observed that when a man is firm on the inside and gentle without, he is a healer. When he is hard outside and soft inside, he is useless.
~ Robert Johnson

The Tao teaches that a person is more whole when balanced within and without, *Ying* and *Yang*. Tibetan Buddhists call this *Yab* and *Yum* (father-mother). I believe all mystical schools believe the more balance of masculine and feminine one has, the more whole and healthy the person is. I certainly believe this myself.

From the age of nine on, I grew up in a house, a dysfunctional house for the most part, with Mom, five sisters and two brothers. Surrounded by so much feminine energy without any father figure, I naturally carried a strong feminine energy, which I believe was stronger than my masculine energies. It is through tantric and energy class work that I now feel my Yab/Yum (masculine/feminine energies) are more balanced. Being in a man's body, I actually feel more comfortable working with masculine energy than I had before starting this work. There is a little part of me that feels as if I am a healer; there is a very large part of me that feels healed.

Best Wishes for Peace Profound
Love for All
Dony Hia

Like a Dream...

Like a shooting star, a mirage, a flame
A magic trick, a dewdrop, a water bubble,
Like a dream, lightening, or a cloud–
Consider all things thus.
~ The Buddha

Buddha supposedly also said, "Life is like a dream, and we can awaken." Most mystical schools also say that this life is like a dream, or as with the Southern Tradition Schools, "We are dreaming this life." I agree with this assumption. The reason I agree is the way that I experience my night-time dreams.

At night, when my body is asleep, my mind, my subconscious mind, and the collective unconscious mind are all communicating. In nighttime dreams I see things as vividly as I do when I am awake. In my dreams while sleeping I get to go to surreal places that I can never experience during the day-time dream we call "life."

As I have mentioned before, if I look back at yesterday's experiences or last night's experiences, both memories seem to have the same clarity, and I get some meaning from both. The only difference in the weight of either memory is that in one I know people would say I was awake; and in the other, I was asleep.

There is the possibility, as some mystics might say, that I was asleep in both. *Somebody pinch me!*

Best Wishes for Peace Profound
Love for All
Dony Hia

A Few Thoughts on Dreams...

Do not spoil what you have by desiring what you have not; remember that what you now have was once among the things you only hoped for.
~ Epicurus

Everything you have, you have earned. Everything you have not, you have also earned. We do dream and imagine our own futures.

Dreams are illustrations . . . from the book your soul is writing about you.
~ Marsha Norman

Some recent Buddhists have adopted the Akashic Record, which is said to be the record of everyone's life on this planet. Other traditions that speak of the Akashic Record say it contains all souls' lives since the beginning. In the Southern tradition, they have the Chuluamahdah-Hey, the keepers of each of our books of life. The thought is that in each of our books of life is the record of what we chose to do in this, and every other, incarnation.

You are never too old to set another goal or to dream a new dream.
~ C. S. Lewis

When I was 17, a lady I was doing work for told me: "You should always keep at least one dream out ahead of yourself. This will help you stay young." I would certainly say I am a dreamer.

The best thing about dreams is that fleeting moment when you are between asleep and awake, when you don't know the difference between reality and fantasy, when for just that one moment you feel with your entire soul that the dream is reality and it really happened.
~ Unknown

The best thing about life for me is that moment when I am between normal waking moments and a true awakening. In these moments, I sometimes feel this is real and is really happening.

In the book that my daughter, Michelle, gave me, *The Lady of the Hare*, I just read something I found interesting. The author, John Layard, who was a dream therapist, stated that when dreaming, if we dream of someone of the same sex, we are dreaming of our conscious and individual subconscious. If we are dreaming of someone of the opposite sex, it is a reflection of the universal subconscious and our soul. Funny, since I have read this I have been paying more attention to those in my dreams. I have noticed when thinking back on the dreams, the ladies in the dream do seem to carry a deeper meaning than the men; of course, they are all reflections of my connection with the All. I wonder if, when we dream of animals, it is a more primordial connection or remembrance from the universal subconscious.

Best Wishes for Peace Profound
Love for All
Dony Hia

Changing Stations…

When you run after your thoughts, you are like a dog chasing a stick: every time a stick is thrown, you run after it. Instead, be like a lion who, rather than chasing after the stick, turns to face the thrower. One only throws a stick at a lion once.
~ Milarepa

Most Tibetans consider Milarepa (1052AD – 1135AD) Tibet's greatest Yogi ever; almost all of them believe he reached enlightenment in his lifetime. I am pretty sure that Milarepa was speaking about meditation in his quote.

When one is first taught meditation, they are often told to try to stop the flow of thoughts. Since one does not really own or possess thoughts, it does not take long until one realizes one can never stop the flow of thoughts.

Then one is taught to see thoughts as big bellowing clouds floating past in a clear blue sky. Whether the thought is beautiful, ugly or neutral one should not chase after it, any more than one might grab a cloud.

Boy, I like that simile which just flowed through me. I know it is not mine; it is just something that was floating in the field.

Since every thought there ever was, or ever will be, is already floating in the field, no human, saint or sinner, can stop the flow of thoughts. What one can do is rewire the receiver (him or herself) through which thoughts pass. Just as radio or TV is a device running on electricity and tuned to pick up different stations from a field, our brains are devices running on minute electrical currents that can be tuned to receive different thoughts from the field.

Best Wishes for Peace Profound
Love for All
Dony Hia

Good and Bad Faces...

There are only two ways to live your life. One is as though nothing is a miracle. The other way is as though everything is a miracle.
~ Albert Einstein

Of course, I may be wrong but I do tend to believe in string theory. String theory states everything in the universe is made up of vibrating energy, which, if one could see it, would look like minute vibrating strings. At least, that is the theory.

To think that everything from the smallest neutron to the largest star is really just a different vibration of the same energy strings is quite miraculous to me. Once you start thinking everything is a miracle, it seems more miracles happen around you.

For me, not only am I thinking more and more that everything is a miracle, but I can look back and think everything that has happened to me is a miracle. Even all those times, which seemed terribly difficult at the time, were really miracles to get me to where I am at this moment.

So miracles come with both good and bad faces. It has always been this way, and it always will be.

Best Wishes for Peace Profound
Love for All
Dony Hia

Becoming Conscious of the Subconscious…

Most of your experiences are unconscious. The conscious ones are very few. You are unaware of the fact because to you only the conscious ones count. Become aware of the unconscious.
~ Sri Nisargadatta Maharaj

    The unconscious mind and reptilian brain are really the ones that keep this thing we call a body going. They are the ones, which, for the most part, regulate heartbeat, breath, chemical distribution, electrical impulses, without us ever paying too much attention to their contributions. They also do a lot more than this: they help us determine which thoughts we receive and which we just let float by.

    The unconscious mind shows parts of itself in dreams but for the most part, for most people, it goes unnoticed. If one wants to change one's world and outlook, one has to work with both the conscious and unconscious minds.

    It seems, and we are taught this in our energy work, that the left brain works more with the conscious mined, and the right brain works more with the unconscious mind. It is said that those who seem to have more psychic powers tend to use both sides of the brain equally.

Best Wishes for Peace Profound
Love for All
Dony Hia

No Memory...

The Conscious mind, in contrast to the Subconscious and Superconscious minds, contains no memory and knows nothing. It is a point of awareness, your sense of "I Am" the viewing point, or eye of the soul. The Conscious mind is also the agent of your free will, a moving point of choice and personal identity – it gives you the experience of being an individual. By choosing different views and identifying with what it sees, the conscious mind determines your experiences. Perhaps this is why Edgar Cayce called it "the architect of our existence."
~ Penney Peirce

When I first read this, a small part of me said, No . . . Then a feeling of deep resonance rose up and said there is truth in this. Yes, if the conscious mind is the mind of Now how could it have memory? This is what Buddhists speak of when they say, when we first sense something for a fraction of a fraction of a second, it is just Now. Then our mind tries to connect this Now, with something from the past or something we want from the future. If we are trying to connect to something from the past we move into our subconscious mind. If we try to connect this Now to the future, we are moving into the Superconscious mind. Either one takes us out of the moment, the Now, and lessons our awareness of Now.

The more we can stay in, and to the extent we can totally *be* in the Now, the more awareness we can have, and the more magical and mystical life becomes. We can even experience that we are a dance of energy and light dancing with all other energy and light in the universe.

Best Wishes for Peace Profound
Love for All
Dony Hia

One Magical Step at a Time…

Mindfulness is the path to immortality. Negligence is the path to death. The vigilant never die, whereas the negligent are the living dead. With this understanding, the wise, having developed a high degree of mindfulness, rejoice in mindfulness, paying heed to each step on the path.
~ The Buddha

Of course, no one can honestly say if this is a quote from the Buddha. For the first few hundred years after Gautama Sakya passed, the teachings were passed on orally. Things were passed down by chants, songs and such as a way to try to keep the teaching as true as possible. Having said this, the quote does have major elements of what one understands as Gautama's teachings—Mindfulness, Immortality, Vigilance, and the idea that life is a journey on a path.

As I understand it, until one reaches Nirvana, merging back into the One, one is forever on a journey. If one is vigilant and mindful enough, one can come to realize this body, and even this mortal mind we have are not who he or she truly is. These are just tools to help us recognize who we truly are.

The awareness we truly are is never born and never dies; it is just here, now and aware. The more one can experience this awareness, the more magical this seemingly endless journey is at each and every step.

Best Wishes for Peace Profound
Love for All
Dony Hia

No Dust…

The presence of space makes it possible for the whole universe to be set out within it, and yet this does not alter or condition space in any way. Although rainbows appear in the sky, they do not make any difference to the sky; it is simply that the sky makes the appearance of rainbows possible. Phenomena adorn emptiness, but never corrupt it.
~ Kyabje Dilgo Khyentse Rimpoche.

There is no Bodhi tree
Nor stand of a mirror bright.
Since all is void,
Where can the dust alight?
~ Hui-neng, the 6th Patriarch of Zen

Both of the above quotes speak to me of Our Witness, Our Awareness. All Phenomena is born from emptiness and returns to emptiness. Emptiness, the cosmic mirror, the One Mind, is never born and never dies; yet it reflects all phenomena. Our Witness, Our Awareness is part of this emptiness, part of the One Mind, and is never born and never dies. In each incarnation, our witness of our awareness is there. Awareness is who each of us truly are. All other parts of our world including our bodies and minds are just reflections of this awareness.

Hopefully, if even only for a moment, you can experience the eternity of The Witness, the Awareness. As Hui-neng says, nothing can tarnish this Witness. No matter what our lives seem to be, the Witness stays pure.

Best Wishes for Peace for Profound
Love for All
Dony Hia

A Few Thoughts on Dreaming Our Lives...

A dream is a little hidden door in the innermost and most secret recesses of the soul, opening into that cosmic night which was psyche long before there was any ego-consciousness.
~ Carl Jung

I can never decide whether my dreams are the result of my thoughts or my thoughts are the result of my dreams.
~ D. H. Lawrence

Is all that we see or seen but a dream within a dream?
~ Edgar Allan Poe

    I do get a deep feeling sometimes; as some mystics say, each of us is dreaming our own life. After awakening from a night of dreaming of elegant parties, boating, fishing, my wife dressed to kill and heading to a party with friends, working, drinking and more, I had a feeling someday I will awaken from this life I dream.

    For most of us it will be after we let go of this incarnation in our next realm, where we will awaken to the understanding we were dreaming in this life all along. I believe there are some sages and prophets that are awake enough they experience this very incarnation as a dream.

    If we are dreaming this life, why should we not dream the best dream possible?

Best Wishes for Peace Profound
Love for All
Dony Hia

Beginnings and Endings...

You live on earth only for a few short years which you call an incarnation, and then you leave your body as an outworn dress and go for refreshment to your true home in the spirit.
~ White Eagle

Die happily and look forward to taking up a new and better form. Like the sun, only when you set in the west can you rise in the east.
~ Rumi

It is better to spend one day contemplating the birth and death of all things than a hundred years never contemplating beginnings and endings.
~ Buddha

Today Luyu turns forty-four. My lucky number has always been four; I woke up with part of me feeling twice as lucky.

At the end of work yesterday, I was thinking my cousin Fred would be sixty-three today. A few moments after that thought, my sister, Virginia, called and said Fred had passed.

This morning part of me woke up with a surreal feeling of some sadness and a surreal feeling of joy that Fred is no longer suffering.

Leaving work with the news of Fred, my thoughts were these: Pick up Yizi from school, stop at Lucky's, out of coffee, dinner tonight with Gayle and Andy.

When Luyu got home, she said, "Poor Fred, one more day to his birthday but the God said No!"

As with yesterday, and the day before, I contemplate the beginnings and endings of things and try to live in the moment no matter what I am feeling.

Best Wishes for Peace Profound
Love for All
Dony Hia

Just Sharing the Magic…

The world is full of magic things, patiently waiting for our senses to grow sharper.
~ W. B. Yeats

    I just want to share the magic. Yesterday, after I heard Fred passed, the song "Freddie's Dead" by Curtis Mayfield started going through my head. I was even singing parts of "Freddie's Dead" last night. I haven't heard the song on the radio for years but was hoping I would hear it today. When I was young, it always reminded me of Fred whenever I heard it.

    On KFOG's *10 at 10,* it was the tenth song they played. The song brought back so many pleasant memories of Fred and me cruising around in one of his old cars in the early Seventies. Yes, we were much like TV's *That 70's Show*, Fred looking cool and me with my bird-nest hair. They just said "Freddie's Dead" tied for "best song of set." Thanks for taking care of that wish for me Fred. Blessings all around us.

Best Wishes for Peace Profound
Love for All
Dony Hia

At the Core…

Inside myself is a place where I live all alone and that's where you renew your springs that never dry up. ~ Pearl Buck

Yes, each one of us has this place inside us where we can go to renew ourselves. The name for it I like the best is, our *Core*. In our energy work, we have been taught our core is in the middle of our body. Mystical drawings often show our core light emanating from an area between our solar plexus and our navel.

The Earth has a core, as does the Sun. Everything in the universe has a core, from the largest stars to the smallest atom.

I believe at the core is where all connects with All and it is where each of us can connect with, draw energy from, and touch the All.

There are many names for this connection with the All: Prana, Chi, Ki, Baraka, Mana, Ruach, light, Holy Ghost, life force and more. No matter what the name we give life force, it is a source we can go to and recharge ourselves. We all naturally go there when we are in deep dreamless sleep.

Take a moment and touch your core, I think you will like it.

Best Wishes for Peace Profound
Love for All
Dony Hia

All Is Magic...

Any perception can connect us to reality properly and fully. What we see doesn't have to be pretty, particularly; we can appreciate anything that exists. There is some principle of magic in everything, some living quality. Something living, something real, is taking place in everything.
~ Chogyam Trungpa Rinpoche

    In Buddhist, Native American, and some other traditions, all matter has life, and matter like all life is born and then dies.

    Rosicrucian thought says all matter contains spirit, the universal essence radiating from the divine source of all creative energies and powers, permeating all matter and giving all matter its vitality.

    Much of our energy work is based on southern traditions (Native American tribes). Not only do we work with the wisdom of plants and animals but with minerals also.

    If one does not believe there is life in matter, just listen to someone playing a Stradivarius Violin. It is not only the life in the player that touches our soul, it is also the life in the violin.

    I do feel the life in all. All is one, One is all; where would there not be life?

    Buddhist thought says if there is an environment, there is life; the environment itself is life. I would add, And All is Magic!

Best Wishes for Peace Profound
Love for All
Dony Hia

Sounds of Silence…

I can hear the deep silence any time I remember to listen. It's right below the noise.
~ Penney Peirce

Most Buddhist centers start off and end meditation periods by striking a bowl, gong or bell. Often one will be told to meditate on the sound of the bowl, gong or bell. One will be asked to meditate on where the sound comes from and where it returns to. The sound comes from the silence and returns to the silence. This silence is also the "emptiness" which Buddhists speak of.

It is often said that it is the silence between the notes that makes beautiful music. Without the silence between the notes, it is just noise.

In meditation one will come to find gaps between the thoughts, these gaps are moments where we can recognize the emptiness in our own being.

Best Wishes for Peace Profound
Love for All
Dony Hia

Feeling the Descriptions…

The real thing is when the body realizes that it can see. Only then is one capable of knowing that the world we look at every day is only a description.
~ Carlos Castaneda

Prey animals naturally see with their whole bodies; they need to do this for survival. While like us they see with eyes, they also see with body perception the energy fields around them. Horses and empathic humans probably do this more than any other animals. Often human empaths don't even know they are doing it. Empath bodies read the energy fields just as horses do. The problem often is their body not only reads the energy; sometimes it mirrors it. An empath can walk into a room where someone is sad or depressed and will start feeling the same way without knowing why.

In energy class, we are taught methods to both feel and also to set boundaries to the energy fields surrounding us. When one is able to do this, one gets and understanding of what Don Juan/Carlos Castaneda spoke of when he says our worlds are only descriptions.

It seems the more energy work I do, the more my body sees something before my brain does. I am learning to trust the body's vision.

Best Wishes for Peace Profound
Love for All
Dony Hia

Feeling Comfortable...

Remember! Trust endings and beginnings; it's your soul changing direction.
~ Penney Peirce

I look back to when I was younger and endings were tough. These days, beginnings and endings seem as natural as the sun rising and setting.

Reflecting on turning sixty-one today, I kid myself: if I had known I was going to live this long, I would have taken better care of myself. Then one of those voices says, "You haven't abused your body too much." Then a deeper voice speaks: "You know you have always enjoyed your mind, and you have worked pretty well at helping it grow." Then a deeper, deeper voice, maybe from my core, says, "You have done a nice job of protecting your soul."

While I know things can change or end at any moment, I have never felt more comfortable living within the body and auric field I live in now. It's a nice place to visit, and yes, I enjoy living here.

Best Wishes for Peace Profound
Love for All
Dony Hia

We Live in Animal Bodies…

You only have to let the soft animal of your body love what it loves.
~ Mary Oliver

While I know my being, "spirit" if you like, is living in a human body, I also know it is living in an animal body.

As humans we may, or may not, be the highest evolved animals on the planet; still, we are animals. I find remembering this brings a lot more compassion towards my own weakness or shadows. As a spiritual being, I try to connect with the higher evolution of the super consciousness. As an animal, I know I am also very rooted in the subconscious mind also. Most of the day is spent making choices that appear to come from our conscious mind, but even these thoughts are rooted in the subconscious mind. I believe our conscious mind is always communicating with both our subconscious mind and the superconscious mind. I think it is from the superconscious mind where we can feel compassion and what our body and the rest of us loves. I feel the subconscious mind may be much more concerned with survival than matters of love…

I have to say, in last night's dream I am not sure what planet the dream was on. There were dark souls living in bodies which were mixtures of plants, insects, and higher life forms. They could take on the appearance of anything they wanted, including humans. I poured Sprite soda on some of the beings when they were taking on the form of grasshoppers and saw it boiled and killed them. When I poured Sprite on the back and left arm of the beautiful woman who I suspected of being an evil alien it boiled. I knew I had to be careful. As leaves started to grow all about her I knew I had to get to safety.

As I was heading for safety I awakened from the dream. One might ask if this awake feeling we experience each day is truly the safer of the two dreams; it seems there may be dark souls in both.

Best Wishes for Peace Profound
Love for All
Dony Hia

Touched by a Dream...

Dreams offer themselves to all. They are oracles, always ready to serve as our silent and infallible counselors.
~ Synesius of Cyrene

What we experience during the day goes into our subconscious mind, mixes with the superconscious mind and rises again as a dream. I believe all dreams have some teaching in them.

Yesterday I went to Kaiser to discuss some neck surgery I need to have at some point. After meeting with the surgeon I went through the new hospital to see how much more work our crew has. While talking to our GF, he mentioned he was told when the new MRI is on the magnets would pull metal tools out of your hand. This set up a powerful dream for me.

Last night I dreamed a healer had a magnetic machine, which she said would remove blockages. I was not sure what she meant. She proceeded to set up a black machine that was about two feet square and two feet high, with a fourteen-inch solid cylinder in the center. She turned it on, and I could feel a pulling sensation on my spine. As the machine spun faster, I could really feel a pull on my heart chakra. I moved right in front of the machine and sat in the lotus position. I felt energy dancing up and down my torso, and then a feeling of warmth and wellbeing came over my entire body. The woman shut off the machine, and I stood up. After I stood up, the woman said to me, "You know this feeling will also fade." I replied, "I know. This is life, and we should not grasp at anything, we should feel and let be."

It was 3:00 AM when I awoke from this dream, and I could hardly believe the warm feeling I had in my heart area. I actually felt as if my heart had been emptied of all past and had no future. Just a real feeling of warmth and Now. I could feel my mind start to grasp at the feeling, saying, "I want this to last." Then my heart would just feel empty and warm. If my mind tried to go to the past, my heart let me know there is only Now.

From 3:00 to 5:00, except for two, short periods of sleeping and dreaming again, I lay there letting my body enjoy the feeling. I also rolled over and held Luyu for long periods. I was enjoying her breathing and the warmth our bodies were sharing in the moment. I also wished I could pass over the warm feeling I was having in my chest to Luyu.

It is over four hours later, and I still feel the warmth. My heart is empty of a past or a future. Still I am not grasping to hold onto the feeling.

I am glad I will be heading to the energy class in a short while. I think the dream represents how the day may go.

Best Wishes for Peace Profound
Love for All
Dony Hia

Listening to the Field…

Identifying equally with body, mind, and spirit immediately opens your direct knowing.
~ Penney Peirce

I remember reading, in my twenties, that people who show more psychic abilities tend to use both their right and left brains more equally. Here, forty years later, I have come to realize it is not that these people are psychic, it is just that they are more aware, more attuned to all the energy fields, which exist all around us. The Fields contains all that ever was or ever will be. And to the extent one can connect with and read the Fields, the more one is capable of direct Knowledge. This ability lies within all of us. It is just for most of us it is still dormant.

I agree with Peirce, the more we use our body (all of our body), mind (all of our minds within our body and within our auric field) and spirit (both conscious and super conscious spirit), the more we are able to Directly Know.

There are a lot of times for me, and probably for most of us, in which we ask ourselves how did I know that? For me I *feel* that I know; my body, mind and spirit have listened to the Field.

Best Wishes for Peace Profound
Love for All
Dony Hia

Never Tarnished...

Your entire personality, both your innermost and outermost self, is your soul taking shape. If you trust your imagination to be the voice of your soul, then the greater your imagination, then the more your true self can become real. You have enough originality within you to last for as long as you live. Consider how we manifest such wildly different realities. Isn't it amazing that some people marry 5 times and others can't find anyone they are attracted to? Or that one person is scrupulously honest and someone else learns by getting caught stealing a car and spending time in prison? Is one right and one wrong? Not at all. Each person's subjective experience is just right for him or her.
~ Penney Peirce

For us, living in relative reality, there are human-made concepts of good and evil.

Buddhism says there is no soul, but I have come to believe there is a part of us that travels from life to life, even if we don't call it a soul. If the mystics are correct, we chose to take on an incarnation for our soul, or whatever you want to call it, to evolve. For this soul, as with the Watcher, there is no good or evil: just *isness*. In Buddhism, the Watcher is never tarnished. In mysticism, the lower soul can be tarnished, but the highest high self, which never takes on an incarnation, never is. I think the Watcher and the Highest High self may be two names for the same thing.

More and more, I get a sense of that part of every being that is never tarnished. Feeling this opens my heart.

Best Wishes for Peace Profound
Love for All
Dony Hia

Lovers of Knowledge...

The true lover of knowledge is always striving after being... He will not rest at those multitudinous phenomena whose existence is appearance only.
~ Plato

What we see in our universe from the smallest atom, to the largest stars is only a small part of existence. For a few thousand years, religious and mystical schools have spoken of several planes of existence. Now, in explaining string theory, physicists speak of several planes of existence.

Watching Cosmos last night, I heard it said that everything in our universe exploded out of a space smaller than an atom. Yet, every bit of energy in our universe was there at this first moment.

Like humans, stars are born and die; all phenomena is impermanent. It seems, and Buddhists say, the only thing which does not come in and out of existence is the emptiness that contains All. Actually emptiness *is* the All, the One. As Plato alluded, one cannot find *being* in physical objects alone.

Best Wishes for Peace Profound
Love for All
Dony Hia

Here, Now...

There is no wisdom higher than present mind itself. The mistaken ideas about the essence arise from fixated attachment that solidifies the present mind as being negative. You believe that noble and positive wisdom will be attained only if present mind is relinquished. This is a mistaken idea in the Mahamudra tradition, because there is no wisdom higher than present mind itself.
~ Dzogchen Ponlop Rinpoche

It sounds like it should be so easy: *just stay in the present mind.* Yet, this is really a difficult task. It seems our minds love to jump to the future or drift to the past. Even sitting on a zafu meditating, it is not easy to stay in present mind. Yet, enlightenment can only be realized in the present moment.

Even after thirty-five years of meditation, I find several times a day, I catch my mind jumping forward or drifting back. I simply smile at my mind and say, "Here, now." Each time we do this, we wake up.

I no longer sit on a zafu to meditate; I meditate all day long in all activities. I do this by coming back to present mind, whenever I notice I am not *Here Now*.

Best Wishes for Peace Profound
Love for All
Dony Hia

Your Home...

Your most important home is your own mind, more important than any other. You've got to come back to that home, to get to know it a little better. And when you rest in your home, even for one moment, it might be the most beautiful rest you ever have. That is the beginning of finding meaning in your life. That is the beginning of making peace with yourself.
~ 17th Karmapa

    Yes your mind, or minds if you prefer, is the only place one can find true peace. Everything outside of your mind, or minds if you prefer, is your guru guiding you to find your way back home. Yes, everything in your environment is a guru to guide you back home.

    How you see everything outside of your mind is a reflection of yourself and are your gurus working to guide you.

    At some point, before enlightenment, sages must become their own gurus. Your own mind is, and at some point, in some life, will become, your best guru. After that, you will let go of your mind, future incarnations, and will be back at your original home.

Best Wishes for Peace Profound
Love for All
Dony Hia

The Great and Rare Mystics...

The great and rare mystics of the past (from Buddha to Christ, from al-Hallaj to Lady Tsogyal, From Hui-neng to Hildegard) were, in fact, ahead of their time, and are still ahead of ours. In other words, they are not figures of the past. They are figures of the future.
~ Ken Wilber, *Sex, Ecology, Spirituality, the Spirit of Evolution*

I rise to taste the dawn, and find that love alone will shine.
~ Ken Wilber

If one becomes familiar with Ken Wilber's work, one will likely come to believe he is also a figure of the future, if not as a mystic, at least as a philosopher.

Wild, the wide disparity of worlds on this planet we inhabit. There are still primitive people living in jungles, and at the same time there are sages leading the way of the future.

If in the future, the average human are to become more like the mystics Wilber lists above, there will be beings as far ahead of the average man as the mystics of two or three thousand years ago were to the average man then.

I know I am somewhere between the primitive in the jungle and the mystic, hopefully heading towards the mystic.

What a great way to rise in the morning. I find these days that I awake from dreaming each morning and feel both blessed and full of love.

Best Wishes for Peace Profound
Love for All
Dony Hia

Renewal, Regrowth and Regeneration...

Greetings and Happy New Year!
As Rosicrucians we celebrate the beginning of a new year on the Spring Equinox when everything that we see around us is in a state of renewal, regrowth and regeneration.
In the words of the founder of AMORC, H. Spencer Lewis:
"On the Spring Equinox we begin a new Rosicrucian year. It is a most logical time for the birth of the year; it is the beginning of the Sun's new journey through the signs of the Zodiac. It is the beginning of spring, the rebirth of life after winter."
In this spirit of renewal, and celebration, we wish you a new year filled with love and joy and Peace Profound!
~ The staff at Rosicrucian Park

When I read the above email in my in box this morning I thought, yes, the last couple of beautiful mornings have felt like the beginning of a new year; more so than last January first. Then again, we don't need to wait for a new year for renewal, regrowth and regeneration. As Buddhism emphasizes: in each moment, we are dying to the last moment and being reborn in the next. The thing is; are we going to be reborn in the next moment pretty much the same as the last, or is there going to be shift in our consciousness with a big change to happen. For most of us, most of the time, we will not have a big shift; yet, each of us do have moments where there are large shifts.

I may not have noticed all the little shifts, but if I look back three or four years, I do realize there has accumulated a rather large shift in my consciousness.

"Best Wishes for Peace Profound" is something borrowed from the Rosicrucians.

Best Wishes for Peace Profound
Love for All
Dony Hia

A Few Thoughts from Ken...

So the call of all Non dual traditions is: Abide as Emptiness, embrace all Form. The liberation is in the Emptiness, never in the Form, but Emptiness embraces all forms as a mirror all its objects. . . You and the universe are One Taste.
~ Ken Wilber, *A Brief History of Everything*

When we come to the point, as stated in the Heart Sutra, where we realize form is emptiness and emptiness is form, the world becomes surreal and magical.

In fact, all things, we might surmise, intuit to one degree or another that their very Ground is Spirit itself. All things are driven, urged, pushed and pulled to manifest this realization. And yet, prior to that divine awakening, all things seek Spirit in a way that actually prevents the realization: or else we would be realized right now! We seek Spirit in ways that prevent it.
~ Ken Wilber, *The Eye of Spirit*

We seek Spirit as if we are not Spirit ourselves. When we realize we are Spirit, seeking can end. Why continue to carry the raft when you are already on the other shore.

Ultimate reality is not an idea, philosophy, experience, proposition, technique, or perspective. It is rather a profound realization, in the deepest seat of consciousness that opens one to a direct identity *with that ultimate non dual Estate, a Reality that in itself can therefore* never *be seen as an object and hence remains purest Mystery shining in the Cloud of Unknowing.*
~ Ken Wilber

I feel the deepest consciousness Wilber speaks of cannot be found in the brain, it can only be realized by going in and passing through our core. I feel if one passes through the core, there is no-mind, only *isness*; a mind would still be a duality.

Best Wishes for Peace Profound
Love for All
Dony Hia

Doing and Getting it Done…

We are here to do. And through doing to learn; and through learning to know; and through knowing to experience wonder; and through wonder to attain wisdom; and through wisdom to fine simplicity; and through simplicity to give attention; and through attention to see what needs to be done.
~ Ben Hei Hei

    It seems to me, if one goes through the steps Ben Hei Hei speaks of, then the doing and getting it done becomes effortless. To me, after many years of doing and learning, it seems most of what I do these days is effortless.

    I don't know why, but when I see this mystic's last name, I laugh inside: hei hei…

Best Wishes for Peace Profound
Love for All
Dony Hia

Why Did I Come Back...

When we have an intuition, a mental image of a possible future, we're actually getting flashes of memory from our Birth Vision.... The intuitions we have, the dreams and coincidences, they're all designed to keep us on the right path, to bring back our memory of how we wanted our lives to unfold.
~ James Redfield

Do I know we had a Birth Vision, a plan, before we choose our present Life? No, I am not blessed with past life remembrance. Do I, deep inside, feel we choose a life meant to help our spirit evolve? Yes. I feel this increasingly, by the moment, exponentially.

I had a dream a week ago, which at some point I would like to write down. I can remember it as I can remember what I did yesterday.

At the end of the dream, in a high-rise building, a distinguished elderly man asked me why I came back. He was not talking about life. He was talking about why I came back to see the lady in the penthouse. He said he was going to take all the money away from his niece and her family. I said I did not come back for the money; the money meant nothing to me. When he was convinced I spoke the truth, he turned, smiled and shook my hand.

Since this dream, this has almost become a Zen koan: *Why did I come back*; twice I have felt an answer: to help.

I don't know if that was my favorite part of the dream or when the lady and I were on the penthouse level, naked just outside the elevator, in the position of Buddha and His Consort.

Best Wishes for Peace Profound
Love for All
Dony Hia

Keep Moving Forward…

I died as a mineral and became a plant, I died as a plant and rose to animal, I died as an animal and I was Man. Why should I fear? When was I less by dying?
~ Rumi

The further we are from our origin, the less we remember it. Most of us don't remember much or anything from four years or younger. And it is a rare being that remembers a past life. Yet, I feel, and believe, Rumi is correct: we have all been evolving for a long time.

Rosicrucians, Buddhists, American Indians and many other traditions believe that all matter is imbued with spirit; thus life.

In energy class, as mentioned before, one of the matrixes we build is the children's twenty-count, based on an Indian tradition. The first five energies we call on are as follows: Grandfather Sun, Grandmother Earth, Sacred Plants, Sacred Animals and Sacred Humans. This follows what Rumi states above; one is built up upon the other.

It is said that in our reptilian brain and our subconscious mind everything we have evolved through is still there. A lot of the way we respond in this life is from these past life experiences still stored within our being.

Best Wishes for Peace Profound
Love for All
Dony Hia

Part of Yourself…

If you hate a person, you hate something in him that is part of yourself. What isn't part of ourselves doesn't disturb us.
~ Hermann Hess

    Also, if you love a person, you love something in that person which is part of yourself. What isn't part of us, we really don't even notice; whatever we notice in some way is part of us.

    It may be a hard concept to grasp, but really, there is nothing outside of us. Anything, yes anything, we think we experience outside ourselves is really inside ourselves. Feeling joy, pain or sorrow outside your body can't be done. Even the lover one sleeps with is really within because how you see the other is really an inner reflection. Think of how many people think of your lover in a different way than you do. Start with your lover's family, and then imagine how friends of your lover see this person. Finally, imagine how people who are indifferent to, or who may not like your lover see this person. From this example, one can come to understand how we see our world really is a reflection of ourselves.

    I love this magical world I live in, and I also love so many people who live here.

Best Wishes for Peace Profound
Love for All
Dony Hia

Truth in the Strangest Places...

Don Juan, once told Carlos Castaneda that well-being was a condition one had to groom; "an achievement one had to deliberately seek. He said that the only thing I knew how to seek was a sense of disorientation, ill-being, and confusion. He laughed mockingly and assured me that in order to accomplish the feat of making myself miserable I had to work in a more intense fashion. . . . 'The trick is in what one emphasizes,' he said. 'We either make ourselves miserable or we make ourselves strong. The amount of work is the same.'
~ Penney Peirce

There is no evidence there ever was a shaman Don Juan Matus, who Carlos Castaneda claimed taught him the shaman ways. This does not mean there are not truths in Castaneda's books.

There is a Russian author, Vladimir Megre, who wrote 11 books on a mystical woman, Anastasia, whom he claimed to be a true person. In the books, she was over 100 years yet looked twenty. Later in a court hearing, when a woman came out claiming to be the Anastasia Megre wrote about, he admitted the books were fiction.

One thing Vladimir's books did do was have hundreds of thousands, if not over a million people start family gardens on their property.

So, while Castaneda's books may have been fiction, they also have truths. One truth I can easily agree with is—it takes the same amount of work to make yourself miserable as it does to make yourself happy. Of course, the results are completely different. Happiness draws in energy and makes one feel light. Unhappiness locks or pours off energy and makes one feel heavy.

Best Wishes for Peace Profound
Love for All
Dony Hia

A Few Thoughts about Art...

Creativity is allowing yourself to make mistakes. Art is knowing which ones to keep.
~ Scott Adams

Art is anything people do with distinction.
~ Louis Dudek

Every artist dips his brush in his own soul, and paints his own nature into his pictures.
~ Henry Ward Beecher

I feel that there is nothing more truly artistic than to love people.
~ Vincent van Gogh

    Last evening, after looking at the room I had just completed adding a craftsman's touch to, I went on Facebook. I saw a picture of my daughter Michelle in her new place. I also saw in the background, in a window, a stained glass of Buddha sitting under the Bodhi tree, next to the Ganges River. I had made this stained glass and gave it to Michelle some years ago. After seeing these two things, it took me back to when I was ten or eleven years of age. I remember going next door to talk to mom (a story in and of itself) at Cliff's house. I told her I wanted to be an artist! I remember her reply: "You don't want to be an artist, you won't make any money until you're dead." That one comment may have killed the courage in me to ever attempt to make a living as an artist; it certainly did not kill the art in me. Over the years, I have enjoyed watching many of the things the hands at the end of my arms have created. When things are flowing right, it is as if I am not the one creating them. It is more that they are creating themselves through me.

Best Wishes for Peace Profound
Love for All
Dony Hia

Don't Hold too Tightly...

Some of us think holding on makes us strong but sometimes it is letting go.
~ Hermann Hess

There comes a time when the bubble of ego is popped, and you can't get the ground back for an extended period of time. Those times, when you absolutely cannot get it back together, are the most rich and powerful times in our lives.
~ Pema Chodron

It is probably letting go that always makes us stronger. Most try to find some type of ground which they can stand firmly upon: family, friends, job, money and such. The thing is, even the firmest ground usually gives away.

For me, this ground falling away has happened so often that life naturally has taught me this lesson. When we are very young we blame ourselves for the falling away, such as when parents divorce, or even die. As we grow older, and hopefully wiser, we learn this falling away, or having the rug pulled out from under us is actually for our growth.

There is nothing I hold on to too tightly these days, not even beliefs.

Best Wishes for Peace Profound
Love for All
Dony Hia

A Few Thoughts from Donne & Dony...

No man is an island, entire of itself; every man is a piece of the continent.
~ John Donne

In John Donne's time (1572 – 1631), without TV, radio and the internet, the world did not seem as small as it does today. But even back then, he intuitively knew we are all interconnected. As humans, we are all connected to the same human superconsciousness, just as dogs are all connected to their own superconsciousness. And outside our own species, all beings are connected to the highest, the superconsciousness, the One.

Reason is our soul's left hand, Faith her right. By this we reach divinity.
~ John Donne

There is a Chinese saying, which is probably a couple thousand years old: "The Right hand doesn't know what the left hand is doing." Both this Chinese saying and John Donne's saying above intuitively showed we have two brains: a right and a left. It is probably only in the last seventy-five years that study of the brain has shown the Chinese and Donne to be correct. Our left brain is the logical and the right is the creative. It is the right, creative side, where faith probably lies. Man is more whole when both the left and right brains are balanced.

No Spring, nor summer beauty hath such grace, as I have seen in one Autumnal face.
~ John Donne

My first thought when reading this quote was, As we age, we can age like a fine wine or we can turn to vinegar. While both serve a purpose, wine is more likely to bring pleasure. I would be lying to myself, if I said I was not entering my autumn years. All I ask is that I can manage to share some pleasure, and that there are people to drink it up.

Best Wishes for Peace Profound
Love for All
Dony Hia

Looking Back, Moving Forward...

Do not go where the path may lead, go instead where there is no path and leave a trail.
~ Ralph Waldo Emerson

It seems life is pretty good, and I only have a bucket list of three items. One was to go to Tibet, and I was able to check that one off a few years ago. There was one point in Tibet where I felt I had returned home. When that happened joyful tears rolled down my face.

Another item on the list is to learn to play the violin. I had always heard that my great grandfather, Nathan Hughes, made violins. This one will probably have to wait for another lifetime. I have also read that Nathan Emery Hughes' artistry as a stonemason was legendary.

The third item is to go to Wimberley Texas; named after my great-great-grandfather, Pleasant Wimberley. I have wanted to go there since I was young and heard stories about the Hughes and Wimberley families. I don't know why the pull, but I kind of sense two things: one, I lived there before; and two, a more recent feeling, I may have lived there as Nathan Emery Hughes.

Next week Luyu, Yizi, and I will visit Wimberley, and we will see the ancestor's house. I am sure that I will experience energy from some of the ancestors who lived there.

Best Wishes for Peace Profound
Love for All
Dony Hia

Ah the Refreshing Airs…

It's the air not the Kite…
~ Pharrell Williams

While on vacation, I saw Pharrell Williams being interviewed. At one point during the interview he made the comment, "It's the air not the kite." He was referring to himself as the kite and all the people who have helped him along the way as the air. Hearing this touched me because I too know the happiness I feel is certainly not just my own doing. My happiness is also due to all those people, and beings, in my life, and those before my life who have laid down the foundation for me to grow into happiness. We are all floating kites, held up by a multitude of airs.

Going to Wimberley was in some ways like going to Tibet for me. In both places, I had a real sense of returning to a home I once inhabited.

Wimberley's slogan is *Wimberley, a little slice of heaven*. I certainly could feel that while there.

Best Wishes for
Peace Profound
Love for All
Dony Hia

Cypress Creek Wimberley Texas

Simply Dancing...

It is better to conquer yourself than to win a thousand battles. Then the victory is yours. It cannot be taken from you; not by angels or by demons, heaven or hell.
~ Buddha

It seems to me the leaders who have conquered themselves before leading others tend to be peaceful leaders; Gandhi and Mandela come to mind. Then I think of leaders who have not conquered themselves; they seem to want to conquer others by force.

I also think on a smaller scale that leaders do the same thing. If we have conquered ourselves, we tend to bring more peace into our environments. If we haven't conquered ourselves, we tend to want to conquer our environment.

Seems to me, the more one conquers oneself, the more magical and surreal the environment becomes; it becomes less solid and more a dance of flowing energy. At least this is my own experience.

Best Wishes for Peace Profound
Love for All
Dony Hia

For the All...

To practice tantra requires even greater compassion and greater intelligence than are required on the sutra path; thus, though many persons in the degenerate era are interested in tantra, tantra is not for degenerate persons. Tantra is limited to persons whose compassion is so great that they cannot bear to spend unnecessary time in attaining Buddhahood, as they want to be a supreme source of help and happiness for others quickly.
~ 14th Dalai Lama, *Meditation on Emptiness*

When one mentions tantra, a lot of people only picture people embraced in lovemaking. While this can be, and often is, part of tantra, tantra is much more. Tantra can be one of the quickest routes for taking charge of our egos. Picture your ego as a wild stallion, this wild stallion can be a scary thing; then again, if one can tame this wild stallion, one can ride swiftly and freely where others might not be able to go.

Tantra is living in the moment; when one is angry, one notices one is angry, when one is happy, one notices one is happy, without becoming attached to either. All activities become ritual and spiritual, yes even lovemaking; nothing is done for oneself alone. Everything is done for the All.

Tantra can also be dangerous if one is not spiritually ready. As the saying goes: Play with fire and you may get burned!

Best Wishes for Peace Profound
Love for All
Dony Hia

Learning from Pleasure...

To finish the moment, to find the journey's end in every step of the road, to live the greatest number of good hours, is wisdom.
~ Ralph Waldo Emerson

Yes, as we learn to live each moment as it is, complete and perfect in and of itself, a certain innate wisdom rises from within. The task is to take and accept each moment as it is, to see what we are to learn in each moment. Often, if a moment is unpleasant instead of living it, looking at it, feeling it, and tasting it, so we can learn from it, we spend a lot of energy trying to escape from such a moment.

In energy class, one teacher made the statement, "Most people on the planet are still at the stage where they learn the most from suffering." He added, "As we evolve, we can learn as much from pleasure as we can from suffering." For me, this is also a tantric path. The danger with the tantric path, I believe, is that if one is not evolved enough, the pleasure one seeks actually becomes a path for more suffering.

I do feel the number of good hours, and wisdom, rising for me. Ah the Wizard!

Best Wishes for Peace Profound
Love for All
Dony Hia

Love Butterflies; They Make My Heart Flutter...

Happiness is a butterfly, which when pursued, is always just beyond your grasp, but which, if you will sit down quietly, may alight upon you.
~ Nathaniel Hawthorne

I love the metamorphisms of the butterfly; egg to caterpillar, caterpillar to cocoon, and finally from cocoon to butterfly. Each of us goes through these metamorphisms several times throughout our lives. In some ways several times a day.

The egg is a thought rising from the void. The caterpillar is the thought as we run it through our minds. The cocoon is the time where we decide to either let the thought just slip back into the void or bring something into manifestation. The butterfly is the thought when it materializes into something in the physical world. At each of these steps there is chance for new birth or death. I am sure not many eggs make it to caterpillars. Even fewer caterpillars live to spin a cocoon. Other than being hidden, there is no protection for the poor cocoon. So when a butterfly does live to fly, it is a beautiful, magical thing.

At this moment, I am trying to push my folded wings against the hardened walls I have built around myself. Oh, how I want to be a butterfly.

As I have said before, it is sad to think how many could have been beautiful butterflies, die still wrapped in their own silk.

Best Wishes for Peace Profound
Love for All
Dony Hia

Just Imagine…

A butterfly lights beside us like a sunbeam, and for a brief moment, its glory and beauty belong to our world… But then it flies again, and though we wish it could have stayed . . . we feel lucky to have seen it. ~ Unknown

Yes, there are many beautiful moments in our lives that we try to hold on to. The thing is, the minute something has passed, it is only a memory, and when we still try to relive that moment, we are not living the moment that we are in. Then there are moments in our lives that are like flies, we try to push away. Again, any moment we are grasping or pushing away we are not living in the present moment.

Unfortunately for most, we spend a lot of wasted hours grasping and pushing.

Every moment I am in the present moment is like the words in John Lennon's song, "Imagine": *Just imagine, no heaven and no hell*. If you can, you too are probably a Buddhist.

Best Wishes for Peace Profound
Love for All
Dony Hia

Me, the Tree...

Everybody who's anybody longs to be a tree.
~ Rita Dove

    Often I've thought when I grow, I want to grow tall, strong, and artistically attractive like the Oak Tree.
    Then there was a time, after studying Buddhism, how nice it would have been to be the Bodhi Tree that held space for Gautama as he reached enlightenment.
    Ah, at last I think I have become the Willow Tree.
    The Oak Tree is strong but not flexible. In a storm the Oak Tree will resist as if saying to the wind, *you want a piece of me?* Thing is, the wind often says yes and takes away a piece, or even sometimes the whole tree.
    The Bodhi Tree is still, I feel, a being much wiser and maybe even calmer than I may ever be.
    The Willow Tree, yes this is me. The older I grow, the more flexible I've learned to be.
    My friend, the Oak resists and fights well, at least to me. The Willow, on the other hand, bends and dances in a storm, which is what I like to see. Even in a wild storm not even a piece of me will flee.
    Oh, I am so happy to have become a Willow Tree. If you have any doubts, come sit in my shade and share time and a thought with me.

Best Wishes for Peace Profound.
Love for All
Dony Hia

A Few Thoughts from Padmasambhava...

The eagle that is flying high in the sky should not forget that it should come down one day to see its shadow.
~ Padmasambhava

If I understand this correctly, Padmasambhava is saying no matter what one's status is in life, one should take moments to look at and understand one's karma.

As soon as one's mind is known to be of the Wisdom of the Voidness, concepts like good and evil karma cease to exist. Seek therefore, thine own Wisdom within thee. It is the Vast Deep.
~ Padmasambhava

We dream ourselves into a relative world where we see good and evil. In absolute reality, there is no good or evil. In the Vast Deep of the void from which all manifestations arise, there is no duality, thus, no good or evil.

Empty cognizance of one taste, suffused with knowing, is your unmistaken nature, the uncontrived original state. When not altering what is, allow it to be as it is, and the awakened state is right now spontaneously present.
~ Padmasambhava

In the Now and Knowing, I awaken and have beautiful glimpses of enlightenment. Then I leave to the past or the future and forget I was awake. Dreaming again I am.

Best Wishes for Peace Profound
Love for All
Dony Hia

Kindergarten...

These are the things I learned (in Kindergarten):

1. Share everything.
2. Play fair.
3. Don't hit people.
4. Put things back where you found them.
5. Clean up your own mess.
6. Don't take things that aren't yours.
7. Say you're sorry when you hurt somebody.
8. Wash your hands before you eat.
9. Flush.
10. Warm cookies and cold milk are good for you.
11. Live a balanced life - learn some and drink some and draw some and paint some and sing and dance and play and work every day some.
12. Take a nap every afternoon.
13. When you go out into the world, watch out for traffic, hold hands, and stick together.
14. Be aware of wonder. Remember the little seed in the Styrofoam cup: The roots go down and the plant goes up and nobody really knows how or why, but we are all like that.
15. Goldfish and hamster and white mice and even the little seed in the Styrofoam cup - they all die. So do we.
16. And then remember the Dick-and-Jane books and the first word you learned - the biggest word of all - LOOK.
~ Robert Fulghum, All I Really Need to Know I Learned in Kindergarten

I have never read Robert Fulghum's book but for some reason, it has often came into my thoughts since I first heard the author talking about his book in 1988. I may come across and read his book someday.

Then again, I never did get to go to kindergarten. I wasn't old enough when we lived in California. Then we moved to Arizona, and I was too old so they put me into first grade. I wonder if I did miss anything I should know.

In Buddhist, and mystical thought, we come into this life already knowing everything we need to know; we just have to remember. I feel we know things in our heart, and depending on our karma, we meet things in our environment that remind us of these things our hearts already understand. If our hearts know truths and we go with them, life is pretty easy. If we fight the truths of the heart, life is usually a struggle.

Best Wishes for Peace Profound
Love for All,
Dony Hia

Thanks for the Reflections...

You may never have proof of your importance but you are more important than you think. There are always those who couldn't do without you. The rub is that you don't always know who.
~ Robert Fulghum, *All I really need to know I Learned in Kindergarten*

Fulghum's quote above reminds me of the magic of all the different worlds we all live. I live in a world in which other people may get a glimpse but can never live. It is the same for each of us. You may see your partner as a wife or husband. Others will see this person as a friend, a stranger, or maybe even an enemy. Each way we see another person is a reflection of our own minds. We see others' worlds from the perspective of how our own mind works, not from how their mind or world works for them.

Fulghum is also correct when he says people couldn't do it without you. Each of us live in a magical dream world where some people love us, some people are indifferent towards us, and others don't even like us; even the sages live this way. Each of us is important, not only to those who know and love us, but also to people we don't even know.

Each of us reflects to the world exactly what others need to see, good, bad, or indifferent, for their growth. Also others see in us the reflection they need for their own growth. None of us ever truly see the true being of another person; we are always seeing a reflection of what our mind needs or wants to see for our growth, our evolution. Other than maybe, and this is a strong maybe, a few sages or prophets, people don't even see who they truly be...

I am looking forward to today's energy class in a few hours.

Best Wishes for Peace Profound
Love for All
Dony Hia

Direction of Your Dreams...

Go confidently in the direction of your dreams, live the life you've imagined.

~ Henry David Thoreau

If the mystics are correct, we can't help but live the life we imagined; unfortunately so many imagine a life of struggle and woe.

When I was young and things were going well, I would look over my shoulder for the trouble about to arrive. These days it is the opposite, if there is a little trouble, or struggle, I look over my shoulder and smile, for I know something good is on its way.

This last month, in the energy class, we were for the first time exposed to the feeling of the Fifth World, the dream world plane. Just a few moments of being exposed to this world and I get a sense of how I have dreamed much of my life into Third World, third plane.

In class I could sense the Fifth World is the first place outside the void. Every possibility already exists in the void, but it takes the Dream World, the Fifth World, to start the movement from the void. Once the Dream World has movement, the Thought World, the Fourth World, is the place where it will be determined if something stays in the Dream World or can be passed into the Third World where manifestation take place.

In energy class it might be said that we start with our Highest of High Self, down through Template of Perfection, through the Dream World, through the Thought Form World, and finally into the Third World.

If we can bring our Template of Perfection, down through the Dream World and the Thought Form World without distorting it, we would truly be doing the work we chose to do in this incarnation. Unfortunately, for the most part we don't know how to maneuver through the thought form world and we distort what we want to dream into existence.

I understand there are many other worlds of existence, but we have only worked with five planes and the void to date.

Best Wishes for Peace Profound
Love for All
Dony Hia

Desire's Tremendous Energy...

It is precisely because our present life is so inseparably linked with desire that we must make use of desire's tremendous energy if we wish to transform our life into something transcendental.
~ Lama Yeshe

Many religious practices try to teach us that the way to happiness is to repress our desires. Tantra, on the other hand, tries to teach us the quickest way to enlightenment is through fulfilling desires with awareness.
I believe all useful desires must come from a core desire, not to just help ourselves but also to help all beings on their own paths. As with the Bodhisattva ideal, our desires should be led by compassion for all being, not just to satisfy our personal needs and ego. The Bodhisattva takes a personal vow not to enter enlightenment until all beings are ready to enter enlightenment.

Tantric practice can be a dangerous practice if one allows one's ego to master them instead of the other way around. In Tantra, one does not try to get rid of the ego. Instead, one masters the ego like taking control and riding a wild stallion. This is what Lama Yeshe speaks of with the words, "desire's tremendous energy."

Best Wishes for Peace Profound
Love for All
Dony Hia

Vajrayana (Tantric) Buddhism...

If you want to sin, sin wholeheartedly and openly. Sins too have their lessons to teach the earnest sinner, as virtues the earnest saint. It is the mixing up of the two that is so disastrous. Nothing can block you as effectively as compromise, for it shows lack of earnestness, without which nothing can be done.
~ Sri Nisargadatta Maharaj

Why is it that whatever we touch we turn into a problem? We have made love a problem, we have made relationship, living, a problem, and we have made sex a problem. Why? Why is everything we do a problem, a horror? Why are we suffering? Why has sex become a problem? Why do we submit to living with problems; why do we not put an end to them? Why do we not die to our problems instead of carrying them day after day, year after year?
~ Jiddu Krishnamurti, *On Love and Loneliness*

Suffering in hopefulness is the externalist. Suffering in hopelessness is the nihilist. Beyond both hopefulness and hopelessness is the Buddhist.
~ Dungse Thinley Norbu Rinpoche, *Magic Dance*

When you arrive at the extinction of reality there is nothing but the spontaneity of pure potential; there is no other way to dance in the sky.
~ Yeshé Tsogyel

I manifested in a dreamlike way to dreamlike beings and gave a dreamlike Dharma, but in reality I never taught and never actually came.
~ Shakyamuni Buddha

The above are a few thoughts on Vajrayana (Tantric) Buddhism.

From the books I have read on Tibetan Buddhism, I believe most Tibetan Buddhism is Tantric.

For me, the energy classes I have been taking merge very well with Vajrayana Buddhism. In many ways, all of the mystical schools are Tantric. Rosicrucian, Kabala, Mystical Christianity, Many American Indian traditions, Many Mid-Eastern traditions, Ipsalu, and so many more have Tantric flavors.

I consider my own practices Mystic and Tantric. The one thing common with all of these traditions is they all teach that you have to find, and walk, your very own path.

Best Wishes for Peace Profound
Love for All
Dony Hia

Stop Searching...

Searching for happiness prevents us from ever finding it.
~ Pema Chodron

For me it is easy to understand what Pema Chodron is speaking of. What she is alluding to is if we are searching for happiness we are not present, not here in this moment. If we are searching, our mind is running off into the future or slipping back into the past.

A lot of religions will take this approach. They will say if you live a good life, heaven awaits you; if we live for a future heaven, we can miss the heaven of this very moment.

In Buddhist teachings, heaven and hell are not somewhere in the future; either of them can be in this very moment. Heaven can be embracing a loved one in this very moment. Hell could be this same loved one leaving you at some point. The thing about heaven and hell in Buddhist thought is that they are both impermanent. If you are in heaven, don't try to grasp it. The tighter you try to hold it, the quicker it will slip away. And if you are in hell, don't try to push it away. The more you try to push, the more it will stay.

In Vajrayana (tantric) Buddhism, one dances with the energy of the present moment.

I am loving this moment. My mind is not in the future, trying to prepare for the next moment; that moment will come naturally.

Best Wishes for Peace Profound
Love for All
Dony Hia

A Few Thoughts to Ponder…

The real voyage of discovery consist not in seeking new lands but seeing with new eyes.
~ Marcel Proust

Most of us are not looking with the same eyes as we looked with when we were children, which may or may not be a good thing. Most children's eyes look with an innocence that so many people lose as they age. I have managed to hold on to some of the innocence. I also try to remember to have fresh eyes each moment.

Work like you don't need money, love like you've never been hurt, and dance like no one's watching.
~ Unknown Author

I feel I can relate to all three of these, but my favorite is "Love like you've never been hurt." It seems to me that just doing any one of these three would bring much joy. I would like to think I often do all three.

Believe those who are seeking the truth. Doubt those who find it.
~ André Gide

One of the reasons we need to doubt those who say they have found the truth is because most truths are time relative. I am sure I will be seeking truths for the rest of this life; I have done this for nearly sixty years now. What I am not searching for is one truth that fits all; I know it does not exist.

Truths are best served individually!

Best Wishes for Peace Profound
Love for All
Dony Hia

A Few Thoughts on Change...

Every possession and every happiness is but lent by chance for an uncertain time, and may therefore be demanded back the next hour.

~ Arthur Schopenhauer

I agree with some of Schopenhauer's philosophy, but from much of what I have read, I am sure if I had met him, I would have thought he was not a very happy man. It is written that he even told his own mother, who was a writer, the only thing she would ever be remembered for was being Schopenhauer's mother. Of course, the story goes, he was right.

Without accepting the fact that everything changes, we cannot find perfect composure. But unfortunately, although it is true, it is difficult for us to accept it. Because we cannot accept the truth of transience, we suffer.

~ Shunryu Suzuki

I have not only learned to accept change, I have realized sometimes drastic change is where I find the quickest emotional growth. If we are not growing, we are dying. Of course, we are heading towards death of the body even if when we are blooming emotionally. Why not keep blooming right to the end?

I put a dollar in one of those change machines. Nothing changed.

~ George Carlin

According to Buddhists, each moment holds a death and a birth. The more we can let the last moment die, the more we can be born fresh in the present moment. Today is a great day to feel fresh and alive, moment to moment all day long.

Best Wishes for Peace Profound
Love for All
Dony Hia

Stuck in Old Samsara Again…

Samsara is mind turned outwardly, lost in its projections. Nirvana is mind turned inwardly, recognizing its nature.
~ Tulku Urgyen Rinpoche

I am convinced the Nirvana Buddhists speak of can only be found by going so deep inside ourselves that we come out on the other side. Even when I was young, lying in bed, turning my mind inward, I would hit what seemed like a dark wall; which kept me from going in further. I still hit this wall, but it is further in than I have ever been. I think maybe the only thing keeping me from going further in is fear. I may just be afraid to cross that threshold.

Oh my Son! Appearances of phenomena do not bind you to samsara, but attachment to them does.
So, Naropa cut off attachment.
~ Tilopa

Not only attachment to, but rejection of phenomena also binds us to samsara. When we have no attachment to or rejection of all phenomena in our environment, our environment becomes more like nirvana than samsara. Our world takes on a very dream-like quality, a dance of the One energy. Even though it only happens occasionally, I know this through experience, not logic.

For some reason Tilopa's quote brought back that old Credence Clearwater Revival song, "Oh Lord, I'm stuck in Lodi Again."

Best Wishes for Peace Profound
Love for All
Dony Hia

God and Goddess…

A unifying factor between the different traditions and lineages of Tantra, is that it is feminine in nature. It acknowledges the feminine as the basis from which all the practices spring. Therefore, Tantra is by its nature, the understanding that all phenomenal existence, the universe, or cosmos that we experience is feminine in nature.
~ Zeena Schreck

According to Ken Wilber, all early religions were Goddess religions, which makes sense because the earth itself is feminine. Unfortunately, many of the Goddess religions also had human sacrifice. This also probably made sense at the time. Before cultivation, everything was seen as a gift from mother earth. So, by giving a sacrifice to the goddess, the hope was that she would return the favor.

Wilber says after cultivation, when there was enough food that men did not have to hunt every day, they had time to start contemplating. At some point, probably at the time of early Greek and Egyptian empires, God religions started to appear. Hermetic thought (Hermes Trismegistus) is often thought of as one of, if not the earliest. Wilber also says the problem with most of the God religions is that instead of merging with Goddess religions, they threw out the Goddess. Gnostic Christianity, Buddhism, some other philosophies and especially Tantra have merged God and Goddess into their religions and philosophies.

Best Wishes for Peace Profound
Love for All
Dony Hia

I Can Hardly Believe It Has Been Nearly Three Years...

Every muscular contraction contains the history and meaning of its origin.

~ William Reich

They say golf is mainly muscle memory. Well, our fight or flight patterns are also muscle memory. If we overreact in the present moment we are in pattern. We are in a fight or flight pattern because of an unconscious memory (energy) locked in our body or auric field. I am not speaking from what I have read or what my mind may think; I am speaking from what I have experienced firsthand.

The body is a self-healing organism, so it's really about clearing things out of the way so the body can heal itself.

~ Barbara Brennan

When Brennan speaks about clearing things out of the way she is also speaking of locked energy in our body, auric field, or chakras. The more we can release these locked and blocked energies, the more energy we can handle running through our bodies.

I can hardly believe there are only three more classes in our third year of energy class. For the last few weeks, I have felt more energy moving in my body, even to the point of extra heart beats PVCs. I have also felt blockage in my sixth chakra.

Funny, several minutes ago I was thinking I needed to talk to one of the teachers in tomorrow's class and work on this. A moment later, he called and we talked about the amount energy I was running. He suggested I put it in dream-time tonight as something the class matrix can work on. I felt a sudden grounding feeling and a moment later he said he was working on grounding me until tomorrow's class. Each time we can release a blockage we evolve a little and can handle running more energy.

Best Wishes for Peace Profound
Love for All
Dony Hia

Which Do You Operate from…

Everyone is welcome to my world, but first they must find the door.
~ Unknown

What a powerful energy class I had yesterday. I released energy that had been locked in my body for probably sixty years. Other than my head not spinning around on my shoulders and not floating above the ground, I am sure my energy release looked somewhat like the movie, *The Exorcist*. It was nice to let that locked energy go.

In the afternoon, we worked with the energies of the five worlds we experience. There is a lot more to these worlds than I spell out below, but hopefully it will give you a taste. In the class the teachers put the vibration of each of the worlds into the room and we could experience each of the worlds.

The First World is the core of the earth. If we can align with the energy of this world it is great for resting and recharging.

The Second World is comparable with the crust of the earth. It is the world of worms, bacteria, fungus and such. The world of composting, where old things are broken down into fertilizer that supports new growth. This is also the world of emotions. When we let old emotions break down here, it also opens us up for new growth. If we don't let old emotions break down here, they get stuck in our bodies and can cause illness, stress, depression and more. It was said in class people often get stuck in the Second World.

The Third World is Third Plane, the world our bodies live in; it is the Material World. It is also the world in which we can really taste the other four worlds. We can take our minds into the other four, but it is our body in Third Plane that experiences the other four worlds. It is the sensual world. As long as we don't get stuck in the Second or Fourth Worlds we bring the experiences of those worlds back into the Third World, Third Plane.

The Fourth World is the world of thought forms. It is the world where we attract things from the Fifth World (Dream World) and start working with them to materialize them into the Third Plane world. This is also a place where we can get stuck. If we get too attached to thoughts of things we want, or too attached to thoughts of things we don't want, we can get stuck in the Fourth World. One can know they are stuck if the same thoughts loop through the mind day in day out. Some people can get stuck in thought loops for years.

The Fifth World is the dream world. If I understand the Fifth World correctly, it is a conduit between the Void and the Thought World, the Fourth World. The Void, while it can't really be described or known, is the storehouse for everything that ever was or ever will be. But for something to manifest from The Void to Third Plane it has to pass first through the Dream World and then the Thought World. I believe the Fifth World is the closest world our human minds can get to the void; a human mind can never enter the Void.

A well-balanced life will have a core running from the First World through the Fifth, and our attention given mainly to First, Third, and Fifth Worlds, passing through Second and Fourth Worlds without getting stuck, without grasping.

Best Wishes for Peace Profound
Love for All
Dony Hia

Shopping at the Gap Again…

When looking at an object, there is no object: it is seen as mind.
When looking at the mind, there is no mind: it is seen as emptiness.
When looking at both, dualistic fixation is freed of itself.
May we realize clear light, the nature of our mind.
~ The Third Karmapa

There may be other methods, but meditation is the only one I know to get a taste of what the Third Karmapa spoke of.

When one meditates, one can come to experience the gap between two thoughts. This gap, this emptiness, is the nature of our minds.

Just as it is the silence between notes that makes beautiful music, it is the gap (the emptiness) between two thoughts that makes our beautiful minds.

For many years I spent time sitting on my cushion meditating. These days I no longer meditate sitting on a cushion. I try to take my meditations along with me out into the world, all day long.

I do notice a lot of gaps during each day.

Best Wishes for Peace Profound
Love for All
Dony Hia

Thoughts Floating By...

No thought has any power, you have power. And when you identify and believe in the thought you give power to the thought.
~ Mooji

Mooji is correct: thoughts have no power until we latch onto them and start to bring them into fruition.

We have two mechanisms we use to latch onto thoughts and they are not always in agreement. We have our conscious mind and our subconscious mind; sometimes they agree and sometimes they disagree. This is why, when we latch onto a thought and try to bring it into fruition, it doesn't always turn out the way we desire.

For instance, our conscious mind may say I am going to succeed at this, but a deeper voice may say you are not going to succeed at this, you have never succeeded before. Whichever mind we give the most power will be the mind which manifests the thought into reality. Of course, it can work the other way, our conscious mind may believe we will fail at something yet the subconscious mind believes we will succeed this time. Again, whichever mind we give the most power will take charge and manifest the thought its way. If both minds are in agreement, the only outcome is to manifest what we believe.

Then there is a third way, if the thought is not a useful thought, don't let the conscious mind lock onto it in the first place; let the thought float by as if it were a billowy cloud in the sky.

Best Wishes for Peace Profound
Love for All
Dony Hia

A Taste of Enlightenment...

Just as every drop of the ocean carries the taste of the ocean, so does every moment carry the taste of eternity.

~ Sri Nisargadatta Maharaj

Every moment also carries a taste of enlightenment. If we look back on our lives, or even a day, we realize how little of each day we can remember. Often, we are out of the moment, not in the here and now and we don't remember where our minds were.

I sometimes think every memory is a moment where we may have tasted enlightenment. Funny, as I was having this thought a song came on the radio that always takes me back to a special moment. The song is "Everybody Wants to Rule the World" by Tears for Fears. This song always takes me back to an Intel plant being built near Folsom.

The year was 1985. I was sitting on the west side of the building during lunch. It was a pleasantly warm spring day with white billowy clouds floating across the sky. During the first part of my lunch, which I was having by myself, I was reading a book, *The Buddhist Bible*. During the second half of lunch, I put on my headphones and was listening to the radio.

With by back leaning up against a wall, I felt the sun warming my entire body. Looking out at the day, I smiled as the green leaves on the oak trees, moved by a light breeze, seemed to be dancing in rhythm with a song I was listening to.

The bright deep blue sky with white billowy clouds slowly rolling by could have been a movie scene. At that moment I felt total bliss arise in me. Just as the blissful feeling was arising, the song "Everybody wants to Rule the World" started playing on the radio. It made me feel as if I were ruling my own world. For that moment, time froze and for a slight moment, I tasted my own enlightenment.

A nice thing is every time this Tears for Fears song plays on the radio, I taste the same enlightenment again. That moment is locked safely inside. I hope by my sharing, you might taste one of your own enlightenment moments.

Best Wishes for Peace Profound
Love for All
Dony Hia

Finding Your Ecstasy…

Find ecstasy within yourself. It is not out there. It is in your innermost flowering. The one you are looking for is you.
~ Osho

Actually, a Buddhist would be more apt to say, when you realize there is no you, this is when you have found it. Buddhists say it is the ego that believes in a separate self; self and other are an illusion created by the ego. Yet, since we are existing, or dreaming ourselves, in this world why not look in, find our own flower and share it with the outer dream world.

In doing energy work I realized, not only had I locked away painful traumatic experiences, I had also locked away joyful blissful experiences. While for me, most of the released locked energy has been from painful experiences, I have also had a few blissful releases. One example is when I was young, maybe two and a half years old. Sunshine was coming through a window into a living room. The sunshine was warm and nourishing my soul, and I wanted to move and dance around. I had lost this joyful and blissful memory until one session when I was working with Alison and was able to relive both the joy and why the joy had to be suppressed.

When we were very small children laughing, being joyful, fully out loud and expressing our bliss, our parents may have yelled at us to stop and be quiet. This simple experience can freeze our bliss within.

Last night in one of my dreams, I was in an energy class. There were a few new funny and joyful characters who showed up for class; I was observing, perhaps being a little too serious. A moment later, a friend who flies out from New York for our class most months asked me if I would like a Clearing. I replied yes. At that moment she placed her hand about four inches in front of the left side of my chest, where the heart is. I felt an energy covering my heart and move out of my body towards her hand as she pulled it away. As the energy left, I felt a nice chill run up my body, goose bumps, and then a feeling of great joy and bliss.

You know, some dreams are just a heck of a lot more enjoyable than others.

Best Wishes for Peace Profound
Love for All
Dony Hia

Moment by Moment…

In your everyday life you always have opportunities for enlightenment. If you go to the rest room, there is a chance to attain enlightenment. When you cook, there is a chance to attain enlightenment. When you clean the floor, there is a chance to attain enlightenment.
~ Shunryu Suzuki

In any moment, if we are fully in the moment, keep our awareness and lose the notion of self; we are enlightened in that moment.

The difference between the average person and those who are said to be enlightened is quantity. Where we might have a couple or a few moments in a day in which we are fully here Now, those enlightened sages probably have just a couple or few moments when they are not here Now.

It really is quantity not quality. One person's enlightened moment is not more or less than another's enlightened moment; it is just how often one is here in the Now.

Best Wishes for Peace Profound
Love for All
Dony Hia

Thoughts from Nisargadatta...

Between the banks of pain and pleasure the river of life flows. It only when the mind refuses to flow with life, and gets stuck at the banks, that it becomes a problem.
~ Sri Nisargadatta Maharaj

Nature is neither pleasant nor painful. It is all intelligence and beauty, Pain and pleasure are in the mind. ~ Sri Nisargadatta Maharaj

The problem is not yours – it is your minds' only. Begin by disassociating yourself from your mind. Resolutely remind yourself that you are not the mind and that its problems are not yours.
~ Sri Nisargadatta Maharaj

    We can easily think we are our minds, but we are not! We never had this mind before and we will never have it again. Like our flesh, we put on a new mind with each new incarnation; and we let go of this mind at death.

    Our spirits have borrowed this great flesh and this great mind, and we should let them work for us, not try and work our spirits.

    Our minds see pain, pleasure and indifference in order for our spirits, souls if you like, to evolve on their way back home. If our spirits remember this mind is just a gift, a tool, for our spirits to grow, our spirits can watch this life as if watching the greatest movie ever.

Best Wishes for Peace Profound
Love for All
Dony Hia

Sacred Mandalas...

The experience of the tantric yogi is like this: The outer world is seen as a sacred mandala circle, and all living beings seen as divine beings. All experiences become transformed into blissful primordial awareness; and all of one's actions become spiritual, regardless of how they conventionally appear. Every sound that one makes becomes part of a great cosmic song.
~ 2nd Dalai Lama

    This seems to me to be a great meditation, which, in many ways, I already do.

    Whatever I am doing, walking, working, talking with family, friends, or strangers, cooking, eating, making love, pooping, bathing, or just watching my breath, these are all done in a sacred environment with sacred beings.

    While all of my experiences may not be blissful, they do have a sacred quality for me. This time and place, which I have chosen for this incarnation, has not always been easy, but it has been a great mandala for my spirit to evolve.

    Each of us lives in and operates in our very own sacred mandala.

Best Wishes for Peace Profound
Love for All
Dony Hia

Thoughts from Rumi...

Be grateful for whoever comes, because each has been sent as a guide from beyond.
~ Rumi

If we can be fully aware, we can recognize how each being who comes into our environment is a guide. Actually not only beings, everything in our environment is a vibrating energy, and affects us on some level. In this sense, everything is a guide if we really pay attention.

If you are irritated by every rub, how will your mirror be polished?
~ Rumi

We each rub other beings, and other beings rub us. We also rub ourselves and others rub themselves. We even rub our environment and our environment rubs us. As Rumi said, this is all to polish us, polish our spirits. The funny thing is, it is often those beings or things that seem to rub us in the worst way that actually polish us the most.

And you? When will you begin that long journey into yourself?
~ Rumi

Buddhists often speak of how precious a gift this human birth is. They say it is the best vehicle for realizing enlightenment. They also iterate how quickly this human life passes. Thus, as Rumi asks, when will you begin that long journey into yourself? Tomorrow, five years, ten years, twenty years?

Best Wishes for Peace Profound
Love for All
Dony Hia

Inside Out (4)...

Where would I possibly find enough leather with which to cover the surface of the earth?
But (just) leather on the soles of my shoes is equivalent to covering the earth with it.
~ Shantideva

Likewise, it is not possible for me to restrain the external course of things but should I restrain the mind of mine what would be the need to restrain all else.
~ Shantideva

Pema Chodron says she was really influenced by Shantideva's writings, especially his writings on the Way of the Bodhisattva.

I really like how Shantideva compares trying to control things outside himself so he is comfortable, to trying to cover the whole earth in leather to make his feet comfortable. No more could we cover the entire world in leather than we could change all things in our environment. We can, though, change our mind to experience the outer world differently. In changing our internal world, we change how we look at, and experience, our outer world. I would like to say this is simple, and for some maybe it is. For me, it has taken years of working with my mind to mold it into my best friend. Now, I like how this friend views his world.

Best Wishes for Peace Profound
Love for All
Dony Hia

Stripping One Layer at a Time...

Warriorship is a continual journey. To be a warrior is to learn to be genuine in every moment of your life. ~ Chogyam Trungpa

It sounds as though this should be easy; just be your genuine self. The problem is that most of us don't even know our genuine self. We all have been layered over with other's ideas of what we should be. The layering starts with parents, then school, then friends, associates and even others we barely know. These days even the airwaves have and an endless supply of messages of what we need to have to be happy, which layers us with others' ideas of how we should be.

If we truly want to find our genuine selves, we have to start by stripping off all the layers of what we are not.

Even though I have always believed I heard the sound of my own drum, I know there were also others drums sounding. I also know that I am more genuine in more moments today than I have ever been. I like this continual journey I am on of stripping away what I am not.

Taking a deep look inside, I believe it is really nice there in the depths where a bright light shines forth. The more layers I remove, which dim the light's ability to shine, the more I hope I can light up the world.

Best Wishes for Peace Profound
Love for All
Dony Hia

Soft or Hard…

Water is fluid, soft, and yielding. But water will wear away rock, which is rigid and cannot yield. As a rule, whatever is fluid, soft, and yielding will overcome whatever is rigid and hard. This is another paradox: what is soft is strong.
~ Lao Tzu

If anyone wonders how strong soft water can be, think of the Tsunami that hit Japan.

I look at some of the people I have known in my life who have acted so hard, knowing all along they were not really that hard or strong on the inside. One who did surprise me though was my own mom. She was always soft on the outside, but I knew she had strength on the inside, having eight kids and making sure they were fed on her own.

It was only in the last few years of her life when she was in a convalescent home that I saw just how strong she was. In this home, she was well respected, and from what I heard, a lot of people would go to her for comfort. I am glad I got more of my mom's softness than my father's hardness. I am flowing more easily than ever.

Best Wishes for Peace Profound
Love for All
Dony Hia

It's a Good Mind After All...

Before we can extend our compassion to others, we first have to extend it to ourselves. How do we do this? We have to look at our own mind and appreciate how our own neurotic expressions – our confused thoughts and disturbing emotions – are actually helping us wake up. Our aggression can help us develop clarity and patience. Our passion can help us let go of attachments and be more generous.
Basically, once we see that this mind of confusion is also our mind of awakening, we can appreciate it and have confidence in our ability to work with it. It's a good mind after all, the mind that will carry us to enlightenment. When we understand this, we can begin to let go of our previous attitude of revulsion toward our emotions.
~ Dzogchen Ponlop Rinpoche

Ponlop's quote above seems to go very well with the request in the energy class, where we worked with our emotions this month.

How often we seem to be such good friends with other people's minds, which we can never truly know, and yet not become best friends with our own. We may think we know how another's mind works, but we don't. For the most part, we don't know how our own mind works. Not knowing how our mind works does not mean we cannot become best friends with our own minds; after all, our own mind is the only one we can dive into completely. Even when therapists try to dive into others' minds they are doing if from their own viewpoints, from their own minds.

Best Wishes for Peace Profound
Love for All
Dony Hia

In and Through, Not Out and About…

Your most important home is your own mind, more than any other. You've got to come back to that home, to get to know it a little bit better. And when you rest in your home, even for one moment, it might be the most beautiful rest you ever have. That is the beginning of finding meaning in your life. That is the beginning of making peace with yourself.
~ 17th Karmapa

Our human mind is not our permanent home; it is a temporary home, just as our body is a temporary body. This temporary mind, though, is our most important possession. For it is only through this temporary mind that we can get a taste of our permanent being, an extension of the One Mind. One has to go *in and through* our human mind to find the One Mind.

So many people seem hardly to be able to spend even a moment with their own mind. They run here and there, doing this activity or that one, anything they can do to keep from spending time alone with their mind. If one cannot spend time alone with one's mind, it is hard to truly get to know it.

Most mornings, I spend several minutes to an hour paying attention to my in-and-out breaths and observing my mind. My mind and I are becoming good friends.

Best Wishes for Peace Profound
Love for All
Dony Hia

One Special Tear…

After your death you will be what you were before your birth.
~ Arthur Schopenhauer

Seeing death as the end of life is like seeing the horizon as the end of the ocean.
~ David Searls

Death is a stripping away of all that is not you. The secret to life is to 'die before you die' - and find that there is no death.
~ Eckhart Tolle

This place is a dream. Only a sleeper considers it real. Then death comes like dawn, and you wake up laughing at what you thought was your grief.
~ Rumi

    This morning when I checked my emails I saw one from my daughter letting me know a friend's husband had let his body go and moved on. The friend was a roommate a few years back. Her energy lit up the whole house. Both Tilo and I enjoyed the time we shared with her.

    My heart goes out to her and all those who knew her husband, and are suffering as they let his soul move on to its next assignment.

    Each person touches so many lives, not just of those we know, but also those we don't know. I believe each of us comes into life to touch each other's souls and to help each other evolve. Sometimes when we do this, people love us. Sometimes when our souls teach, some people hate us. Yet, loved or hated, we all help each other's souls to evolve.

    The last teaching any of us do, in each incarnation, is to let go of this life. As one lets go, each person who knows the one moving on is touched in the way they need to be.

Nichole, I never met your husband, yet today he is showing me there is one special tear in my heart. This tear is trying to take on some of the suffering you are feeling so you might suffer less.

Much Love, Dony.

Best Wishes for Peace Profound
Love for All
Dony Hia

This Month Is Emotions Month for Me...

I don't want to be at the mercy of my emotions. I want to use them, to enjoy them, and to dominate them.
~ Oscar Wilde

Letting an emotion move through you is healthy. Letting an emotion define you is not.
~ Chip Conley

Unexpressed emotions will never die. They are buried alive and will come forth later in uglier ways.
~ Sigmund Freud

This month's homework in the energy class is to work with emotions and let them follow their course. Being such, I thought a few thoughts on emotion would be appropriate. This month in class we were told emotions are our souls trying to bring something into manifestation.

While I agree with Freud that emotions don't die if we don't let them move through us, I don't agree they need to come out in ugly ways. While some emotions may do this, others may arise in joyful ways. I am speaking from experience here. We don't only bury darker emotions; we also bury light, blissful emotions.

When working with Ipsula Tantra, I released emotions, which caused some very intense physical pain. I also released some that brought up some of the most blissful experiences I have ever had. I knew these blissful ones were from joy I had hid when I was a baby and small child.

I am beginning to believe emotions have no feelings of their own; it is how we let them rise or how we suppress them that bring forth feelings.

Best Wishes for Peace Profound
Love for All
Dony Hia

Working with Our Fears…

Courage is resistance to fear, mastery of fear, not absence of fear. Except a creature be part coward, it is not a compliment to say it is brave.
~ Mark Twain

He who is not every day conquering some fear has not learned the secret of life.
~ Ralph Waldo Emerson

Every person on the planet, with a healthy mind, has some fear about something. Some people have more fears than others, but none are without fear.

I have said in the past that I feel I am today more from fear than from courage. Having been agoraphobic for forty-four years, I learned to survive with fear. Also, for my early years, there was a fear of not surviving life with Shorty.

As I grew older, there was a fear of failure. There was even some fear in relationships. Today, most of these fears have been overcome, but I know I still have a few.

One of my deepest fears is a fear of heights. This is so deep, and I have had it as far back as I can remember. The fear is so deep I think I may have brought my fear of heights with me from a past life.

This weekend I faced fear as I painted on the front of our house. I placed a twenty-foot ladder on the stairs, strapped it down and proceeded to spend hours prepping and painting. While I was shaky and fearful the whole time, I held with it and actually felt pretty good that I could do it.

As I painted I never overcame the fear of heights, I just made friends with it and held it. I thought of it as part of energy class homework working with emotions.

Best Wishes for Peace Profound
Love for All
Dony Hia

Never So Alive…

Your distress about life might mean you have been living for the wrong reason, not that you have no reason for living.
~ Igor Stravinsky

I have to admit Robin Williams's death touched me and made my heart feel a little sad. Any feeling we have in our heart is good; it shows we have a heart.

These days, I am more open to feeling. I even feel sorrow for William's wife, who may be questioning herself whether there was anything she could have done. Of course, there wasn't.

Growing up in a house on welfare, being agoraphobic, insecure, afraid of girls, lonely in a house full of kids, I would be lying if I said that I did not think death would have been easier a few times. But I thought we pick up where we leave off. Bailing was not the answer, and deep inside I knew this. I knew what I felt to be problems were my problems and I had to work on my own problems; no one else could do it for me. So I spent the next forty-five-plus years working, and am still working, figuring out who I am and what I came here to do.

I've walked a lot of paths to get to the energy work I am doing now. I feel the journey is paying off. I have learned to feel so much in the last four years. I have never felt so alive; even in those few moments when I suffer I still feel so alive!

Having known suffering, it makes me want to relieve others' suffering. I think my journey is finally moving me towards being able to help others in some way.

Best Wishes for Peace Profound
Love for All
Dony Hia

Just Ordinary, or Ordinary Magic…

Anyone can love a rose, but it takes a lot to love a leaf. It's ordinary to love the beautiful, but it's beautiful to love the ordinary.
~ Unknown

The whole world is a series of miracles, but we're so used to seeing them that we call them ordinary things.
~ Hans Christian Anderson

What is normal? Normal is only ordinary; mediocre. Life belongs to the rare, exceptional individual who dares to be different.
~ V.C. Andrews

I remember when my daughter, Michelle, was about one and a half years old. I took her for a walk on the block we lived on. As I walked her, I showed her how to hug a tree and see beauty in ordinary things. As we walked along on the sidewalk I pointed out clover flowers, dandelion flowers, and a host of other so-called weeds. Her whole body lit up with excitement at all this ordinary magic.

I don't know if what I tried to implant held true, if she still gets excited by ordinary things. I do know sixty years after I was that young age, I still do. I can still find, and hopefully now create, beauty in ordinary things. I have always been a little different; it is only in the last few years that I have felt so blessed with being different.

Best Wishes for Peace Profound
Love for All
Dony Hia

Fresh Morning Breaths

Dreaming the Dream...

We are like children building a sand castle. We embellish it with beautiful shells, bits of driftwood, and pieces of colored glass. The castle is ours, off limits to others. We're willing to attack if others threaten to hurt it. Yet despite all our attachment, we know that the tide will inevitably come in and sweep the sand castle away. The trick is to enjoy it fully but without clinging, and when the time comes, let it dissolve back into the sea.
~ Pema Chodron

If one truly understands, and can experience everything is impermanent, one naturally loses strong attachments and even aversion to things, even one's own body. This does not mean one cannot enjoy things that come into one's presence. It can be just the opposite, one can learn to enjoy and appreciate things more because one knows he or she may not be around for long. Even aversion can lessen when one understands even things that we dislike may not be around long.

Best Wishes for Peace Profound
Love for All
Dony Hia

Feelings, Nothing but Feelings…

When we stop distracting ourselves, and courageously dive into the heart of any feeling, positive or negative, right or wrong, we rediscover the vast ocean of who we are. Every feeling is made of unspeakable intelligence.
~ Jeff Foster

We tend to pull away from unpleasant feelings. More often than not, this pulling away is what intensifies the pain of an unpleasant feeling.

I remember some years back when I was feeling very sad in my heart and was trying to pull away from an unpleasant feeling. Of course, in trying to pull away, I was actually focusing on the pain. At one point, I decided to just dive in and feel all I could feel. At that very moment, a warm feeling arose, along with a feeling that I have a good heart.

My first fight or flight pattern is Rigid. One of the things rigid pattern needs to learn is it is okay to feel. People with a rigid pattern tend not only to avoid having unpleasant feelings, they tend not to feel joyful ones, either.

Since I started the energy work, I have probably let myself feel more in four years than I had in forty.

Best Wishes for Peace Profound
Love for All
Dony Hia

From the Core...

Meditation is not the pursuit of pleasure and the search for happiness. Meditation, on the contrary, is a state of mind in which there is no concept or formula, and therefore total freedom. It is only to such a mind that this bliss comes unsought and uninvited. Once it is there, though you may live in the world with all its noise, pleasure and brutality, they will not touch that mind.
~ Jiddu Krishnamurti

Meditation really gives us nothing! Everything we think meditation could give us, we already have. It is not what meditation gives us; it is what meditation strips away that makes it such a useful practice. At the core, we are all already Buddhas, we already have Buddha Mind. In meditation we start stripping away at the outer edges everything that is not Buddha Mind. Think of it like stripping away layers of an onion. If one can manage, like some before us, to strip all the layers away until it seems only emptiness is left, one will have become enlightened.

While most of us may never reach enlightenment, still the closer we get to our core, the more bliss can naturally rise. Bliss will never come from the outside because everything outside is subject to birth and death, including our body, which is also on the outside of our core. Bliss only rises from the core.

From an experience I had at a Tantric retreat in Kentucky, I would say bliss happens when heaven and earth connect through our core.

Best Wishes for Peace Profound
Love for All
Dony Hia

Labor or Play, Sleep or Awakened...

A person who is a master in the art of living makes little distinction between their work and their play, their labor and their leisure, their mind and their body, their education and their recreation, their love and their religion. They hardly know which is which and simply pursue their vision of excellence and grace, whatever they do, leaving others to decide whether they are working or playing. To them they are always doing both.
~ Zen Poet

With Labor Day weekend upon us, I thought labor would be a nice topic.

Sometimes, when working at home Luyu tells me: "You are working too hard!" My view on working too hard is, if it's too hard, I can't do it. If I am doing it, it can't be that hard. Not being able to work with the tools at work, the work I do at home is actually more meditation and play than it is work.

As the Zen Poet stated above, there is little distinction between the different aspects of my waking hours. I would even add there is little distinction between my waking hours and dreaming hours.

I guess, if there is one place where there is a distinction, it is when I am in deep sleep. I really have no idea what my conscious or subconscious minds are doing in deep sleep. I have a feeling that this is the time we truly connect with the All and recharge.

Some Tibetan Buddhists say, if one can be aware in deep sleep, one would realize the clear light of enlightenment. I just don't know.

Best Wishes for Peace Profound
Love for All
Dony Hia

A Few Thoughts on Doubt…

In Zen Buddhism, the greater your doubt, the greater will be your enlightenment. That is why doubt can be a good thing. If you are too sure, if you always have conviction, then you may be caught in your wrong perception for a long time.
~ Thich Nhat Hanh

Learn to be still. When in doubt do nothing.
~ White Eagle

When your footsteps and thoughts carry you down the same path your heart and soul are directing you, you will know without a doubt that you are headed in the right direction.
~ Molly Friedenfeld

On the beginning of any spiritual path, Doubt is our best friend. Without doubt, we may just take what others are telling as the truth. We should not accept anything as truth until we have exhausted our old friend, doubt.

When we have looked high and low, inside and out, even sideways and worn out our old friend, doubt, then we can accept something as true. And even then, we need to realize it may be a relative truth with a true meaning for only our self.

Lying awake at four o'clock this morning, I decided to meditate on my sore neck; I had been working so hard painting our house. As I meditated, I realized the tension was doubt, not overwork. My inner voice was saying you need to let go of the last little doubt you are holding before you put the *Fresh Morning Breaths* out there. Seems that the doubt is melting on its own.

Best Wishes for Peace Profound
Love for All
Dony Hia

Natural Flow…

A quiet mind is all you need. All else will happen rightly, once your mind is quiet. As the sun on rising makes the world active, so does self-awareness affect changes in the mind. In the light of calm and steady self-awareness inner energies wake up and work miracles without effort on your part.
~ Sri Nisargadatta Maharaj

    A mind full of chatter not only wastes energy, it can actually stop the natural flow of energy. We tend to think the energy we have in our body is only in our body and is created from the fuel (food) we feed it. This is not the case; energy also flows down from grandfather sun and up from grandmother earth. This energy flow is a connection of heaven and earth, masculine and feminine, and the more this energy flows naturally, the healthier we are in body, spirit and mind.

    In energy class, by quieting the mind and placing awareness on our different chakras, we can actually open up blocked energy channels. I feel it is a little different than Nisargadatta has stated. The energies do not wake up; the energies were never a sleep. It is more that the body wakes up, blockages are removed, and once again the energies flow naturally as they should.

    With a quiet mind, besides one being able to observe one's mind more easily, one can also observe, and tame, that little frisky monkey we call Ego.

Best Wishes for Peace Profound
Love for All
Dony Hia

The Man in the Gray House

The Man in the Gray House is one of my very favorite memories of my youth. The memory is from 1962 when Mom, my seven siblings and I were living in the tiny one-bedroom house.

The memory starts one day when Ginny and I were walking home from a park. We reached the back alley that led to the back of our house. The alley was narrow and not paved. It really just consisted of dirt, weeds, and two ruts made from an occasional car that drove the alleyway.

At the edge of the alley, Ginny said, "I can beat you home if you take the alley and I run up the street and down the block." I knew I could beat her because I had far less to run.

I took the wager, and off we both went running, Ginny up the street and I down the alleyway. I had no idea where Ginny was when I was about to reach the back of our house. Just as I closed in on the house, my foot caught a board that was sticking up out of the dirt and tripped me. I was running so fast when the board tripped me that I flew through the air several feet and landed face down. The right side of my face hit the ground first. I am sure I let out one hell of a scream.

Mom heard me scream and ran to the alleyway, where I was still lying face down in the dirt crying. Mom asked if I could move my leg, which I could.

Later, Mom said with as far twisted around as it was, she thought I had broken it. My leg was fine, and so was everything else, except for the right side of my face, which had already started swelling. My face hurt so much. I remember I cried for some time.

I was never taken to the hospital to see what damage there might be to the right side of my face. I ended up with a black eye, which lasted for five or six weeks before clearing up.

To this day, I can feel a crease in my right cheekbone where I must have smashed it.

Me running, tripping, flying through the air, and landing on my face happened just a few days before my ninth birthday.

On the morning of my birthday, Harry built a *Little Rascals* sort of wagon out of some wood, four different sized small hard tires, some round bars, and a rope he had scrounged up from somewhere.

Even at a young age, Harry started bringing stuff home and building things.

Later in afternoon, Harry said, "Since it is your birthday, I will pull you around the neighborhood."

It was a great, old, tree-lined neighborhood. One elderly neighbor said she had lived in her house for over 60 years. Other than me and my siblings, I don't remember there being any kids living within several blocks of our house. I am sure many of the oldest households probably had two generations of children grow and move away. For even the newest houses probably one generation of kids had grown and moved away.

So there I was feeling special as Harry started pulling me up the street. He pulled me to the end of our street and made a right turn. Once on Stockton Boulevard, a block away, he made a left turn. He had just pulled me across the street, heading in the direction of the Coca Cola plant, where sometimes we would get a Coke for a nickel. Right after we were back on the sidewalk, a man stopped us. He looked at Harry and asked, "What happened to him?"

Harry replied, "It's his birthday present."

The man asked, "What do you mean?"

Harry replied, "It's his birthday and his black eye is his present."

The man looked at me and asked my name. I said, "Donny."

After I told the man my name, he took out his wallet, opened it, pulled out a dollar, handed it to me, and said, "Happy birthday!" Back then a dollar was enough to buy candy for all eight kids and Mom too.

Turns out there was more kindness to come from this man. He looked at me and said, "See that gray house up the block? I want you guys to come there next Saturday morning." After that, he turned and started walking down the street.

Harry and I went to the little market, which was just a little further up Stockton Boulevard. I used the dollar and bought everyone in the house candy.

When we returned home with the candy, Mom asked where we got the money for it all. We told her a man gave it to me for my birthday. We told her he also said to come to his house next Saturday morning.

Instead of Mom getting upset for me taking the dollar, she said, "It was nice of the man to do that." Then she said, "You don't go to anyone's house on the weekend before ten in the morning. A lot of people like to sleep in."

We saw the man on a Sunday. All the following week I could hardly wait for Saturday to come.

Come Saturday morning, Harry and I were up early. We waited right until 10:00, then headed out the back door and up the alley, crossed the street, and were at the gray house.

When we walked up to the house, the man was in his garage, sitting on a stool at a workbench. We said hi to him. He asked if we would like a soda. We both said yes. Next, he asked, "Root beer or orange soda?" Harry and I both said root beer. He then called to his wife, "Ma, bring out a couple of root beers for these boys."

I think it was about this time I noticed a brand new Red Flyer Wagon in the back of his garage. The man saw me look at it and asked if I liked it. I am sure I lit up when I said yes. He then said, "Happy birthday. It is yours." I hardly believed what he said. Here we didn't even know him and he says the wagon is mine.

Harry asked the man his name, and he replied, "Puddentame. Ask me again, and I'll tell you the same." We had heard that phrase before, so we knew this was not his name. We also heard his wife call him Pa, but we knew that wasn't his name, either.

I know we stayed and talked to the man while we finished our sodas. Of course, it was so long ago I have no idea what we talked about.

When we were leaving, he told us to stop by once in a while for a soda, which we did. There were a couple times Virginia went with

Harry and me.

One time when I went, the man noticed I had a hole my shoe. I remember him saying to come by the next Wednesday after four thirty and to bring my mom. We must have told him at some point our parents had divorced.

The next Wednesday, Mom and I walked to his house and knocked on his door. When he answered, he told my mom he was going to take us to Oak Park to buy me a pair of shoes. The three of us got in his car, and he drove us to a shoe store. Sure enough, he bought me a brand new pair of shoes.

Again, such an act of kindness! I still did not know his name. If he told Mom his name that day, she certainly never told us.

I don't remember how many times we went to his house for sodas. At first, we went just once a week. Then Harry talked me into twice a week. Harry wanted me to go more, and I said no. I told Harry to go by himself, but Harry said, "He likes you more." Hum, just the opposite of our Shorty, our father.

Harry was older and already kicking my shins all the time, so I let him push me into going more and more. Harry figured out what time the man got home in the afternoon. Harry would push me to head into the alley, hide behind a fence, and wait till we saw the man show up. Then, just a few moments after the man got into his house, Harry would say, "Let's go."

At some point, and rightly so, the man had had enough and said, "You can't come every day." I'm not sure if I ever went back again. I was so embarrassed. I look back from today and feel we must have looked like feral cats waiting in the alleyway.

Often, as I grew older, in my teens and twenties, I wished I had the courage to go back to that gray house and both thank and apologize to this man who had shown me such kindness. Unfortunately, with my agoraphobia, I never had the courage.

I mentioned The Man in the Gray House was one of my best memories from my childhood. In actuality, it is one of my favorite memories of my life. I often think of The Man in the Gray House as my first guru. He showed me great acts of kindness and never *wanted anything in return.*

I don't believe The Man in the Gray House was kind to me because he felt sorry for me. I think he did it because he saw something in me. I remember him saying something like, "You will do something good someday."

Whatever he said, the man did teach me that if you have a little extra, share it. Throughout my life whenever I have been able to share something, I feel not only am I thanking The Man in the Gray House, but I am also doing as he had wished. Probably every act of kindness I do, or have done, has a little flavor of this man's compassion in it.

Dony Hia

www.ingramcontent.com/pod-product-compliance
Lightning Source LLC
Chambersburg PA
CBHW040106120526
44588CB00039B/2750